The Fantasy of Globalism

The Fantasy of Globalism

The Latin American Neo-Baroque

John V. Waldron

LEXINGTON BOOKS
Lanham • Boulder • New York • Toronto • Plymouth, UK

Published by Lexington Books
A wholly owned subsidiary of Rowman & Littlefield
4501 Forbes Boulevard, Suite 200, Lanham, Maryland 20706
www.rowman.com

10 Thornbury Road, Plymouth PL6 7PP, United Kingdom

British Library Cataloguing in Publication Information Available

Library of Congress Cataloging-in-Publication Data

Waldron, John V., 1960-
The Fantasy of Globalism : the Latin American Neo-Baroque / John V. Waldron.
pages cm
Includes bibliographical references and index.
ISBN 978-0-7391-7776-1 (cloth : alk. paper) -- ISBN 978-0-7391-7777-8 (electronic)
1. Latin American literature--History and criticism. 2. Globalization in literature. 3. Baroque litera-
ture--Influence. I. Title.
PQ7081.W326 2014
860.9'98--dc23
2013041444

∞™ The paper used in this publication meets the minimum requirements of American
National Standard for Information Sciences Permanence of Paper for Printed Library
Materials, ANSI/NISO Z39.48-1992.

Printed in the United States of America

To Lester Eugene Waldron and Betty May Waldron
Now you can stop asking

Contents

Acknowledgments

As I sit down to write this, thinking of all who have left their mark on me and in turn on this book, I realize that this section could be longer than the book itself. It goes without saying, and it has often been said, that a project of this or any length is impossible without a large and perhaps infinite network of assistance. Though the name of one person appears on this work, many others prop up that name. I would like to take an all too brief moment here to thank some of them.

The NEH Summer Seminar led by Andrew Debicki and Jill Kuhnheim at Kansas University was key in my development. I was surprised to be accepted to the seminar and am still thankful for the support they and other participants gave and still give me.

I presented many of the ideas developed here to the students in various iterations of WLIT 020, Spanish 142, and during an Independent Study with Emma Sector at UVM. Their doubts and questions helped me clarify many of my ideas.

Thanks to Sabah Ghulamali for her patience and enthusiasm. She, along with the readers' comments, was of immense and unquestionable help in shaping the final product now in your hands.

My research would have been impossible without the constant, cheerful, and well-informed support of the librarians at the University of Vermont. I would in particular like to thank expert book sleuth June Trayah as well as the librarians at Interlibrary Loan and Acquisitions who quickly and happily responded to my many requests.

Much of what I have written here was inspired by conversations I had years ago—more than I want to count—at the Moo Shi Factory with Tom Waldemar (don Tomás), Francisco Souza, Eleuterio Santiago-Díaz and Claude Mallory. The usually heated debates we had watching the sunset over the UCSB bike-path challenged me to think and see the world differently. Though years have passed, I'm still trying to work out many of the things we talked about there. To Rolando Romero, Carl Good, and Marcus Embry, I am thankful for the laughs, good food, and friendship. I'm particularly thankful to Rolando, whose frequent phone calls encouraged me to continue when I felt all was lost. Equally I am grateful to Yvette Aparicio, who read and commented on early, non-sensical, drafts of the manuscript that eventually became "the book." I am deeply thankful for the community, the *compañerismo*, (dare I say friendship?) of Joseph Acquisto, Todd McGowan, Hilary Neroni, Bea Bookchin, and Hyon Joo Yoo. They have created a "universe if not a university" that I always dreamed existed.

Without the "red pen," intelligent, sharp comments, *agudeza* and "cheerleading" of Emily Hind, what you have in your hands would still be an even more vague and muddled file on my desktop. Gracias, Emily.

I would also like to thank my parents who, even though I wish they had, never tired of asking me, "How's the book coming?" They, along with my siblings, Pamela and Christine, and my other parents, *mis suegros*, José D. González, Myrna Rivera, Gustavo González, and Wendye Li, provide the loving support of family that is difficult to explain, but impossible to live without.

Finally and most importantly, I would like to thank my wife, long-time friend, and life-partner, Kathryn González. Kathy knows me better than I do. She knows when to give me *un patatús*, when to leave me alone, and when to tell me to go do some home repair project that I hate doing. She gives me the balance, grounding, and love I often underestimate, but constantly need. I'm not sure what I give her, but then you know what they say about gifts . . .

Introduction

There are many scholars who have dealt with the philosophical and political problems caused by globalization in Latin America. Walter Mignolo, Alberto Moreiras, George Yúdice are just a few of the important theoretical thinkers connected to the topic. Similarly, famous literary critics such as Lois Parkinson Zamora and Wendy Faris have studied the neo-baroque and magical realism. My book combines theories related to globalization and its results in Latin America and the Caribbean with literary theories to show how the neo-baroque can be understood as a strategy that allows artists to rearticulate the imperial, colonialist gaze of globalization.

For many, the advent of globalization brought with it an end to the way that the world had been viewed previous to the fall of the Berlin Wall. Among the many endings the one that most concerns my book is the perceived foreclosure of alternatives to the capitalistic ideology that structures globalization. Even criticisms of globalization are bounded by its limits since the theoretical models that critics use cannot conceive of a space outside its homogenizing discourse. Against the final limits that shape most interpretations of globalization, I show how writers and thinkers on the periphery of the Globalizing North, through the development and deployment of neo-baroque imaginings, offer a different possibility to the totalizing gaze of globalization. I show that the baroque, and now the neo-baroque, is a way of resisting and reconfiguring the colonial gaze in Latin America since the time of the first encounter to the present.

A central point to my argument is the difference between the imperial gaze, as defined by Mary Louise Pratt, and the gaze, as Severo Sarduy and psychoanalytical theory understand it in general. Both definitions offer important avenues for exploration of the relationship between the Global North and its periphery. I argue that the imperial gaze observes the ravages committed in the colonial and globalizing process. The imperial gaze is one that totalizes the scopic field ignoring any fissures in the ideological fantasy it constructs. The gaze, as Sarduy and Jacques Lacan understand it, unsettles the mastery that empire would wish to exert by showing that there is a constitutive lack in any totalizing fantasy. Within the totalizing structure, there is always an element that cannot be fully assimilated to its fantasy. The element that is left out haunts the totalizing regime, reminding it of its own incompletion, thereby unsettling it. I argue that the neo-baroque and magical realism are artistic tools that unsettle the various narratives of colonialism and globalization.

In the first chapter called, "Globalization, the Neo-Baroque, and the Gaze," I introduce the reader to the key theoretical issues that will inform my argument. Here I contextualize the two theories of the gaze—proposed by Pratt and Sarduy—and put them within the larger, global context. In the second chapter called "*El reino de este mundo* and the Ghosts of Haiti" I analyze Alejo Carpentier's novel, *El reino de este mundo*, and show the relationship between Haitian history and globalization. I argue that Haiti haunts colonialism and globalization because it forms the underside to the modernizing project and progress in general. Haiti's revolution is something that the Enlightenment inspired and yet wanted to forget. I show how the ghosts of the Haitian Revolution stare back at the Global North even today, unsettling its claims of totality. In chapter 3, "The National Symptom in Three Puerto Rican Authors: René Marqués, Ana Lydia Vega, and Judith Ortiz Cofer," I analyze how Puerto Rico first tried to fend off colonialism by proposing resistance narratives based on the exclusionary practices of Spanish colonialism. I then show how two writers, Ana Lydia Vega and Judith Ortiz Cofer, make their readers aware of the constitutive lack in the colonialist models and the various responses. Their work unsettles any attempt at mastery or illusion of totality. I argue here that the lack of mastery is a negative that can actually become something positive. Where totalizing discourses want to define and limit subjectivity rendering them dead in Antonio Viego's words, by engaging lack, the subject actually becomes a subject. Chapter 4 called, "An Interlude: Magical Realism and Failed Incorporation," functions as a bridge between the first two chapters that deal with the neo-baroque and the last two that emphasize magical realism. This chapter connects magical realism to the neo-baroque and confronts criticism about magical realism. Here I argue that, while it is true that magical realism has been rendered an artistic form devoid of critical power by globalized capitalism, depending on the critical perspective employed, it can offer a great deal of potential with regard to globalization. In chapter 5 titled, "The Vanishing Real: Magical Realism's Political Swerve in García Márquez's "La increíble y triste historia de la cándida Eréndira y su abuela desalmada," I analyze García Márquez's story given the theoretical framework set out in the previous chapter. Here I argue that García Márquez uses magical realism to bring into the symbolic order things that would otherwise be erased from it. In this way magical realism and what it tries to represent haunts the closures and ends that globalization would like to affect. In the sixth and final chapter called, "Engaging the Darkness in Mayra Montero's *Tú, la oscuridad*," I return to the topic of Haiti, the neo-baroque, and magical realism. Montero's novel tells a more recent story about Haiti that shows how it still exists on the periphery of the Global North. Her story is a cautionary one that enjoins us to encounter our other as our equal rather than trying to colonize or otherwise control him or her. In her novel Montero shows how magical realism can work both ways, by showing how the Haitian character, Thierry, looks at Western culture as something that is magical. By reversing the traditional relationship of magical realism—where the Global North looks at the periphery as something magical—Montero destabilizes mastery.

The overall project engages artistic modes that have been practiced in Latin America and the Caribbean for quite some time. These artistic modes have been used to arrive at what Alejo Carpentier calls a "limit state" when he speaks of "*lo real maravilloso*." By arriving at the limit state, it is also possible to do something else that he was concerned with, actualizing history. By a reengagement with history and the constitutive lack in all representation, it is possible to reinitiate the dialectical relationship that can help move society and to vivify us as subjects. In one of its many implicit declarations, globalization has declared an end to revolution and an end to the dialectic. The result has been that we are left in a state of cynicism where we can only believe in technological "progress," or consuming as much as possible. By reinitiating the dialectic, it is possible to bring what Fukayama called "the end of history" to its own end.

Chapter One

Globalization, the Neo-Baroque, and the Gaze

This book analyzes the deployment of two modes of representation, specifically the neo-baroque and magical realism in Latin America and the Spanish-speaking Caribbean. It studies these two types of representation as responses to colonialism, neo-colonialism, and its latest iteration, neoliberal globalization. The colonial relationship that has divided the globe into a "center and periphery" is one that has not ended with other major historical events that, for many critics, have signaled epochal changes. The premise of the book rests on an assertion that is not new; the Global North exerts an imperial gaze in its encounters with the Global South. The central thesis is that the neo-baroque and magical realism destabilize the mastery projected by the Global North by making readers aware of the inherent lack in the imperial gaze itself. The neo-baroque and magical realism are the result of colonization from its earliest times to the present. They remind the colonial project of its underside. In chapters subsequent to this one I show how the neo-baroque and magical realism form a blot, stain, or imperfection in the North's masterful gaze by analyzing several canonical and not so canonical texts such as works by Alejo Carpentier and Mayra Montero among others. In what follows here, I will provide an outline of the theoretical framework that I will use in my analysis of those texts. The primary concern of this chapter is to delineate two types of gaze, the imperial/male gaze as described by Laura Mulvey and employed by feminist and post-colonial critics and the Lacanian gaze as described in Lacan's *Seminar X* and *Seminar XI* as well as by Severo Sarduy in his *Simulación* and *Barroco*. It is my contention that the understanding of the gaze proposed by Lacan and Sarduy offers the possibility for subversion of the colonial paradigm. First I will begin with a brief descrip-

tion of my interpretation of the current epoch as a continuation of colonialism and from there will define the general framework for this project.

Terms used to name different epochs of the colonial project are important
because they denote key technological, economic, historical, and perhaps
geographic shifts in its scope. The latest iteration of the colonial project, the
one I am currently living in as I write this book in the second decade of the
twenty-first century, is one of neo-liberal globalization. It might be argued
that this particular period is different from previous colonial moments due to
historical shifts such as: the end of the Cold War, the rise of a neo-liberal
China, the "flattening" of the globe due to technological advancements including the important rise of the Internet and other means to share data
instantly. Many who support this view would say that globalization and
attendant neo-liberalism offer an opportunity to "lift all boats." They would
point to economic indicators that would show that the standard of living has
increased in areas where neo-liberal reforms have been enacted as a key
example favoring their argument. However, this positive understanding of
globalization/neo-liberalism is only possible if what Walter Mignolo calls
"the underside" of colonialism is ignored. I can only conceive of neo-liberalism as a positive force if I am able to forget the fact that my T-Shirt was
made in a Bangladeshi factory that collapsed and killed over 1,000 workers;
workers who made less than 40 dollars a month.[1] Across the breadth of
several books Walter Mignolo has argued that perceived racial differences
that colonizers in the Global North used to justify its division of the globe
into hierarchies has created a "colonial difference" and an underside to modernity that has not ended with the advent of globalization and the fall of the
Berlin Wall in 1990 or Tiananmen Square protests and subsequent crack-
down in 1989, which marked the shift of China to a neo-liberal powerhouse
and the real end of the communist regime. These two events, the fall of the
wall and Tiananmen Square, marked for some people the end to an official
ideological opposition to capitalism.

The proclaimed end of colonial difference and the underside of modernity
is a key component in the ideological structure asserted by the Global North.
However, these "ends" are products of the ideological fantasy constructed by
the Global North itself, which removes references to labor and the stain of
oppression that provides the products that allow the North to revel in its
advancements. It could be argued that capitalism began much earlier than
1492 and was an important, driving force behind European expansion. However, Aníbal Quijano and Immanuel Wallerstein argue that, "The Americas
were not incorporated into an already existing capital world-economy. There
would not have been a capitalist world-economy without the Americas"
("Americanity as a Concept" 549). 1492 marks an important moment for
Latin America, the Caribbean, as well as the Hapsburg Empire for the obvious reason that it was when those two systems came into contact. The com-

ing into contact of these two worlds that were previously unknown to each other created a capitalist world system that continues to this day. The world system is how the world is divided as part of the project of modernity; a project that has as its reciprocal function colonization. Mignolo, describing the world system says, "Coloniality of power underlines the geo-economic organization of the planet that articulates the modern/colonial world system and manages the colonial difference" (*Local Histories* 53). However, the Global North seeks to erase the connection between coloniality and its much-heralded "progress" through economic expansion. From the perspective of the Global South the idea that colonialism has come to an end simply because it has a different name—such as globalization or postmodernism—is yet another example of how the North imposes its hegemony over the South. The relationship created by the inequities of modernizing progress and consequent colonization seems to work quite well for the Global North. The fact that the world system works so well for the Global North may be one reason why it chooses to continue ignoring the results of its own processes. The goal of this book in some respects is to observe the modernizing machinery of occlusion that is at work as part of the Global North's instrumental reason.

The imposition of power, whether economic, military or cultural brings along an ideology that confirms the Northern ideation of reality. That is to say that divisions are part of and implicit in the ideological fantasy that structures the world system. Anibal Quijano describes this relation as follows: "The coloniality of power and historical structural dependence both imply the hegemony of eurocentrism as a perspective of knowledge" ("La colonidad" 141).[2] Two things are implied with this statement: first, that knowledge rests with the colonizer and second, since knowledge is power, the colonizer is therefore able to ignore or defeat any propositions to the contrary. This is an example of the imperial gaze, or how the Global North asserts its mastery over the globe.

I: THE IMPERIAL GAZE: IDEOLOGY, DISTORTION, AND THE "INVENTION" OF THE AMERICAS

I am using the term "imperial gaze" as Mary Louise Pratt develops it in her landmark book, *Imperial Eyes: Travel Writing and Transculturation* (1992). In that work Pratt shows how sixteenth-century explorers wandered the world and, using a scientific system of classification developed by Carl Linné (Linnaeus) in his *System of Nature*, tried to systematize everything they came upon. Linnaeus' work held that it is possible to classify anything existing in nature into his invented system of knowledge. This systematization of the world into pre-established categories leads to what Pratt calls a "planetary consciousness." The "imperial eyes" armed European explorers with a scientific ordering that allowed them to gaze out at the unknown world with a sense of mastery. In a very real sense, Linneaus' system allowed the scientist to feel as if he knew the world even before he saw it since a category existed for everything in the predetermined system. The imperial gaze allowed the European and others of the Global North[3] to look out at the world with a sense of mastery over it.

Pratt emphasizes the importance of Linneaus and the scientific reason that supported the segmentation and hierarchization of the globe. Similarly, in his book *The Idea of Latin America* (2005), Mignolo points to the T-in-O map as a starting point for the division of the globe that results in placing Europe in a position of power with relation to other locations and peoples. With the T-in-O map the reason that supports the construction of divisions emanates not from science, but from religion. According to the Bible, the tribes of Israel were divided after the flood when Ham laughed at or ridiculed Noah's nakedness after a drunken party. Ham and his offspring were condemned to forever be the servants of the descendants of the other brothers. This created a world system that justified slavery and viewed the globe as divided between northern peoples who were generally of lighter skin and southern, African people. Mignolo relates in his *The Idea of Latin America* that:

> St Augustine, writing in the early fifth century, contributed significantly to continental racialization. Although the *term* "race" in today's sense is from the eighteenth-century, the *idea* of superiority imbedded in the Christian classification of the people by continent was already in the T-in-O map. (27)

The division of the globe based on religious belief into racial categories that set up a hierarchical power structure is one that predates and shapes the conquest itself. It forms an essential part of the "imperial eyes" with which Europe looked at the lands they were invading and colonizing. This is to say that the basis to the scientific system of rational categories used by science is a primordial division of the globe into a hierarchical structure based on perceived racial differences.

Mignolo and Pratt's study show that the sensed state of mastery is only possible as the result of a distortion. Linnaeus' system, like the T-in-O map, distorts the globe. Using the scientific and racist framework in their encounters with the unknown, the position of the European explorer as knowing, masterful subject will be affirmed rather than upset or questioned. Knowledge then is a distortion of reality. This is a clear example of how ideology functions and, in fact, how it has worked and continues to work in global, planetary relations. As Jorge Larrain says in his analysis of Marx's conception of ideology, "Human beings do not contemplate reality as something already formed, they represent it as they construct it" (65).[4] Understood in this way, ideology is a distortion that we create that shapes and limits our ability to understand the world around us. In *The German Ideology*, Marx says, "Men, in the development of their material production and their material interactions, alter, along with the world around them, as well as their thoughts and the production of their thoughts" (47). The imperial gaze, like any ideological framework or fantasy, distorts reality according to its own limited understanding. As I will show, a crucial difference between the imperial gaze and the gaze as studied by Joan Copjec via Lacan, is that it accepts its own fantasy as real.[5] That is, the colonial, imperial gaze is completely unaware—and does everything it can to remain unaware—of the limits of its own system. As Slavoj Žižek says whenever speaking about ideology, in the first stage of ideology, "we don't know what we are doing and we're still doing it." This self-deception is entirely necessary if one is to maintain and assert a sense of mastery over the world. Part of the self-deception is that we don't understand that the illusion, the fantasy created by the distortion, is on the side of reality itself. That is to say, reality as we can only know it is already a distortion.

Expounding on the relation between illusion, ideology and fantasy, Žižek says that in the current age we are no longer in the first stage of ideology in which we were unaware of the illusion or fantasy created by ideology, but that we are in a second stage: "We know very well what we are doing and yet we are still doing it." For example, most of us are entirely aware that our consumption of inexpensive products is linked to abuses of workers and the environment on the other side of the globe, and yet we still consume them. For example, I still buy T-Shirts made in sweatshops even if they aren't in Bangledesh. Or, as is happening as I write this, I might still watch the Confederation Cup football tournament in Brazil even as there are protests in the streets reminding me of the reasons I shouldn't: money is being given to sports rather than feeding and education the underprivileged. Or, I—living in the Global North—try to overcome my guilt by purchasing something that will make me feel as if I am making a change. Maybe I will buy coffee at Starbucks because it will send money to some poor farmer. Or perhaps I will buy Tom's Shoes since in purchasing the shoe, I am told a shoe will be purchased for someone in Africa who doesn't have shoes. These are all ways that we in the Global North have of dealing with the guilt the capitalist system causes us. None of them actually do anything to change the system itself. Detailing how the relationship between ideology and fantasy work Žižek says the following:

> They know very well how things really are, but they are doing it as if they did not know. The illusion is therefore double: it consists in overlooking the illusion, which is structuring our real, effective relationship to reality. And this overlooked, unconscious illusion is what is called *ideological fantasy*. (*The Sublime Object of Ideology* 33)

The point of criticism and this book is to try to see the illusion for what it is and to understand how it forms the reality in which we function. Several Latin American critics have already done work in this area, pointing out the illusion is created by the colonial ideological fantasy.

The imperial gaze and how it functions in the Latin American context is studied by Enrique Dussel, in particular in his *The Invention of the Americas: Eclipse of "the Other" and the Myth of Modernity* (trans 1995). Here Dussel studies the relationship between the European explorer and his native other by studying representational models. Similar to Pratt's understanding of the imperial gaze, Dussel shows how the European never really saw anything that he had not already invented or imagined before coming to what he called "The New World." To the European explorer, this place of newness was not really new, but rather a repetition of already formed models. Dussel defines a relationship between the European "I" and its Other as being one of "the same" rather than one of difference. That is to say that the European in its encounter with the radically different others he found in the Americas is unable to see or interact with his others as other because he is constantly trapped in his own perceptions and the limits of his own representation. The European for Dussel is functioning within the limits of an ideological fantasy. As Dussel says, "This Indian was not discovered as Other, but subsumed under categories of the Same. This Indian was known beforehand as Asiatic and re-known in the face-to-face encounter and so denied as Other, or covered over (*encubierto*)" (32). The force of his will and worldview are so great that the European discoverer is unable to view, interpret, or interact with his others as other. Dussel underlines this by means of play on words in Spanish. Rather than *descubrir* a word that at its root means to literally "uncover or reveal," Dussel says the explorers *encubrieron* or covered over their others, making it impossible to ever see them. This activity of "covering over" the other will underlie all interactions between powerful, colonizing countries and their others, from the conquest until the present. In this way the power of representation, the power to be and say, in the new world created after Colón's journey, is removed from those who are ethnically, racially or sexually different from cultures at the center. This activity of converting all differences into identity is one that continues until today in globalization.[6]

Perhaps one of the best and most startling examples of how this functions is in Bartolomé de las Casas' transcription of Cristobal Colón's[7] notebooks. In Colón's third voyage as transcribed by Bartolomé de las Casas, he tries to explain why stars seem to change their position in the sky and his measuring instruments no longer work as they do elsewhere. His way of finally dealing with the problem that causes his instruments to fail will set a precedent for how Europe, and in the future the United States, will interpret Latin America and other continents such as Africa. Though, perhaps since what he does merely conforms to the pre-established ideological framework that divided the globe, what he does cannot really be called a precedent, but more of a continuation of a project that was well underway. Colón says that he had always believed that the world was round as Ptolemy and others had proven via scientific observation, but now he has seen such "Deformity [. . .] and for that reason I began to think this of the world, and I found that it was not round the way they write about it, rather it has the shape of a pear and that it is round except there where the nipple is at the highest point, or like someone who would have a real round ball and in place of it were the shape of a woman's tit placed there, and that part that is the nipple is the highest part, closest to the sky" (238).[8] Such an image might come as something of a shock to us now as we live in a post-feminist age, but in the history of Western representation depictions of the female body often arise during times of anxiety and are often used to depict the threshold figure between one world and the next. Though she is presenting her study on women in nineteenth-century England, what Anne McClintock says could easily be applied to the times that Colón or Las Casas were writing, "In myriad ways, women served as mediating and threshold figures by means of which men oriented themselves in space, as agents of power and agents of knowledge" (*Imperial Leather* 24). Here, Colón feels disoriented as he returns for the third time to what will be called *América*, and he reacts to that feeling of loss of control through an act of representation.

It might be said as others have already done, that he names the world in order to control it in an act similar to those of the scientists using the Linnean system described by Pratt. The picture Las Casas via Colón draws now of the world is of a woman who is in repose since, in order for the nipple to be the highest point the woman would necessarily have to be reclined. So she is in a defenseless position welcoming, or at least not defending herself against European exploration. This welcoming portrait will be repeated often as is the case with the famous woodcut of Vespucci coming to America and in the language used by the early discoverers and conquistadors. What the male conquistadors decide to do with this welcoming image is evident in the language of rape and violent penetration, which pepper any text written by a chronicler of discovery who follows Colón into America. As they relate their stories of conquest, they don't explore so much as penetrate the jungles of what they call the New World. This is not to say that because of Colón's text rape happened during the period of colonization—rape and other violations certainly did happen abundantly—but rather that his text forms a mode of representation, a way of viewing the world; an ideological fantasy. It not only shows how the colonialist ideological fantasy functions when it relates to the unknown, but the Las Casas translation of Colón's voyages become a text that produces the same ideology. Colón's text and others give some insight into how the representation of woman's body is used to exert control over an experience that creates anxiety and offers the possibility for change and difference in perception and even being. It shows how representation is used not just to relate information, but also to exert control or mastery over an unknown and perhaps uncontrollable situation. As a cultural text that is reporting events seen and experienced by the colonizers, it is also one that reproduces ideology adding another text to the archive of facts that assert mastery. The ideological fantasy is as racist as it is sexist.

The weird image that Las Casas forms is so strange and distorted to those of us reading it two hundred years after its composition that it generates a lot of different questions. What creates the anxiety in Las Casas' transcription of Colón's text is that he sees that the world is no longer round; better, it is no longer a perfect sphere without hierarchies. The "deformity" he sees is that the shape is not one of an orb, or an apple, but rather one of a pear; a shape that is more narrow at the top than it is at the bottom. One way of reading this is that Las Casas is mashing the round shape of the globe into the more triangular, hierarchical shape of the Great Chain of Being. This would allow the King and Queen, who are his audience, to be able to be more accepting of the heretical round shape since it allows them to maintain their space of dominance at the time of the pyramidal, or pear-shaped structure.

As the third voyage continues, Las Casas' reason for his seemingly strange and problematic structuring of the globe becomes evident. He notices that the people living in the more northerly areas of the pear-shaped breast of his newly envisioned globe have a lighter complexion and that the farther one gets from the *pezón* the people become darker. His recognition gives reason to his journey:

> And now that your Royal Highnesses have commanded that the globe be navigated and searched and discovered, it is shown very evidently, because I was on this journey to the *septentrión* twenty degrees from the equinoctial line, there was on the right of Hargin and those lands and there the people are black and much burned. And later I went to the islands of Cabo Verde, and there in those lands the people are a lot more black, and as I went lower to the Austro, even more do they arrive at the extreme [of blackness]. (239)[9]

The perceived increasing degree of blackness as one travels farther from the north or the nipple gives Colón, via the transcription of Las Casas, a reason for his travels. Also, in a way that is reminiscent of travel novels as well as the quest or spiritual progress tales, Colón finds the true reason for his journey after he has been lost. It all makes sense to him now. The panic that so troubled his men in earlier voyages when the North Star appeared to move and was eventually lost is now fully explained; he is able to find the words to explain it and to locate himself and difference within the order of things. The North Star's movement is also relevant to the degrees of blackness he finds in the people, "Where the North Star rose during dusk five degrees, there the people are extremely black" (239).[10] Eerily, the North Star's location now becomes a means for finding the "most extremely black" people. The people closer to God have lighter skin, the farther away from God you get, the darker your skin. Indigenous people are in some intermediary stage between black and white, which allows them to be saved or converted to Christianity. Africans are the darkest, and therefore the farthest from God. Their distance from the divine means that conversion would be impossible, so it is perfectly justifiable to enslave them and treat them like animals. As this racist understanding of the global world system's structure enters into order and language it becomes knowledge and that knowledge forms part of the colonial machine that will be lubricated by the blood and sweat of African slaves. Here we see a clear case of how the ideological fantasy functions.

As Las Casas tries to make sense of the world Colón is seeing, he is also organizing the knowledge, based on what he already knows, into the system he already has: The Great Chain of Being. This organization of knowledge also serves several functions. First of all it calms the nerves of anyone reading the text, rather than being so frightened by the new and radically different, the reader will be able to see how his pre-existing worldview already has a place for what is seen within the system they already know and master. While it may be upsetting momentarily for the colonial reader to see these new things, it is also comforting since the new organization of the globe still leaves Europe at the top and in a position of power. The Chain of Being is a hierarchical organizing structure that gave order to the world by using the body as a metaphor for the organization of the cosmos. Generally speaking the King/Queen along with the Pope were at the top of the body, the nobles beneath them, and the lesser nobles beneath them, and so on forming a pyramidal body in the form of a hierarchy. As Las Casas through Colón looks at the world—now round, he maintains the round shape along with the hierarchy by giving it the form of a pear. Rather than allowing it to be a perfect sphere where there would be no up or down, he imposes the figure of the pear/breast on the round shape and thus incorporates the new discovery into the pre-existing hierarchy. This also allows him to give support to his argument of the importation of slaves to America. For, if the indigenous people are lighter, they are also in a place higher up on the breast/pear/Great Chain of Being and if Africans are darker, they are farther away from the top and so farther away from God and much closer to the base elements. Following the rationale here, for this reason it is a morally correct decision to enslave the "extremely dark" rather than the lighter "Indians" since Africans are farther away from the top. The conclusion to the syllogism based on the ordering of the world had a powerful and horrible effect.

It is important to make clear that the text I have been referring to is translated by Bartolomé de las Casas and not the original as written by Colón. Las Casas translated or transcribed Colón's text into a Spanish that was more easily digested by the Spanish public. Living up to his role as *traductor*, *traídor*, he changed the language and he also changed the story in a way that confirmed and produced imperial ideology and mastery. Colón's original text is rather tedious and straightforward in its description of his various journeys. Las Casas' text captures the emotion of travel and the wonderment of the traveler, Colón, but it is also written with specific audience in mind, the Spanish nobles and the courts, for a particular reason. As many know, Las Casas is the famous defender of the indigenous people of America and wrote against their enslavement. A problem with his argument in defense of the Indies created was that the vast mining and agricultural practices during Spanish colonialism worked more profitably with cheap, slave labor. If the indigenous people could not be used, then the Empire had to look elsewhere. Las Casas' translation of Colón's journals views the shape of the world through a lens that allows him to justify the protection of Native Americans and the enslavement of Africans. As we all know, his argument had terrible effect, Africans were kidnapped and sold into bondage in America. What may seem to us as Las Casas' odd way of perceiving the world—as a pear or breast not only showed the new European discovery within the order of the old, but also showed the way, by following the North Star, to what would be the future.

This is the way that the imperial gaze functions. It supports the ideological fantasy of the Global North in its encounters with others. It is similar to the gaze as discussed by Laura Mulvey in her essay, "Visual Pleasure and Narrative Cinema." This important essay informed feminist criticism of cinema and formed the basis for many cultural studies interpretations of cinema and the power dynamics represented on the screen. Other important cultural critics, such as bell hooks, employ an understanding of the gaze or the look that is similar to Mulvey's as they write about the construction of racial and gender hierarchies. Though Las Casas is obviously not a film director, it is possible to understand his way of looking at the world as one that is "scopophilic." According to Mulvey, Freud in his *Essays on Sexuality* discusses scopophilia where he locates looking as a type of pleasure that also implies control. As Mulvey says, Freud "associated scopophilia with taking other people as objects, subjecting them to a controlling and curious gaze" (485). As Las Casas looks out at the Americas and the world in general, he, like other explorers and conquistadors, looked out at the recently discovered territories and peoples with a great deal of curiosity; however, this look also subjects them to a type of control that assures his mastery. As Mulvey further argues, "In a world ordered by sexual imbalance, pleasure in looking has been split between active/male and passive/female. The determining male gaze projects its fantasy onto the female figure, which is styled accordingly" (487). The power imbalance puts the person in power; the male or the colonizer in the active position and the disempowered figure is "styled" according to the desire of the person in power. That is to say that the representation itself is shaped or distorted in order to conform to the desire of those in power. Clearly, the way Las Casas imagines the globe shows how he styles it according to his own desire and his own ideological fantasy.

Mulvey's understanding of the gaze is, as will be discussed below, a partial one based on an understanding of Lacan that was not informed by his *Seminars*, which would be made public after her essay was written. It is helpful, however, to employ her understanding because it gives a clear picture of how the ideological fantasy is constructed by the male or imperial gaze and it makes evident that something must be left out, or *encubierto* in Dussel's terms, in order for the fantasy to continue functioning. In what follows, I will show how the baroque and neo-baroque reveal the limitations of the ideological fantasy through an expanded understanding of the gaze via Lacan.

II: THE STAIN IN THE PICTURE: THE FOUCAULDIAN AND LACANIAN GAZE

Mulvey's interpretation is important and has led to a lengthy bibliography of studies that has revealed the functioning of the male/imperial gaze. However, as important as studies subsequent to hers have been, they are based on a partial understanding of the gaze in psychoanalysis. This is an important point because the Lacanian understanding of the gaze denies mastery of the subject over the object. Years after Mulvey's article was published, Lacan's *Seminar XI: The Four Fundamental Concepts of Psychoanalysis* became available in which he adds an important dimension to the gaze.[11] Lacan's understanding of the gaze shows how the gaze contains within it something, a spot or stain, that is un-representable that he called the *objet petit a*. This stain or blot that is entirely unassimilable by representation or the symbolic order has the effect of undermining our mastery of the thing we look upon. The subject, already split or "barred" by language, looks at the object and asks "*Che vuoi?*" what do you want? As a result of this question, his or her preoccupation becomes one of trying to satisfy the desire of the Other. In large part, the difference between Mulvey and Lacan is that Mulvey's understanding of the gaze is influenced by Foucault's interpretation of power, which places a primacy on the visible; it seems to avoid the understanding that subject cannot see everything or that there is always something in the picture or what the subject looks at that escapes its ability to contain it. Lacan on the other hand, emphasizes the mis-recognized, non-representable spot or stain that is in the gaze.

In Joan Copjec's detailed analysis of the gaze in *Read My Desire: Lacan Against the Historicists*, she shows how critics grounded in Foucault's understanding of the panopticon have interpreted it. Copjec argues that:

The panoptic gaze defines *perfectly* the situation of the woman under patriarchy: that is, it is the very image of the structure that obliges the woman to
monitor herself with a patriarchal eye. (17)

In this type of structure some other sitting in a tower looks at and can see
everything. In addition, what is looked at must conform to the law imposed
by that look. In Mulvey's and subsequent formulations, this Other is the
patriarchal male subject who sits in a position of power and is able to survey
and master the world. An understanding of the gaze grounded in Foucault
emphasizes the visible denying the existence of the invisible. In fact, the
panopticon eliminates any possibility for the hidden, anything that might be
invisible to the other sitting in the tower. As Copjec argues, "The perfection
of vision and knowledge can only be procured at the expense of invisibility
and nonknowledge. According to the logic of the panoptic apparatus, these
last do not and (in an important sense) cannot exist" (*Read My Desire* 17).
The understanding of the gaze Copjec articulates here has important implications on several different levels for criticism in general and for my understanding of it here in particular.

The importance of the visible can be traced back to the Cartesian *Medita-*
tions in which Descartes attempted to find what he could truly know. For
Descartes the visible is valued as knowledge and as reality itself; for this
reason he limited his inquisitions to what he could clearly and distinctly
perceive. His emphasis on the visible and the capacity for reason to arrive at
a clear and distinct perception in turn gave rise to the scientific method of
which Linneaus was a part. For those who followed Descartes' *Meditations*
the perceiver is able to grasp reality through clear and distinct perception and
then is also able to fit everything into a predetermined set. Using this system
of analysis, the critic of power employs his or her ability to perceive and
know reality to bring to light inequities and problems within the social structure. Similar to film criticism after Mulvey, critics are able to locate the male/
imperial gaze and its functioning in cinema and bring to light the way that
power is structured. In this understanding everything is determined by visible
relations of power. Though it is possible to point to conflicts and differences
within this structure, they are still, nevertheless, contained within the limits
of the visible and power's functioning. As Copjec argues:

Not only is it the case that at each stage what is *produced* is conceived in
Foucauldian theory to be a *determinate* thing or position, but, in addition,
knowledge and power are conceived as the overall effect of the *relations*
among the various conflicting positions and discourses. Differences do not
threaten panoptic power; they feed it. (*Read My Desire* 18)

With globalized capitalism examples abound to prove the final phrase in the above quote. One of the unique abilities of globalization is that it absorbs and commodifies difference.

In his analysis of "McDonaldization" Jan Nederveen Pieterse shows how Burger King, KFC, and other multinational food corporations adapt menus to "local conditions" saying that "it would make more sense to consider McDonaldization as a form of intercultural hybridization, partly in its origins and certainly in its present globally localizing variety of forms" (51). He concludes his argument saying, "Accordingly, the clash between cultural diversity and globalization may well be considered a creative clash" (58). But if it is creative, it is so only in the most visible and even superficial way. A counter argument would show that the "clash" between McDonalds and vegetarian local culture in, say, India may have resulted in a veggie burger on the menu, but has not resulted in the same type of systemic change that McDonalds and the presence of other multinationals has effected in India. The encounter with difference is incorporated and hybridized into the company's structure making it an even more profitable enterprise, but nothing substantial has changed in the way the corporation operates on the local or multinational level.

Similarly, George Yúdice in his study *The Expediency of Culture: Uses of Culture in the Global Age*, analyzes among other things hip-hop music produced in Brazil that is radically critical of globalization and neo-liberalism. The music originally was self-produced and sold without the intervention of recording studios. However corporations became aware of this music and offered contracts to the artists, thus incorporating this radical critique into the very system that it was and still is criticizing. As Yúdice says:

> Consequently, the failure to repeat normative behavior as the constitutive feature of subversive performativity may actually enhance the system rather than threaten it. The system feeds off "disorder." (33)

Difference, the more radical the better in some cases, sells. This is an evident statement to anyone who has seen a commercial advertising something that is "new and improved." No one wants the same old thing, so manufacturers give us the appearance of difference. In fact, global capitalist enterprises find a way to "sell to" the revolutionary impulse many might have, as Yúdice's example makes evident. The music industry doesn't change, quite to the contrary.

As much as we have contact with the "different" we also see how the system—in Yúdice's words—feeds off and incorporates difference. What room is left then for criticism or even art other than to show how power functions? But, after seeing the horrors of power, there is always the question, what to do? That is met with depressing cynicism. The relationship between cultural analysis and its resultant cynicism drives at the heart of the problem with the Foucauldization of the male gaze and the importance it places on the visible. I would argue that a way to avoid cynicism is to look awry at the multinational, capitalist edifice by taking another look, and another approach to the gaze.

The Foucauldian interpretation of the gaze and culture in general is quite different from the Lacanian proposition. As Copjec argues, difference or conflict in the Lacanian understanding would not be the result of "the clash between two different positions but from the fact that no position defines a resolute identity" (*Read My Desire* 18). It points to the invisible and to "the incompleteness of every meaning and position" (18). The ramifications of this difference are important: "Incapable of articulating this more radical understanding of nonknowledge, the panoptic argument is ultimately *resistant to resistance*, unable to conceive of a discourse that would refuse rather than refuel power" (18). Like Yúdice, Copjec notices how the system is "resistant to resistance." For Copjec the reason that critics are unable to articulate a refusal to power is because criticism is trapped in the visible and not concerned with what she terms "nonknowledge." Nonknowledge is labeled as such because it resists articulation within the economy of the visible, symbolic order. It is part of the register of the Real.

For Lacan the subject is not a subject of knowledge—a subject supposed to know—but is always constructed in relation to language and the unconscious. To become a subject one must enter into language and that journey results in the split or barred subject. This splitting of the subject creates a lack that the subject will always want to fill unsuccessfully. The subject enters into an anxious relationship with the Other since the subject feels that it is being observed or gazed at by the Other. It looks at the Other and asks "What do you want?" Rather than mastering the other via the gaze, the subject is, on the contrary, determined by the gaze of the Other. As Lacan relates, "What determines me, at the most profound level, in the visible, is the gaze that is outside. It is through the gaze that I enter light and it is from the gaze that I receive its effects" (*Seminar XI*, 106). In this way it is the subject that is constituted by the gaze of the Other and not the reverse.

In a reversal, the gaze is not something we or I control; rather it is something that peers out at us, like the figures in Velázquez's *Las meninas*, from the object revealing to us our own lack. In this way the "Real effect" of representation is engaged by full and unreserved encounter with the object. As I will discuss in the next section, this is something that both Sarduy and Lezama understood as they undertook to write an expression of "nuestra América."

III: SARDUY AND THE GAZE

José Lezama Lima begins *La expresión americana* and Sarduy starts *La simulación* by analyzing European painting. It could be said that the two Cuban authors "look back" or "return the gaze" of the hegemonic colonizing culture as they analyze and criticize its representational practices. However, it is evident that the two Cuban writers study the gaze in ways similar to those articulated by Lacan.[12] Sarduy's analysis of the Hans Holbein painting *The Ambassadors* is strikingly similar to the one given by Lacan of the same painting in *Seminar Book XI* in the chapter "Of the Gaze as *Objet petit a*." Sarduy moved from Cuba to Paris in 1960 and became part of the *Tel Quel* group. He cites Lacan's work and it is even possible that he attended the seminars where Lacan spoke about the gaze since Sarduy spent a great deal of time in Paris and worked on the critical magazine *Tel Quel*, where figures like Julia Kristeva, among others published their works. Sarduy's *La simulación* is not a mere repetition of Lacan's essay. In fact, ironically enough, the Cuban writer develops the Lacanian understanding of the gaze in order to explain the difference between copy and simulation. In this way he attempts to add another twist to the understanding of the gaze while showing that his text is not a copy of Lacan's work, but rather a simulation.

For Sarduy, a copy would presuppose an original that the copy reproduces in mimetic fashion. The original would hold some sort of power over the copy since it would be thought to be closer to some sort of truth, essence or authenticity than the copy. Simulation for Sarduy and Lacan is rather a chain of signifiers constructed over the empty space separating me from my other. As Sarduy puts it:

> *It is not a vacuum that germinates whose metaphor and simulation are visible reality* and whose life and understanding are liberation. It is emptiness, the initial zero, that which in its mimesis and simulacrum of form project a one (a singularity) from which will issue the entire series of numbers and things [. . .] a pure non-presence that transvests into pure energy engendering the visible with its simulacrum. (20)[13]

What he says here with regard to simulation underlies his and Lezama's understanding of culture as a point-counterpoint relation that has no primary and secondary term resulting in a final overcoming. That is to say, while it does create a dialectic of sorts, it is not one that results in a final synthesis or overcoming of tensions.

The symbolic order, or language, can only function with laws such as grammar and other social codes of grace and etiquette we are all taught to follow. When someone asks us "How are you?" we say "Great!" and even put on a big smile in spite of the fact that our life is in ruins. We know that our interlocutor really does not care how we are, and to tell him or her the inside scoop would be against the law or normative social codes in some respects. The crucial point that Sarduy is making, along with Lacan, is that we are duped into believing in the primordial, original nature of these laws. That is, the symbolic order and the ideological fantasy it constructs has tricked us into believing in its virtual reality as well as its history.

As with all legal structures, in the symbolic order a tremendous amount of importance is given to precedence, or what came first. If the symbolic law can make us believe that *it* came first, then we also feel as if we must follow that law because that is all there is. As Žižek argues, whenever we speak to another we always have in mind the big Other, the law of the symbolic authority. It watches over us in all we do and say. What is more, "it is sustained by our continuous activity" (Žižek, *How to Read Lacan* 11). Our speech and engagement with the symbolic order gives life to the big Other, the law watching over us all the time much like Orwell's Big Brother, "It exists only in so far as subjects *act as if it exists*" (Žižek, *How to Read Lacan* 12). What Sarduy is pointing out in the quotation above is the provisional or virtual nature of the symbolic laws governing language and social interaction. He is also pointing to the void, the lack that is part of the construction of the symbolic order itself. If Europe and coloniality can be said to be the big Other since it is takes the place of the (colonial) law that gazes at Latin America, Sarduy points out the fact that within this law itself is a devastating emptiness.

Sarduy is arguing that there is no such thing as an original signifier that grounds all discourse. Rather, the symbolic law emanates from "el cero inicial." Similarly, Lacan argues that the "master signifier," the originary, primordial symbolic node, is "supported by some 'pure,' meaningless 'signifier without signified'" (97). The original moment that structures culture, that gives nations and their citizens their identity, is based on a symbolic law and a master signifier that is stretched over "el cero inicial," in an effort to hide its own lack. For Sarduy it is the *horror vacui*, the fear of lack or absence, often spoken about in relation to the baroque that initiates and is interwoven in signification. It is this fear of the Real trauma, fear of lack or the void that causes us to create symbolic structures. The mistake that we all commit is to think that there is some primordial, essential signifier from which all culture, all language emanates; that there is some answer that will fill the lack or absence we feel or solve our trauma once and for all. This is an important point for Sarduy and for any thinker wishing to pose a counterpoint to European culture.

Though it is evident in Lacan that we are all, in a sense, victims of language or as Žižek argues, "Language is a gift as dangerous to humanity as the horse was to the Trojans: it offers itself to our use free of charge, but once we accept it, it colonizes us" (Žižek *How to Read Lacan* 11). We are all colonized by language; however it is also possible to find some respite from authority in the symbolic order. Throughout Sarduy's essay *La simulación* he analyzes how butterflies, as well as artists, reformulate the image or symbolic order to create a hiding place for themselves. Strategically, language can create a camouflage where it is possible to hide from the view of those more powerful such as state censors and so on. As Lacan argues, "the human subject, the subject of the desire that is the essence of man—is not, unlike the animal, entirely caught up in this imaginary capture. He maps himself in it. How? In so far as he isolates the function of the screen and plays with it" (*Seminar XI*, 107). The human subject, a subject of desire created by the lack in the big Other, is able to "play with" representation and in this way avoid being captured by it. This is an important point for Sarduy and other Latin American writers since it shows how the neo-baroque artist can evade the repetition of and capture by the colonial law. However, for Sarduy, what seems to be even more important is what the big Other hides. What is important in the Lacanian economy of the gaze is the dimension totally absent from Mulvey and her followers—the absence, the vacuum, the lack that exists at the very heart of the gaze.

To show his understanding of the gaze, Sarduy analyzes the *trompe l'oeil* and anamorphosis available in some paintings, particularly *The Ambassadors* by Hans Holbein. When seen straight on, this painting seems "realistic." The problem is that there is a blot or stain at the bottom that stirs our curiosity. As we move to make sense of this shape, or as we look at it awry, we can gradually make out that the skull at the bottom of the canvas. Our movement to make sense of the picture, as Sarduy says, implicates us in the picture itself, "the subject is implicated in the reading of the spectacle, in the decipherment of the discourse, precisely because of that which he or she is unable to hear or see what concerns the subject directly" (28).[14] We become implicated in the picture because we know something is hidden and we want to know what it is. Our desire is initiated by the blot or stain in the picture and our need to make sense of it; we want to be able to contain the entire picture to control it and to "know what it means." Sarduy says of this phase:

> Among the concepts with which the pragmatics of communication operates, anamorphosis corresponds without residuals to that of *disinformation*: "obstacles, impasses and illusions, which on the contrary tries to deliberately dissimulate it." (31)[15]

The picture escapes our ability to totalize and make complete sense of it. This destabilizes our sense of mastery over the object as well as over discourse. The relation is reciprocal. The picture controls us by initiating our desire, by gazing out at us and beckoning us to enter into dialogue with it, and revealing to us its lack as well as our own lack. That is, what captures our attention, and generates desire, is the stain that signals absence or the void. The fact that we find the skull as the *horror vacui* of death puts us face to face with the trauma of the Real, our own loss of control and our own lack.

The reciprocal relationship Sarduy describes here refigures the bond between subject and object so that neither has mastery over the other. What does happen is that they both show each other their own lack—we see the lack in the painting as the painting makes us aware of our own lack—and that our dialogue with each other is constructed over the empty space revealed by absence. No one is in control and no one is first. What is revealed is the empty space in the law of the big Other. Speaking of this same occurrence in Lacanian theory, Žižek says:

> The most radical dimension of Lacanian theory lies [. . .] in realizing that the big Other, the symbolic order itself, is also *barré*, crossed-out, by a fundamental impossibility, structured around an impossible/ traumatic kernel, around a central lack. Without this lack in the Other, the Other would be a closed structure and the only possibility open to the subject would be his radical alienation in the Other. (*"Che Vuoi?"* 122)

Since both I and my other are subjects in the symbolic order and that order, the big Other, is also structured over an absence, "el cero inicial," then neither I, nor my other, nor the big Other can claim mastery.

Going back to Las Casas, we can see how he reacts to his inability to master the world by establishing an order that conforms to an ideological fantasy. However, he doesn't recognize the fantasy as such and therefore is not aware of its limitations. For Las Casas and others functioning under the order of the imperial gaze, there is no lack, there is no absence. Everything can be explained within the colonial order itself. Within that order, functioning under the imperial gaze, subjects are completely unaware of the constitutive, traumatic lack that is at the center of the ideological fantasy they create.

Understanding the relationship between subject and other as one based on lack, whose origin is a "cero inicial," Sarduy envisions all interactions as elliptical rather than dialectic. Imagining an elliptical structure rather than a circular one is an essential point in Sarduy's articulation of a discourse of *contraconquista*. As Sarduy says of the ellipsis, "The shift from Galileo to Kepler is a movement from the circle to the ellipse, from a shape that is drawn around a One to what is drawn around the plural, the shift from the classic to the baroque" (*Barroco* 19n3).[16] The relationship here between the representational practice of the baroque and the scientific understanding of the universe is not just a nice image. By drawing this comparison, Sarduy shows that just as the planets have always moved in an elliptical pattern even before Kepler discovered that fact, so too has Latin American discourse and culture existed in an equal, parallel relationship to Europe and other hegemonic discourses. The fact that Latin America is different from but equal to Europe is one that has been obscured due to the same political, social and cultural assertions of power that obscured the heliocentric theory and caused astronomers like Galileo to be branded heretics or worse. It is also a fact that has been obscured by the ideological fantasy that reigned at the time, a fantasy that would not allow for an elliptical conception of the universe.

As Sarduy and Lezama write of the baroque as a discourse of *contraconquista* they reveal that Western history and representation is based on a repression of the fact that there are two equal terms in the relationship. The second term was repressed or obscured because it was ideologically impossible for the second term to be accepted as a possible reality. Given the reigning ideological structure of the time, and of our time as well, it was or is only possible to assert a singular, monologic understanding of the world and representation. As Sarduy argues:

> The ellipse, in baroque rhetoric, is identified with the mechanics of obscurity, repudiation of a meaning that is expulsed from the symbolic universe, [. . .] "the ugly, the uncomfortable, the disagreeable" disappear by means of an "adept whisking away or cover up" that allows for "the disgusting name and the horrible detail" to flee. (*Barroco* 70) [17]

The second term in the elliptical relationship is largely obscured or repressed by traditional representational practices. If it does appear, as it does in the Spanish baroque, it is repudiated as something undesirable and lesser than the primary, unifying term supported by dominant culture.

Sarduy's assertion of the ellipsis brings to light and valorizes the second term placing it on equal footing with the other. The planets revolve around both terms, not just the singular, visible one. Eleuterio Santiago Díaz argues for the importance of this theoretical understanding in the creation of a *discurso de contraconquista* when he says:

> Of course, in the context of the neo-baroque, the ellipsis is already a figure of superior complexity. An expression of a new cosmology, the most radical neobarroque ellipsis is articulated like a proliferation that signals the rupture of the homogeneity of logos and lack as an epistemic foundation for the subject. (85) [18]

By bringing to light this second term, Sarduy forces a reconsideration of the relationship between colonizer and colonized, between the Global North and the Global South. Rather than viewing the interaction between Europe/United States and Latin America as a dialectic that initiates from a first term and seeks unification in a final, third term, he re-inscribes an interrelationship of the *contrapunteo*. Since there is no unifying ideal to strive for, or to be judged against, the dialectic then moves in an indeterminate direction; like the symbolic order, it is stretched out over the void.

The shift to the *contrapunteo* also requires a move away from the master/ slave dialectic that has characterized much criticism concerning Latin American culture, particularly that emanating from United States and British academe. Sarduy and Lezama's essays are part of a chorus of Latin American and the Caribbean critics who have described culture in a way that does not repeat the colonial dialectic in the traditional way established by European invaders and their intellectual legacy. In what the Puerto Rican critic, Arcadio Díaz Quiñones, has described as *el arte de bregar*, Puerto Rican and other Caribbean cultures have "dealt with"[19] the incursion of foreign cultures in a way that avoids the master/slave dialectic that structures the colonial relation. This master/slave or colonial dialectic that forms such an important part in the way that many study Latin American culture through a prism a center/periphery relationship, where Europe and the United States are at the center, and the periphery is a place where all other cultures and peoples are located. This relationship is one that understands culture from the guilty position of the master looking out at his other. The guilt often results in self-righteousness since it initiates a salvational desire—and salvational theories—with respect to the other who is in bondage. Though the intention in studying culture from such a perspective is to uncover colonial abuses and free people from oppression, it nevertheless has the effect of condemning the very people the master critic wishes to free to the role of colonized in a closed dialectic. As Rubén Ríos Ávila says:

> Perhaps there is no fantasy that is more frequent and more venomous in coloniality than the one that gives freedom to the one who is structurally defined from subordination. The most onerous condemnation that the master imposes on the slave in the colonial structure is that of freedom. (*Raza cómica* 31–2)[20]

It should be underlined here that the "liberation fantasy" is imagined by the master, not the slave, and comes as a result of a dialectical view of reality informed by modernist principles and abuses. The master views the colonized/slave as being closer to nature and therefore nearer to some real, essential truth that would liberate the master from his self-created alienation, an effect of his technological or modern progress. What underlies this relationship then is the colonizer's smug attitude that the colonized is in some way undeveloped while the colonizer's culture is complete. As Ríos Ávila explains, "the colonized is always the body *in development* [. . .] with respect to an Other that defines itself from the beginning as *previously developed*" (32).[21] The Other in the colonial fantasy presents himself as whole, not lacking in contrast to the master. On the other hand, the colonial subject is judged by its distance from the Other. Sarduy's analysis of this relationship shows that both are lacking or incomplete thus upending the relationship between master and slave. Sarduy's understanding of our relationship with the Other is one of *contrapunteo*. The aim is no longer toward a singular ideal, but rather toward the constitutive lack. The object cause of our desire is the absence, void, or lack that we sense and wish to resolve. However, resolution is impossible. Lacan says, "the function of the hole is not univocal" (*Seminar X,* X 3),[22] meaning that what we draw around the lack, the surface or topology that we create in our efforts to come to terms with it, are not definitive or complete. This means that we engage in a dialectic with this absence, this hole, that can never be completely symbolized.

Though the Hegelian dialectic is usually thought of as one that results in a final overcoming, Žižek offers a different understanding in his introduction to *The Sublime Object of Ideology,* when he says:

> [. . .] far from being a story of its progressive overcoming, dialectics is for Hegel a systematic notation of the failure of all such attempts—'absolute knowledge' denotes a subjective position which finally accepts 'contradiction' as an internal condition of every identity. (6)

That is to say there is no final overcoming in the dialectic resulting in an unfragmented identity or a subject that is not barred. At best there is a realization of how distant one is from the perfect unity implied by the imagined synthesis. This leads me to the second problem related to subjectivity and the location of the critic. In order for critics to exert the type of closure they want, they cannot accept the premise that the subject is split and unable to obtain absolute knowledge of its object. Rather, on the contrary, the critic in this case must claim absolute knowledge for himself. For criticism that emphasizes visibility over lack, the critic rushes to end the anxiety created by our relationship with our other and answer the question, "What does the other want?" by creating a final overcoming resulting in a satisfactory (at least to the critic) answer.

As satisfying as any ending is, especially if it is an apparently ethical one that offers liberation to oppressed minorities, Sarduy sees the danger in any such closure. If one were given to overgeneralizations and grandiose assertions, it might be said that the history of Latin America is a story of the attempts made by many to assert ideological closure. This manifesto-like statement underlies criticisms of coloniality and might conceal one essential fact regarding all encounters and language itself: It is necessary to have closure, and in fact we cannot live without the illusion of closure. Like the big Other of the symbolic order, closure allows us to make sense of our world with language. However, as Sarduy argues with his discussion of anamorphosis and simulacra, we have to recognize that closure is constructed over a void. The void, hole, absence, lack, and so on are words used to describe what Lacan calls the Real.

I would argue that as critics, the best we can do is to perform our function, to appropriate without reserve in an effort to keep alive the trauma of the Real. In this way we bring knowledge up against its own failure, risking ourselves and discovering our own lack in the process. The fatal error we would commit as critics would be to try to circumscribe this effect, to frame it in our own critical guillotine, or by placing the subaltern or some other figure in its place, thus removing the Real effect from our relation to our other. As Todd McGowan argues, "interpretation—or appropriation without reserve—must keep alive the trauma of the Real in the interpretation. This is the reason why absolute interpretation can never be fascist interpretation. Fascism wants no part of the Real; instead it wants symbolization 'returned' to a harmonious balance, without the threat that the Real constantly provides" ("Condemned" 126). As critics we are charged with the obligation to keep alive the trauma of the Real no matter how painful or unsettling it is. In fact, I would argue that it is necessary to keep the trauma of the Real alive precisely because it upsets any claims of mastery we might have. As Sarduy argues, rather than search for an assertion of the One, we should recognize the second term that has always been there and place it in relation to the other. Not in order to allow one term to assert its hegemony over the other, but so it might engage in a *contrapunteo* with that other. In this way a dialogue without reserve and without end begins. In this book, I argue that the encounter with the other in magical realism and the neo-baroque allows for a such a dialogue with Latin American culture and with racial and ethnic others in general.

IV: LEZAMA LIMA AND THE BIFOCAL BAROQUE

Lois Parkinson Zamora begins her massive and comprehensive study, *The Inordinate Eye: New World Baroque and Latin American Fiction* (2006) with a quotation by Leonardo Da Vinci on bifocalism: "Objects seen with both eyes appear rounder than objects seen with just one" (xiii). Placing Da Vinci's quote next to Saturnino Hernán's painting *Coatlicue Transformado* (1918), she begins her convincing argument that describes the baroque as a truly transcultural and transatlantic art form. It might even be argued that European contact with the Americas caused a revolution in seeing on both sides of the Atlantic, perhaps resulting in a bifocalism that is so important to the baroque. The central argument to Parkinson Zamora's book is that the bifocal baroque way of seeing was always present in the Americas, even before European contact. Bifocalism is when the artist encounters an ideological fantasy entirely different from his or her own and, rather than asserting mastery or control, attempts to represent both visions of the same event at once. In the chapter on Carpentier, I will show how he does this in *El reino de este mundo.* The effect of the American, baroque, bifocal way of looking at art and the world literally de-centered the vanishing point that was so important to European classical art and thus affected a revolution in European representation and ways of seeing. With the baroque the vanishing point took up a position that is either far from the center of the painting or, as is the case in Velazquez's *Las meninas,* with its multiple vanishing points and eyes gazing out from that painting, the vanishing point can be located at a place beyond the canvas, somewhere between the viewer and the eyes gazing out at her or him. As the painting's gaze looks out at the viewer, it unsettles her or him rather than letting the viewer feel mastery over the painting that a single focal point would allow.

This interplay between viewer and viewed in the baroque is quite different from the relationship that is allowed and even invoked by the classical placement of the vanishing point around which the entire painting is ordered. The symmetry of classical painting places the viewer in an objective position removed from the painting itself, which creates the illusion of control or mastery over the object of representation. Baroque art, as Parkinson Zamora so frequently argues, places the viewer in the work itself and erases the boundaries between viewer and work as well as between the work of art and its referent. In this way, she argues, baroque art adopts a particularly American perspective, one it absorbs from pre-conquest indigenous practices. By emphasizing the element that destabilizes mastery, Parkinson Zamora finds a different way of looking at the relationship between Europe and America by appropriating it. For her, in terms of indigenous American cultures, "[T]here was no dichotomy between presence and absence, no assumed separation between the image and the object. The image was not distinct from its referent, but integral to it according to culturally determined systems of analogy" (13).[23] Whether or not Indigenous people really thought this way is unknown. Parkinson Zamora, however, commits a neo-baroque or "New World Baroque" act herself as she appropriates Indigenous representation.

What is important in her formulation of the interplay between Europe and America is that the baroque emphasizes multiple perspectives that have the effect of blurring or even obliterating boundaries that other ways of thinking, perhaps more classical ways, would like to keep in place. In this way, the baroque causes the viewer to doubt his or her own position with regard to the art object and the world where the classical work reaffirms mastery and stable, rooted location. By doing this, Parkinson Zamora shows how the American gaze, looking back at the European, has the ability to unseat colonial mastery. The subject's mastery over himself,[24] his object, and the world are all unsettled by the American bifocalism. Though the European colonizer might try to exert a single gaze, the multiple perspectives looking back at him will always unsettle his attempts.

José Lezama Lima emphasizes the bifocal, transnational interplay between America and Europe in his essay, "La curiosidad barroca" (an essay that forms part of the collection *La expresión americana*) by quoting an unnamed critic who said, "land was classic and the sea is baroque" (33).[25] This quotation was meant as a criticism of baroque art and intends to recognize an irresolvable dichotomy between the two forms and perhaps even between America and Europe. Showing how false this dichotomy is, sea/land, baroque/classical, and how representative it is of European thinking, Lezama says, "we see that here his (the unknown author's) dominions arrive at the height of arrogance, since the baroque hispanic folksongs [or sheds] travel through a sea tinted with ink equally baroque" (33).[26] Making a play on words with "galeón" the ship and "galerón"—a shed or folksong—Lezama shows how even what is thought to be the most national, local, or rooted in the earth, the folk song, is also influenced by the American baroque. With the quotation of a critic who sees the sea/baroque/America and land/classical/Europe as separate and his criticism of it, Lezama emphasizes the *contrapunteo* between Europe and America as he did in "Mitos y cansancio clásico," the essay that precedes "La curiosidad barroca" in *La expresión americana*. However, in "La curiosidad barroca" he makes a conscious effort to distinguish the baroque as a particularly "American expression." Rather than being a mere mimicry or repetition of European forms, for Lezama the baroque is "un arte de contraconquista" (34).[27] Similar to Sarduy in *La simulación,* by situating the American baroque as an "art of counter-conquest" he distinguishes American baroque from the European in part by showing how American baroque is not related or built on top of previous European forms. The instability in European mastery caused by the discovery of the American baroque, is one phase in the "contraconquista" Lezama talks about. Because of its position as descendent of the more classical renaissance, the baroque, like American art, is often denigrated or left in a marginal position.

For many European critics and, perhaps even some artists, the baroque is often characterized as an ugly, degenerate form that is built on top of the more symmetrical classical forms. One etymology of the term makes this evident by showing how the word for a deformed, undervalued pearl—the baroque pearl—is also the one used for the artistic movement called baroque. Seen this way the baroque is not only the continuation of the more classical renaissance, it is also its crumbling, devolved death. As Gonzalo Celorio says in, "El barroco en el Nuevo Mundo, arte de contraconquista," an essay appearing in his *Ensayo de contraconquista*, "such a solution of continuity propitiated that a structural figuration of its own was given to the baroque, it was considered a variant, deformed or hyperbolic, of classical structure" (78).[28] This might be true for the way the baroque developed in Europe, but in America the classical influence is not so preponderant. The connection between the classical and the baroque in Europe led to a baroque that is, in

Lezama's words, an "accumulation without tension and asymmetry without plutonism" (Lezama "Curiosidad" 34).[29] And according to Parkinson Zamora, the baroque sensibility existed even before the European invasion so it is not a mimicry or a deformation of a previously existing form; it becomes something that is not able to be fully digested by the structural limits of European representation. Lezama argues that Latin American baroque maintains "plutonismo" that breaks "los fragmentos y los unifica." There is also a dynamic, explosive tension in baroque art which, like *el contrapunteo*, results in a dialectic of opposites that does not result in a final overcoming (34).

There are several issues brought up in Lezama's characterization of the baroque that are important as they relate to globalism and the presumed tension between the local and the global that are necessary to investigate further. They are all problems rooted in how the relation between opposites is perceived. One possibility views the dialectic in a way that maintains one of the values as more powerful than the other and also that this dual relationship will result in a final overcoming of opposition. The other best described by Fernando Ortiz in his study, *El contrapunteo cubano del tabaco y del azúcar*, sees the relation of opposites based on Caribbean models of the "contrapunteo" or point, counterpoint. In this dialogue between opposites, the two values interact with each other, affecting and changing each other. As characterized by Lezama, the relationship between opposites is one that does not end with any finality; it simply goes on and on. The relation of "contrapunteo" is one that is proposed by American baroque thinkers and artists and it effects how the relation between global and local is articulated in their works and those that come after.[30]

VI: MAGIC REALISM, THE NEO-BAROQUE, AND LACK

By locating magical realism and the neo-baroque with lack as I do in the subtitle above, it is not because I understand either as in some way deficient. Quite to the contrary, they are works that are all the more engaging precisely because lack is apparent in them. The central reason that the dialectic or *contrapunteo* is without end is precisely because in the process of symbolization something must be left out. The absence of this missing piece causes desire in the subject for completion. The desire for completion creates a dialectical movement that I, in agreement with Lezama Lima and Ortiz, have been calling a *contrapunteo* because totality is a structural impossibility. The nature of this relationship is that the symbolic order creates lack in the process of symbolization and this lack sets it off on a journey to try and achieve wholeness.

To take a simple example we can think of the roles that society has made for us—professor, husband, wife, father, mother, coach, cook, cable installer, and so on—when I inhabit the role of professor for example, I never feel entirely comfortable in that role because it doesn't completely define who I feel that I am. There is always something left out, such as my abilities as a cook, my fanaticism for the Minnesota Vikings, and so on. Lacan calls this missing piece the *objet petit a* cause of desire. This missing object is the blot on the picture that reveals the insufficiency of the structure itself.

When the viewer or reader becomes aware of the blot in representation, he or she becomes implicated in the work itself. Todd McGowan talks about this in relationship to *The Ambassadors* saying:

> The skull says to the spectator, "You think that you are looking at the painting from a safe distance, but the painting sees you—takes into account your presence as spectator." Hence, the existence of the gaze as a disruption (or a stain) in the picture—an objective gaze—means that spectators never look on from a safe distance; they are in the picture in the form of this stain, implicated in the text itself. (*The Real Gaze* 7)

We are implicated in the picture through the function of desire. The stain in the picture or text, the thing that does not quite fit, signals to a lack or a hole that we feel the need to fill. It is my contention that magical realism and the neo-baroque create the possibility for readers and viewers to engage with texts in this way. Such a type of reading or understanding of texts evades the totalizing male/imperial gaze. I argue that the way magical real and neo-baroque texts do this is by several means of destabilizing vision. One way that magical realism and the neo-baroque engage the viewer is through "bifocalism".

In the chapters that follow I will try to show how the gaze functions in neo-baroque and magical real texts through various narrative techniques, especially bifocalism. My argument is that the gaze in the texts I analyze is not only a way of looking back at empire, but that they also resist any desire we might have for totalization. In this way the texts I analyze make us aware of the ideological fantasy that we currently inhabit. By pointing out the lack or void at the very center of the fantasy's construction, and by inviting our participation in the creation of the art object itself, the authors also disrupt our sense of mastery and invite us to imagine alternative futures. By reading in this way we can start to avoid the cynicism that is such a necessary part of the perpetuation of the current fantasy supported by neoliberal globalization.

NOTES

1. I am referring here to the recent building collapse in Bangladesh on April 23, 2013, http://query.nytimes.com/search/sitesearch/#/bangladesh+factory+collapse.

2. "La colonidad del poder y la dependencia histórico-estructural, implican ambas la hegemonía del eurocentrismo como perspectiva de conocimiento" (ALL translations from Spanish are mine).

3. From 1492 on, the Global North would have included largely European nations as they expanded their connections throughout the world, by the twenty-first century, the term can be used to characterize northern cultural and economic centers including the United States, China, Russia, as well as Europe.

4. "Los seres humanos no contemplan la realidad como ya formada, la representan a medida que la construyen."

5. As I will detail below, the essential difference is that for Mulvey and Pratt, the gaze is the way the subject exerts power over his other. He imposes his gaze on the other assuring his place, his control, his mastery. For Lacan, the gaze is in the other and as a result, the subject has no control over it. In fact, the gaze destabilizes the subject.

6. There isn't room here to compare and contrast differences between colonial projects. It is true that there were and are differences and that I am, perhaps, over generalizing here to make a point. Essentially my point is that there is a commonality between colonial projects and throughout time that has not ended in spite of the many differences and apparent revolutions we have had.

7. I use "Colón" instead of Columbus to avoid the appropriation of Colón by the United States.

8. "[. . .] disformidad [. . .] y por esto me puse a tener esto del mundo, y fallé que no era redondo en la forma qu'escriven, salvo que es de la forma de una pera que sea redonda salvo allí donde tiene el peçon que allí es más alto, o como quien tiene una pelota muy redonda y en lugar d'ella fuesse como una teta de muger allí puesta, y qu'esta parte d'este peçon sea la más alta e más propinca al cielo."

9. Y agora que Vuestras Altezas lo an mandado navegar y buscar y descobrir, se amuestra evidentíssimo, porque estando yo en este viaje al Septentrión veinte grados de la línea equinoçial, allí era en derecho de Hargin e de aquellas tierras e allí es la gente negra y muy quemada. Y después que fui a las islas de Cabo Verde, allí en aquellas tierras es lagente mucho más negra, y cuanto más baxo se van al Austro, tanto más llegan al estremo.

10. [. . .] adonde se me alçava la estrella de Norte en anocheciendo cinco grados, allí es la gente negra en estrema.

11. To readers of Spanish, Lacan's understanding would have been available much earlier in Sarduy's essay on *Simulación*. I will discuss Sarduy's approach later in this section.

12. As is well known, Sarduy was part of the *Tel Quel* group in France, which included the likes of Julia Kristeva, Michel Foucault as well as many others. The group studied the revolutionary impact of Lacanian theory as well as Marxism and other lines of thought.

13. [. . .] no [es] *una vacuidad germinadora cuya metáfora y simulación es la realidad visible* y cuya vivencia y comprensión son la liberación. Es el vacío, o el cero inicial, el que en su mímesis y simulacro de forma proyecta un uno del cual partirá toda la serie de los números y de las cosas [. . .] una pura no-presencia que se trasviste en pura energía, engendrando lo visible con su simulacro. (20 emphasis in text)

14. "[. . .] el sujeto está implicado en la lectura del espectáculo, en el desciframiento del discurso, precisamente porque eso que de inmediato no logra oír o ver lo concierne directamente en tanto que sujeto."

15. Entre los conceptos con que opera la pragmática de la comunicación, la anamorfosis corresponde sin residuos al de la *desinformación*: "obstáculos, impasses e ilusiones que pueden surgir cuando se está *volunatriamente* en busca de una información o que al contrario se trata *deliberadamente de desimularla*." Here Sarduy quotes Paul Watzlawick, *How Real is Real? Communication, Desinformation, Confusion*. New York: Random House, 1976 (6).

16. "El paso de Galileo a Kepler es el del círculo a la elipse, el de lo que está trazado alrededor del Uno a lo que está trazado alrededor de lo plural, paso de lo clásico a lo barroco."

17. La elipsis, en la retórica barroca, se identifica con la mecánica del oscuricimiento, repudio de un significante que se expulsa del universo simbólico [. . .] desaparece "lo feo, lo incómodo, lo desagradable" mediante un "hábil escamoteo" que permite huir "el nombre grosero y el horrendo pormenor."

18. Desde luego, en el contexto del neobarroco latinoamericano, la elipsis ya es una figura de una complejidad superior. Expresión de una cosmología nueva, la elipsis más radical del neobarroco se articula como una proliferación que signa la ruptura de la homogeneidad del logos y la carencia como fundamento epistémico del sujeto.

19. For the word *bregar* or the expression *bregar con* the best translation is to "deal with" something as it comes up. Sometimes it is possible to hear in response to the salutation, "How are you?" or "¿Cómo estás?" the simple reply "Bregando" or "Estoy bregando," which means a lot of things, such as that I am dealing with the adversities that life throws in the way. Díaz Quiñones devotes an entire book to talking about the subtle meaning of this phrase and its importance to Puerto Rican culture.

20. "Acaso no haya fantasía más recurrente y venenosa en el coloniaje que la de su liberación, que la de la liberación de aquello que se define estructuralmente a partir de la subordinación. La condena más onerosa que el amo le impone al esclavo en la estructura colonial es la de la libertad."

21. [. . .] el colonizado es siempre un cuerpo *en desarrollo* [. . .] con respecto a un Otro que se define de entrada como *previamente* desarrollad.

22. I am citing from a recent translation of this *Seminar*. Each day of the seminar has its own pagination. In this case the X 3 refers to day 10 (X) page 3.

23. It should be kept in mind here that this is decidedly the critic's point of view regarding Indigenous, American art. Parkinson Zamora is performing a neo-baroque or New World Baroque act by appropriating Indigenous discourse and redirecting it.

24. I use the masculine here because it is most often the male who is seen as being in a position of mastery over himself and those he encounters and attempts to dominate.

25. "[. . .] la tierra era clásica y el mar barroco."

26. "[. . .] [v]emos que aquí sus dominios llegan al máximo de su arrogancia, ya que los barrocos galerones hispanos recorren un mar teñido por una tinta igualmente barroca."

27. For more on Lezama and the art of *contraconquista* see Brett Levinson's *Secondary Moderns Mimesis, History and Revolution in Lezama Lima's* American Expression.

28. "[. . .] [t]al solución de continuidad propició que al barroco se le negara una configuración estructural propia, pues se le consideraba una variante, deformada o hiperbólica, de la estructura clásica."

29. "[. . .] acumulación sin tensión y asimetría sin plutonismo."

30. Recent studies have pointed out many of the problems with Ortiz's model and, in particular the silencing of the work of Lydia Cabrera. For more on this see Edna Rodriguez Mangual's *Lydia Cabrera and the Construction of an AfroCuban Identity*.

Chapter Two

El reino de este mundo and the Ghost of Haiti

Alejo Carpentier's novel, *El reino de este mundo* (1949) is still one of the only and best known novelizations originally written in Spanish of the Haitian Revolution. Given Carpentier's pedigree as a well-educated white male who was conversant in the literary "classics" of the Western World, his novel can be read as an attempt to incorporate the representation of one of the most important events in World history into the collective consciousness of the Global North. As Susan Buck-Morss argues in her book, *Hegel, Haiti and Universal History*, the Haitian Revolution had wide-reaching effects in global history; nevertheless, even to this day, it does not form part of the information dispensed in most history books. It is absent from the ideological framework forming the basis for globalization and the Global North's ideological fantasy. As Buck-Morss argues, slavery is part and parcel of the Global North's so-called progress and modernizing project. As Buck-Morss says: Haiti, which was the most profitable of all slave colonies, paradoxically facilitates "the global spread of the very Enlightenment ideals that were such a fundamental contradiction to it" (21). The money colonial France made from the most successful colony in the world, Haiti, essentially funded the Enlightenment. Slavery is, after all, the underside of the Enlightenment just as modern forms of labor that all but enslave workers are the underside of Globalization. As Buck-Morss and Michel Rolph-Trouillot argue, Haiti forms an absence in the retelling of World history and the glorification of Western dominance. For that reason I choose to focus this chapter entirely on the single most important narrative in Spanish written about one of the most important and forgotten events in World history: the Haitian Revolution.

Though Carpentier's novel may be the only extended treatment of this important historical event in Spanish, it is not without its problems. Perhaps the most glaring of all of the difficulties he presents to any reader the least bit knowledgeable of Haitian history are the absences of key figures of the Revolution combined with the hyperbolic and one-sided representation he offers of Henri Christophe. I will analyze the silences and exaggerations, first taking into consideration the way other critics have responded to them. Ultimately I conclude that the silences in the Cuban author's text are constitutive of the ideological fantasy in which Carpentier, colonialism, and globalized capitalism function. The silences form a lack that is at the very center of the symbolic order that forms the basis for the ideological fantasy first of colonialism, and now for globalized neo-liberalism. My conclusion concerning Carpentier's position with regard to the Haitian Revolution is somewhat ambiguous. I see the silences in his narrative as an invitation, or at the very least an opportunity, for future readers to investigate them in an attempt to arrive at a more complete understanding of an important historical event.

Alejo Carpentier was born of a Swiss mother and a French father. Though many critics accepted his own assertion that he was born in Havana, Cuba, it has been recently revealed that he was born in Lausanne, Switzerland, and taken to Havana by his parents when he was still an infant. He grew up in Cuba where he attended excellent schools and was entirely fluent in French and Spanish, which he spoke with a noticeable French accent. In 1928 he fled the Machado dictatorship for Paris where he stayed until 1939 and became a member of the Surrealist movement. He published his first novel in 1933, *¡Ecue-Yamba-O!*, where he attempted to portray African culture in Cuba by echoing the popular movement at the time of *negritud* of which he formed a part. In 1939, when he returned to Cuba, he took a trip to Haiti where he became aware of the Haitian Revolution and began research on it for what would be his second novel, *El reino de este mundo* (1949). In 1944 he traveled to Venezuela and took a journey down the Amazon. He said that he wrote drafts of a novel to retell this experience, but it was never published. Many critics consider his third, and most popular novel, *Los pasos perdidos* (1953) to be based on his impressions of his journey since it is told from the perspective of an unnamed "I" who travels down the Orinoco. In 1959 he returned to Havana after the victorious Cuban Revolution and remained loyal to Castro until his death in 1980. As Roberto González Echeverría notes, "Carpentier lived, and certainly died, in Paris, as an ambulatory Minister of Culture for the Revolutionary government. Significantly, however, he spent long periods of time in Havana, staying in the Hotel Nacional or Free Havana (formerly the Hilton) as if Cuba were not his *patria*, but rather a place that he visited on a tour or on vacation" ("Ultimos viajes del peregrino" 120).[1] Similarly, many of his protagonists are wanderers through important historical events and across the globe. Over the course of his career he published several significant novels in addition to those mentioned as well as essays on music and the aesthetics of the novel.

Alejo Carpentier has almost what can be categorized as an obsession with revolution, discovery, and African culture. In three of his first four novels, *¡Ecue-Yamba-O!*, *El reino de este mundo*, *Los pasos perdidos*, *El siglo de las luces* (1962), and *El arpa y la sombra* (1979) either the theme of discovery, revolution, or both are portrayed. In the first novel, *¡Ecue-Yamba-O!*, he narrates historical events taking the perspective of Africans in the Caribbean. He shows the poverty that confronts Afro-Caribbeans as well as the inner turmoil it causes. In his first novel he reveals a theme that will unite at least three of his novels, namely the frustrated desire for revolutionary change. His second novel, *El reino de este mundo*, tells of the events leading up to the Haitian Revolution, its explosion, and its aftermath. The novel relates the story largely through the eyes of Ti Noel, an African slave, who struggles with revolutionary changes and the shifting allegiances they bring. This novel also seems to show the failures rather than the successes of revolution ending with a stark, existentialist pronouncement. In *El siglo de las luces*, Carpentier tells the story of a little known hero of the Guadalupe revolution, Victor Hugues, and the young, fictional, Esteban, who follows Victor from Cuba, to France, Spain, and Guadalupe where he witnesses revolutionary events first hand. *El arpa y la sombra* shows the failed beatification process of Cristobal Colón as told from the perspective of those involved as well as a middle chapter that relates of his life told in interior monologue.

I: CARPENTIER AND HISTORY

Carpentier was a history buff, and it could be said that much of his work serves to uncover the forgotten moments and heroes in Caribbean history. Forming part of the Afro-Cuban movement, of which Nicolás Guillen is the most famous member, Carpentier writes about African culture, which had been present in the Caribbean for centuries, but which was also the object of oppression, silencing, and occlusion. Many of his narratives are concerned with the history of oppression in the Caribbean and the interrelations between the different races and ethnicities in the area. However it is impossible to understand his novels from a critical perspective that only includes the postcolonial rubric of resistance narratives. Though his books do present some of the same problems found in later postcolonial narratives, Carpentier is concerned with the impasse that occurs when we meet our other and how we attempt to overcome that point of antagonism and the violence that often results in any attempt to do so. Unlike a positivist-inspired understanding of history that imagines and seeks progress through a series of historical overcomings, Carpentier is more concerned with re-marking the closures caused by close repetition of any period or endpoint at the finish of any historical event. Carpentier examines the wreckage left in the wake created by Western histories forging ahead.

As Roberto González Echeverría's landmark work, *Alejo Carpentier: The Pilgrim at Home* (1977) shows, an antagonistic relationship underlies Carpentier's encounter and experience of culture that shapes his narrative and his representation. Some of the oppositions in his work and in his life are Europe and America, white culture and black, spoken word against music, present and past, man and woman, foundations and decay, just to name a few. Carpentier's interest in history and dissimilar cultures could stem from his own interpretation of Oswald Spengler's work. As González Echeverría argues, Oswald Spengler's *The Decline of the West* influenced Carpentier as well as his contemporaries Guillén and Fernando Ortiz among others throughout the Caribbean. González Echeverría goes to great lengths to show the connection between Carpentier's worldview and Spengler's work through an extensive analysis of Carpentier's bibliography in *Alejo Carpentier a Pilgrim at Home*. In addition to Spengler's work, González Echeverría argues that José Ortega y Gasset was equally important in the Cuban writer's formation.[2] González Echeverría's study links Carpentier to Spain and Hispanism as well as an important Western understanding of history. By connecting him to Ortega y Gasset, and the *poesía pura* movement, he also emphasizes the mythic elements of Carpentier's storytelling that distances his narratives from historical and real world events. From this perspective, what happens in the world is used as fodder for the "greater work" of art; an art that is objective, cold and distant from the emotions and turmoil of the real world.

Given Carpentier's interest in Spengler he saw that the Americas, particularly Latin America, was a place of ascendency in contrast to what Spengler saw as a declining Europe. But this concept of ascendant cultures conflicts with another aspect of Spengler's philosophy that is also evident in Carpentier's representations. Spengler's thought, perhaps like the fragmented, multicentered concept of history and culture he promotes, is also multilayered and at times contradictory. On one hand, Spengler points out, there is not one single center for culture. Rather, cultural centers are multiple and shift over time. However, his conceptualization of historical movement is ultimately relativistic since, in order to perceive and judge ascendancy and decline, one would have to have a fixed standard by which to judge where a given culture sits on the scale of decline or ascent. According to Spengler, Europe had achieved ascendency and was in a state of demise. Carpentier saw in America the possibility for the creation of a new culture and even perhaps the birthplace where a new symbolic structure would be made as González Echeverría shows (*Pilgrim* 59–61). But Carpentier also had to be aware that, given the Spenglerian conception of history, birth also leads to decay; that the formation of new symbols often results in the return of similar structures or patterns of oppressive hierarchies. This cyclical conceptualization of time, that Spengler justified basing his conclusions on observations of natural processes, leaves little room for progress or change.

At the risk of reducing his very complex narratives to a single series of sentences, it might be conjectured that Carpentier's novels, particularly the first five, portray the possibility of revolution that often quickly decays into a return of the same patterns. He frequently occludes or avoids representing moments or figures that might herald change or real difference from the past, oppressive models. For example, after the turmoil in *¡Ecue-Yamba-O!* nothing seems to really change; there is nothing but devastation. In *El reino de este mundo*, Ti Noel is left to contemplate the results of the Haitian revolution and observes that newly freed and victorious former slaves were enslaving Africans during the reign of Henri Christophe. As he transforms himself into different animals living first in ant society and then, finally, in goose society, he notices that the same hierarchies and the same oppression, exclusions and practice of marginalization exists in all cultures. In *Los pasos perdidos*, the least historical of the first four novels, the protagonist—an unnamed "I"—literally loses himself in the jungles of South America to find a new music, a new essential sound. But he winds up losing everything because he does not have enough paper to write down his music. He returns to civilization thinking he can go back to Santa Monica de los Venados, but he can never find the waterway to find the town again. As in his other novels, the protagonist "I" is presented as a border character in the sense that he feels at home with the indigenous Americans where he "speaks the language of his mother," which is Spanish and not a native American tongue, as well as in the unnamed large, Northern city where he speaks a different language from Spanish. In the end he is both at home and not at home everywhere. In *El siglo de las luces*, the young Esteban follows Victor Hugues to Spain and Guadeloupe where they try to help spread the French Revolution. Esteban only sees the disastrous consequences as each revolution fails to live up to its ideals resulting in systems that reflect the earlier, oppressive regimes. There is no real change and all the characters can hope for is that they won't get fooled again, to somehow find a place that is outside of history and its violent changes.

It is possible that one reason for this pessimistic view of history and change had to do with Carpentier's understanding of Spengler as well as with his chosen form of expression: narrative. In poetry, such as that by Nicolás Guillen and other Afro-Caribbean poets, it is easier to incorporate the musicality of non-European signs into the texts; in narrative this is much more difficult. It is, in part, for that reason that Carpentier, along with many critics, see his first novel—*¡Ecue Yamba O!*—as something of a failure since he tried and was unable to capture the musicality, the difference of Afro-Caribbean speech in that novel. As González Echeverría points out, the scarcity of novels that have come out of the Afro-Caribbean movement is proof that "in

narrative the problems were much more complex. The linear, temporal flow
of narrative possesses a historical dimension that is contrary to instantaneous,
ahistorical nature of conversion [. . .] Carpentier's narrative in the thirties and
forties will be a struggle with this problem and a search for a theology of
history, for a teleology that will endow the signs of his narrative with new
meanings within a continuum" (*Pilgrim* 61). González Echeverría concludes
that Afro-Cuban religion will be the place where Carpentier finds the "symbolic plenum within which to inscribe the flow of such a history" (*Pilgrim*
62). That may be true, but what seems more evident is that in his discovery of
Afro-Cuban or Afro-Caribbean culture, Carpentier did not necessarily find
one that was in a stage of growth that was somehow lagging behind that of
Europe, but one that was parallel to it and in a dialectical opposition. In this
way he follows Spengler, whose philosophy advocated for a conceptualization of history that would create a Copernican revolution in terms of how
history and different cultures were understood in relation to each other. Even
though there is latent Euro-centrism in his argument, Spengler argued that,
rather than judging the development of other cultures based on how well they
conformed to the Western model, they should be understood on their own
merits. Spengler proposed that each culture was its own center that had a
uniquely particular history and evolution. Instead of conforming to one model of linear progression, Spengler argues that each culture had its own story
that was entirely dissimilar from others. This radical difference between
cultures and the results of their intersection is something that Carpentier tried
to work out in his novels and with his formulation of "*lo real maravilloso*."

As González Echeverría points out, many thinkers in Latin America
latched on to Spengler's ideas since they allowed them a philosophical
ground on which they could construct their own history. That is, if they
ignored the implicit euro-centrism in his argument, they could establish their
own difference without the concern of living up to a European standard of
development. Though Spengler did have a vision of history that could be
categorized as reflective of "cultural relativism" there remains within his
relativism a residual euro-centrism. Added to the fact that Spengler saw
Europeans as more advanced, he considered them detached from culture
(what we would call nature or his natural self). Due to their detached, objective posture with regard to the world, Europeans were therefore better able to
experience culture intellectually. This element in Spengler's thought coincides with Ortega y Gasset's conception of *poesía pura*, which González
Echeverría asserts is important to Carpentier's aesthetic.[3] For Spengler, the
American, particularly the Latin American, is not detached from his culture/
nature and therefore his consciousness is fused with it. Following this mode
of thought, eventually Latin Americans would reach the evolutionary state
now lived by Europeans, but they would still not attain as high a level of
ascendency since they were not naturally distanced from their circumstances.

That is to say, according to this highly problematic understanding of the world and historical change, Latin Americans are incapable of the objective distancing necessary for philosophical and scientific thought. In fact, much recent criticism of magical realism—which many see as emanating from Carpentier's definition of "*lo real maravilloso*"—is seen by its critics as an example of the Global North's nostalgia for a past that it never had.[4] Readers in the Global North long for a time when they were not distanced from nature like people from the Global South. In spite of the many problems his thought presents Latin American intellectuals such as José Vasconcelos,[5] Carpentier and others welcomed Spengler's assertions because they seemed to signal a shift in cultural centers from Europe and the North to Latin America and the South.

As obsessed as the Cuban writer was with history, he was also concerned with how to represent history and how to shape it into myth. Ethnologists and anthropologists such as Mircea Eliade, Fernando Ortiz, and Lydia Cabrera were studying and writing seminal works on the relation of myth to culture during the time Carpentier was composing *El reino de este mundo* and earlier. Since the essential form of myth is one of repetitive, closed cycles it would seem a perfect fit for someone enthralled by Spengler's equally closed and repetitious system. As Carpentier converts history into the closed, cyclical mythic structure, he also erases anything that will upset its closure. In his studies, *The Myth of the Eternal Return or Cosmos and History*, Eliade shows how historical events become myth by conforming to narrative structures and by shaping the historical event to the preexisting mythic form. Similarly, Hayden White in his monumental *The Tropics of Discourse* and *Metahistory: The Historical Imagination in 19th Century Europe,* published years after much of Eliade's work was finished, studied how the very writing of history itself took on narrative shapes in its telling that were reflective of the ideological limits of the authors and the times they wrote in.

In *Alejo Carpentier: The Pilgrim at Home*, Roberto González Echeverría offers a detailed analysis of *El reino de este mundo* showing how Carpentier fits the events of the Haitian Revolution into a numerological and mythic structure. Echoing the title and thesis of Eliade's book, González Echeverría says, "All of the repetitions and Christian rituals are an attempt to make the action fit into a cycle like that of the liturgical year—an attempt, in other words, to fuse the dynamics of the cosmos and writing" (144). Given an understanding of myth and history where the historical event is gradually absorbed by cyclical, mythical structures, Carpentier takes an important event in Caribbean and even American history, the Haitian Revolution, and fits it into the cosmic, mythic structure given by shaping it to conform to a pre-established European frame. In this sense, European, Judeo-Christian myth form an ideological fantasy that distorts history in its retelling.

As I argued in the previous chapter, European narratives and myths give rise to or form part of an instrumental reason that has racism as one of its keystones. If Carpentier were to use a European mythic structure to shape his telling of history, then this framework itself would result in a repetition of representational violence that would distort reality to conform events to the author's own imperial gaze. González Echeverría justifies this violence by relating Carpentier's project to Dante, "The numerical concordance between history and the cosmos represents—as in medieval literature, as in Dante—a fusion between the latter and nature, between history and the work of an omnipotent divinity who has created the universe perfect in measure, number and weight" (145). When read from this angle, Carpentier's project is to write Latin America and the Caribbean into the great Western Canon even if it means eliminating historical events that would force Europe to confront racism and the limits of its own ideological fantasy. By mythologizing historical events in this way, he conforms them to a European, imperial gaze.

II: ABSENT HEROES

For anyone the least bit knowledgeable about the Haitian Revolution, it is possible to be immediately aware of at least two glaring absences in the text. Carpentier makes little mention of two of the most important heroes of the Haitian Revolution, Jacques Dessalines and Toussaint Louverture (or L'Ouverture). He only shows us another important hero, Henri Christophe, in passing as having closed his restaurant to join the revolutionary army and later as a madman enslaving his own people to build his grand palace and fortress. Lizabeth Paravisini-Gebert studies the absence of Dessalines and others in her astute, "The Haitian Revolution in Interstices and Shadows: A Re-reading of Alejo Carpentier's *The Kingdom of this World*." As Paravisini-Gebert argues, Dessalines is perhaps the most important hero of the Revolution, still considered a *lwa* or a Spirit in Voodoo by the Haitian people. In fact, unlike Christophe, Dessalines "challenged the taxonomies of enlightenment so articulately systematized by Moreau de Saint-Mézy" (124). As Paravisini-Gebert shows through Joan Dayan's history of Haiti, Moreau's taxonomies are similar to the Linnean system studied in the previous chapter that European explorers used to understand and categorize the world; they functioned on two vertices, "color and blood, what ostensibly can be observed and what is visible" (Dayan 231). So, it can be argued that Dessalines' absence from the text is due to a distortion in the ideological fantasy that will not admit the possibility of something or someone that is so contrary to its own designs.

In fact, as Michel Rolph-Trouillot has famously argued, "The general silence that Western historiography has produced around the Haitian Revolution originally stemmed from the incapacity to express the unthinkable, but it was ironically reinforced by the significance of the revolution for its contemporaries and for the generation immediately following. From 1791–1804 to the middle of the century, many Europeans and North-Americans came to see that revolution as a litmus test for the black race and certainly for the capacities of all Afro-Americans [. . .] Haiti mattered for all of them, but only as a pretext to talk about something else" (97). It could, then, be argued that with Carpentier's text we are seeing another example of how the Haitian Revolution is used to "talk about something else." What this "something else" is can be debated endlessly. Perhaps it is the integration of Latin American culture into the larger literary canon via conformity to the Judeo-Christian mythic structure and allusions to Dante, Lope de Vega, and other authors considered great. His engagement with Haiti could also be seen as a way of showing the impossibility of historical change following Spengler. Perhaps Carpentier is taking an historical event that many have argued caused momentous change—the first slave revolution led by slaves—and showing how it conforms to a cynical, closed structure of eternal decline. If this is the case, then his novel is yet another example of the imperial gaze that props up the ideological fantasy of colonialism.

As Paravisini-Gebert argues, Carpentier fills the absences created by his erasures in curious and questionable ways that it would lead us to believe that it is at least part of an ideological fantasy that rests its foundation on racist, exclusionary categories. Paravisini-Gebert says that:

> The vacuum left by Dessalines—those very pages of the novel on which one would naturally have expected to find the narrative of his military feats—is filled, somewhat paradoxically, by Pauline Bonaparte. (125)

In the section of the novel where some of the most important and decisive events of the Revolution take place, Bonaparte is seen in relation to her slave, Solimán. In the section that Parvasini-Gebert refers to a plague occurs that decimated the French troops and eventually ended the life of Bonaparte's husband, Leclerc. However, Carpentier decides to show Solimán performing a healing ritual that saves Bonaparte's life.

Carpentier's invention of Solimán's relationship with Pauline Bonaparte has no verifiable basis in history. However, it occurs during Leclerc's invasion of Haiti. The plague that forms the backdrop to Solimán's cure of Pauline was an important event in Leclerc's campaign against Haiti. The plague decimated the French troops and their allies. As Laurent Dubois relates, "In mid-1803 two regiments of Polish troops disembarked in the town of Tiburon; ten days later more than half were dead of fever." "They fell down as they walked," a planter noted, "the blood rushing out of their nostrils, mouths and eyes." By late 1802, "an average of one hundred men a day died. The disease killed the entire crew of a Swedish ship harbored in Le Cap" (281). Among the many things that lead to the expulsion of French troops and eventual victory for Dessalines, Louverture, and the Haitians was that disease, such as malaria and other maladies, affected newly arrived Europeans much more than it did slaves and others who were more accustomed to the Caribbean environment. The other event that led to the ultimate collapse of the French was that the Haitians employed battle tactics used in Africa—similar to what are known now as guerilla tactics—that frustrated the French and European tradition of fighting set battles on open fields. Guerilla tactics combined with disease led to the defeat of French forces in Haiti. The death of Leclerc—emissary of Napoleon himself—was a major turning point that led to Haitian victory. Yet, there is no mention of his death or its importance in Carpentier's novel. Instead we read about an erotic interlude between Pauline Bonaparte and her slave, Solimán.

Though the novel is told largely in third person omniscient with Ti Noel—a slave of Count Lemorand de Mézy—as a witness, in the section on Solimán and Bonaparte, Ti Noel is absent from the action. We see Pauline as a seductress who enjoys inflaming male desire and simultaneously disallowing any sexual contact due to her elevated status. On the ship from France to Haiti, she goes on deck to sleep avoiding the heat below wearing very little. One morning a sailor sees her and "Believing that he saw a chambermaid, was on the point of slipping toward her. [. . .] But a gesture from the sleeping woman, an announcement that she would soon awaken, revealed to him that he was looking at the body of Pauline Bonaparte. She rubbed her eyes laughing like a child" (65).[6] Once in Haiti she tortures her masseur and houseboy, Solimán, by creating an unquenchable desire in him. Her relationship with him adds another dimension to the "mírame pero no me toques" of the erotic tradition. In fact, Pauline pushes the game one step further because Solimán is allowed to touch her, but only as her masseur. Carpentier says, "When she let herself be bathed by him, Pauline felt a malignant pleasure rubbing the hard flanks of that servant she knew was tormented by desire beneath the pool's water" (67).[7] Later we see Solimán's continued desire for her when after leaving Haiti for Italy, he comes upon a statue garden and is enraptured by a sculpture that seems to be made in her likeness. As critic Eleuterio Santiago Díaz points out, "Solimán's rituals [do not] allow him to revive Pauline Bonaparte (from a statue)" (502). Contrary to the depiction of Mackandal, Solimán is a eunuch whose culture and manliness is ineffectual and questioned, he is "a black man yearning for whiteness. His tragic end confirms the elusiveness of whiteness and the irreparable loss of links to his original culture" (502). In the very space of one of the greatest moments of the Haitian Revolution, Carpentier has placed the image of an impotent, African slave.

Paravisini-Gebert remarks that Carpentier decided to fill the void created by Dessalines' absence with the sequence featuring Pauline and Solimán. Speaking of the scene where Solimán saves Pauline's life with Voodoo, Paravisini-Gebert says,

> This caricturesque metamorphosis of Pauline into a Vodou *serviteur* is indeed more significant that (sic) her surrender to indolence and sensuality in the tropics. Inspired by terror and not by faith, it speaks of the practices of Vodou as superstitious mumbo jumbo. (126)

Since Solimán is impotent as Santiago Díaz argues, his Voodoo is also relieved of any power beyond a representation that exoticizes it and turns it into "mumbo jumbo." Paravisini-Gebert's criticism is similar to others that see magical realism or "*lo real maravilloso*" as a practice similar to Orientalism, where the Latin American or Caribbean culture and its subjects are exoticized to the point of caricature. For example, Michael Moses Valdez argues that magical realism fuses culture spheres of the Global North and South, but that it "manages this fusion on the terms of and within the parameters established by global modernity" (14). As it brings cultural artifacts from the Global South into representation magical realism conforms them to the stereotypes and beliefs that the Global North has about itself and its others. It is, to say the least, curious that Carpentier would decide to narrate this exotic tale eliminating entirely the Haitian generals stunning defeat of the French troops and Leclerc.

Dessalines is an important and often problematic figure. Like Louverture, he turned himself in to the French and even fought on their side for a period of time. When the French became weakened by disease and battle with the guerilla fighters who refused surrender, Dessalines became one of Haiti's first leaders. Notably, after ordering a massacre of whites he thought were conspiring with the French against him, Dessalines "explained that a "handful of whites" who had "professed the right religion"—the rejection of slavery—were under his personal protection" (Dubois 300). He went even farther by officially abolishing the category of race that had created a hierarchy in Haiti even before the Revolution. Before Dessalines there were strict, official social categories based on race. Whites were at the top, followed by people of mixed race with Africans on the lowest rung. The constitution of 1805 declared that no white could be a property owner, but the constitution also "went on to declare that, in the interest of eliminating all distinctions of 'color' in the nation, all Haitians would henceforth be known as "'black'" no matter the skin color or country of origin (Dubois 300). The elimination of racial categories is an incredibly important moment not only in the history of Haiti, but of the world in general. It goes entirely against the division of the globe based on racial differences that have structured the Global North's interaction with the South since medieval times or before.

Despite the historical importance of Dessalines and the changes he brought to Haiti, he is entirely absent from Carpentier's narrative: A narrative that both he and his critics say was based on a meticulous study of historical events. For example in the introduction to the novel where he defines for the first time "*lo real maravilloso*," Carpentier says of the historical events the novel recounts that the events he relates have:

> [. . .] been established based on an extremely rigorous documentation that not only respects historical truth of the events, the names of the people—including secondary figures—of places and even streets, but also hides, beneath its apparent atemporality, a minute comparison of dates and chronologies. (18)

Carpentier points to the rigor with which he has studied the events and says that they are hidden beneath the atemporal, mythic structure that he uses to tell the story. Affirming the detail and rigor of Carpentier's historical knowledge, González Echeverría says, "Anyone who has read Carpentier with some care will not hesitate to take these words [his affirmation of his historical knowledge] seriously" (*Pilgrim* 131). The Yale scholar goes on to say that, "And in fact even a cursory knowledge of the historical circumstances narrated in *The Kingdom of this World* seems to confirm his statements" (*Pilgrim* 131). It is true that there was a Count Lenormand de Mézy and that he had a slave named Ti Noel. Other events that Carpentier narrates are also verifiable, but what is also evident to anyone who "even has a cursory knowledge of the events" of the Haitian Revolution, is that there are glaring absences. The question is; if Carpentier was so knowledgeable and so rigorous, how can we as readers of his novel explain the apparent gaping absences of Dessalines and Louverture? Is it enough to simply say that he is part of the paradigm in which he was writing and therefore is entirely incapable of granting the existence of such noble and notable figures and events as the Haitian Constitution? Though it is quite possible that Carpentier is a racist, that conclusion seems a bit too easy.

Seymour Menton in *Latin America's New Historical Novel* (1993) claims of Carpentier's novel that it is "*the* pioneering New Historical Novel" since it has some historical figures and uses other techniques that characterize the sub-genre (20). Menton uses Carpentier's novel complete with its attributes and silences, to define the subgenre of "New Historical Novel" that his book proposes. He says of *El reino de este mundo* that, "in keeping with the New Historical Novel is the distortion of history through the absence of such important Haitian historical figures as Toussaint L'Ouverture, Jean Jacques Dessalines, and Alexandre Pétion" (20). Where González Echeverría argues that Carpentier fits his story into a mythic structure given by Western culture,

Menton argues that the structure the Cuban writer creates forms the basis for an entirely new genre, one that Menton claims to have discovered.

Both Menton and González Echeverría argue that what took precedent in the creation of *El reino de este mundo* was the structure of the story over and above any concern—whether ethical or otherwise—for relating historical events. History conforms to fiction's circular, mythic structure. Though, when handling such an important moment in history and in particular one that has been erased and forgotten from the official history of the Global North, it is difficult to accept the erasure of not only the important figures of that revolution, but also the radical change that it brought with it as anything but yet another example of how a white, European male (who questionably constructs a Cuban identity for himself) eroticizes and silences his other; in this case Afro-Caribbeans. As Susan Buck-Morss shows this silencing of the Haitian Revolution and its heroes is something that continues even today saying that:

> Strikingly, the topics of slavery, the slave trade, and slave labor are never discussed in [Simon] Schama's *The Embarrassment of Riches* [. . .] One would have no idea that Dutch hegemony in the slave trade (replacing Spain and Portugal as major players) contributed substantially to the enormous "overload" of wealth that he describes as becoming so socially and morally problematic during the century of Dutch "centrality" to "the commerce of the world" (23–4).

Buck-Morss points out another example of how Haiti is still erased from the success story that Europe and Europeans as well as the rest of the Global North continue to tell. Carpentier's work, then, could be seen as participating in this ongoing silencing even as it revolutionizes narrative by creating a new genre (the New Historical Novel) and a new aesthetic, "*lo real maravilloso*," which will influence the Latin American "Boom."

III: INTERPRETING THE ABSENCES

Though the actions of the famous figures of the Revolution are erased from his novel, there still remain marks of their existence. Carpentier mentions the names of famous figures, Dessalines and Louverture, but they appear as traces, as anamorphic marks, within the story he tells. For example he mentions a "Toussaint," but the important historical actions of this hero of the revolution are entirely absent from the narrative. Carpentier mentions in passing a, "Toussaint, el ebanista (woodworker)" (38). However, the historical Toussaint was not a woodworker but an unspecialized slave on the Breda plantation, and not that of Lenormand de Mézy like the one in the novel. So, although the name is the same, this is not the historical Toussaint.

Verity Smith in her article dealing with Louverture's absence called "Ausencia de Toussaint: Interpretación y falseamiento de la historia en *El reino de este mundo*" says that the appearance of the names Toussaint and Dessalines name in the text could be what Julio Cortázar called, "una guiñada del ojo al lector" (280). But what do we as readers and critics make of this winking? Smith offers possible reasons for the absence of the three main characters in the revolution saying that, it could be due to the "Marxist or collectivist interpretation of history" which would mean that historical movements should be seen as the result of a collective mass rather than the work of two or three "great men." Smith quickly dispatches with this argument using as proof the fact that Aimée Césaire, the Martiniquean poet and Marxist, argues that, "Toussaint is really the center. The center of the Haitian history, the center, undoubtedly, of West Indian history" (quoted in Smith 277). Noticing other moments in the novel that create "winks" to the reader regarding historical events she says that,

> As all fans of his (Carpentier's) work know, he is very given to parallelisms, counterpoints and symmetry, something that is not just due to his musical and architectural erudition, but also to the minute attention that he gives to the structure of his works. (281)[8]

Smith points to an example of parallelism in the novel when Breille's immurement is similar to Christophe's. After committing suicide, Christophe was buried in the walls of the Sans Souci.

The recognition that in Carpentier's novels it is possible to notice "winks," parallelisms, and counterpoints with the actual historical events leads to a reading traces of otherwise absent historical events and people that does not leave them immured hermetically within a formalist, mythic structure. Studying the linkages between Carpentier's narratives and history, Antonio Fama says that, "Carpentier establishes an unbreakable connection between the current historical situation and the ability of the novelist to capture it" (137).[9] What is more, Fama argues that Carpentier sees himself in the line of the "cronistas," the original history writers of the conquest whose stories are often as fictional as they are historical.[10] Fama argues that for Carpentier, "the work actualizes [or makes present] the past making it part of the present" (142). The traces of the past that Carpentier leaves in his work invite the reader to investigate the historical events that the novel is supposed to represent so that the reader may understand the retold occurrence more fully.

One of the reasons that Carpentier "invented" "*lo real maravilloso*" was to reject the realist and social realist novels that reduced Latin American narratives, in his opinion, to quaint folkloric studies. The other reason was to distance himself from the flighty "artimaña literaria, tan aburrida" of the surrealists (Prólogo 15). Though the "magical" is often seen as being on the side of Latin America while "the real" is on the side of Europe, Carpentier reverses that binary by rejecting the "elogios a la locura" of surrealism and the emphasis on realism in Latin American writers and artists (Prólogo 15). As Theo D'haen argues, Carpentier and his text are hybrid. He lived the life of an exile. When he was at the place he called home, he stayed in a hotel, and though he claimed birth in Havana, in reality he was born in Switzerland. He wrote in Spanish, and yet it was not his first language. He fuses the European with the American, the past with the present; fiction with history and the reader must make sense of all of it.

Critics such as Kathrine Thomas argue, "Carpentier uses the language of myth to form a baroque metaphor which enkindles the surprise of difference within the illusion of sameness, creating such a parodic intertext" (48). In her important article she shows how in *El reino de este mundo* Carpentier combines mythic models from both African and European traditions to create his story. I would argue that the surprise of difference is only possible if readers are fully cognizant of the history that Carpentier is trying to relate. In his attempt to conform history to mythical structure, a structure he chooses to imitate given to him by anthropologists of the time and perhaps based on European ethnographic studies, he leaves out key elements. It is by looking at history in relation to his novels that the novels "actualizan," or update history, making past events come alive and as problematic as ever. Rather than becoming enamored of his skill at mythologizing history, it might be advantageous—and do more service to Carpentier's recognized rigorous knowledge—if we looked critically at his use of myth in writing history. It is as if by absurdly leaving out the most important figures of the historical event he is showing the reader how history is shaped by the prejudices of those who write it. He shows how events are fashioned to fit a pre-established form; it is only in questioning the limits of that form that we begin to understand history, not by accepting them.

It needs to be underlined that Carpentier argued that there is no transparent relationship between language or art and reality. In his *La novela latinoamericana en vísperas de un nuevo siglo y otros ensayos* (1981), Carpentier says that he is looking for an idiom that, without being strictly "typical (folkloric) accepts the Latin American turns for that which it has of ellipsis and metaphors or plastic" (15).[11] He finds an expression that is baroque with its ellipsis, metaphors, and plasticity. In his novel, *El reino de este mundo*, the most awful deaths are those that are in some way connected to mimicry. For example, after the first uprising Lenormand de Mézy's wife is killed and in her death pose, she mimics a painting hanging on the wall (56). It is possible to read mimicry here as a warning to anyone who might think that literature duplicates reality or that art can copy history. In the novel Christophe is shown mimicking the slave system to build his Sans Souci fortress. He becomes a practicing Christian who dresses like French generals and adopts European customs. In the end he kills himself and is immured in the fort he built to defend himself and Haiti from enemies.

The walls that Christophe builds ironically are those that immure him, closing him up in representation. As readers we have to question the limits of the walls and as critics we have to look for cracks in them. If Christophe is the only one of the several Haitian Revolutionary heroes Carpentier chooses to represent, he does so in a way that criticizes anyone who would mimic foreign customs, rather than investigating his or her own truth and reality. Christophe represents a betrayal of the Revolution and its principles. With Christophe, Carpentier represents and criticizes a return of the same—slavery, brutality, European forms—and a denial of African and Latin American difference.

As we investigate history further, it is possible to come up with some rather startling facts. For example, Sans Souci, Christophe's fort, is named after the one Haitian Revolutionary who never once made a deal with the French. While Christophe is considered a *gens de couleur*—and therefore would occupy a social status just below the white French in the pre-Constitution racial hierarchy—Sans Souci had recently made the Middle Passage from Africa and is labeled a "Congo insurgent" by historians. It could be argued that the Haitians defeated the French in large part because of Sans Souci's efforts and the tactics he and other Africans brought with them to Haiti. While Dessalines, Louverture and Christophe surrendered to the French and, in fact, fought against Sans Souci and other Haitian insurgents, Sans Souci remained in the mountains with his army.[12] When the French were defeated, Christophe saw Sans Souci as a threat to his authority and had him assassinated (Dubois 294).

Michel Rolph-Trouillot discusses at length the history of Sans Souci as emblematic of the erasure of Haitian history from the global, planetary consciousness. In a section he calls "Silences within Silences" Rolph-Trouillot argues that Henry I (Christophe) "kills Sans Souci twice: first, literally, during their last meeting; second, symbolically, by naming his most famous palace Sans Souci. This killing in history was as much for his benefit as it was for our own wonder. It erased Sans Souci from Christophe's own past, and it erased him from his future, what has become the historians' present" (59). As Žižek has argued, in order to kill an idea—like the monster in any horror movie—you have to kill the monster not once, but twice (*Sublime Object of Ideology*). First you kill the body and then you kill the idea, the ideological function, that the person or thing represents. Though, anyone who has seen the *Friday the 13th* horror films knows, the monster or the thing you want to kill never really dies, it lives on haunting you.

Rolph-Trouillot's argument raises a question: How is naming a fort after someone an act of erasure? It would seem that naming the fortress after his most feared adversary would rather have the effect of creating a monument commemorating his name. Rolph-Trouillot shows that the name Sans Souci eventually becomes connected with a place in Poland, thus completely by-passing its link to Sans Souci the hero and entirely erasing his name from memory. Rolph-Trouillot argues that in many "non-Haitian circles, the disap-pearance of Sans Souci the man tied the entire significance of the palace at Milot to Sans Souci-Potsdam" (61). In fact one decade after Christophe's death, the name of the palace is connected to Potsdam rather than the Haitian warrior. Further study of the historiography surrounding the place name Rolph-Trouillot notes how subsequent historians in stressing the connection to Potsdam strengthen the representation of Christophe as connoisseur and imitator of European history, culture, and customs while remaining entirely ignorant of the other connection. By connecting him so strongly to Europe, they deny "Christophe's own attempt to silence Sans Souci the man" and in fact join Christophe in his enterprise by eliminating Sans Souci from histori-cal records (65). By eliminating Sans Souci they bolster the association to European culture while disregarding African culture. For Rolph-Trouillot, Jean-Baptiste Sans Souci is "the Congo par excellence. He was the most renowned of the African rebels and the most effective. [. . .] He is a ghost that most Haitian historians—urban, literate, French speakers, as they all are—would rather lay to rest" (67). They wish to silence Sans Souci's ghost because it reminds them of the "war within the war" between the *gens de couleur* (mixed race) and the newly arrived, African *bozales*. I would argue that the fortress itself stands as an anamorphic mark on Haiti and the World's historic and geographic landscape. It marks the place of traumatic violence that was necessary in order for the World Order to constitute itself and exert its hegemony. The "violence" here is the war after the war, the war of the archive, which the Global North has won by largely erasing Haiti and impor-tantly its most African hero (in Rolph-Trouillot's estimation) from memory. As a location of such violence, it functions as a place of lack like the *objet petit a*. It is the absence or void at the heart of the symbolic order and as such it cannot be fully articulated in that order even though it hauntingly stares out at us. Whether Carpentier intended it or not, this is how I want to read the absences and erasures from his text: as anamorphic marks in the historical narrative created within the symbolic order of colonialism.

IV: READING LACK IN CARPENTIER

In his study on Carpentier's fiction, Fama concludes that "for Carpentier language is a vehicle that serves as a means to communicate what is real and it has to be the true image of the reality that it represents" (141).[13] But, at the same time, the reality that it represents has to be constantly "actualized," made real to the reader throughout time. The only way for that to happen is to invite the reader's participation in the creation of the "reality" that the text creates. This aesthetic attitude of inviting viewer participation is one that Carpentier may have picked up with the surrealists, since it was such an important element in their and other modernist movements. It certainly is also part of the baroque and neo-baroque aesthetic. By reading the traces, the anamorphic stains, in his text, it is possible to create a dialectic between his novel and history, one that is never satisfactorily brought to an end or "over-coming," but one that opens up the seemingly closed textbook of history to allow other voices and other perspectives to bear witness to its truth.

For starters, let us return to the fleeting mention made of *un tal* Toussaint in Carpentier's novel. In that brief moment Carpentier says of him: "he had crafted some magi in wood, too large for the collection, that never found a place above all because of the terrible white cornea that Balthasar had—carefully realized with a fine brush—that seemed to emerge from the night of ebony with tremendous accusations of a drowned man" (38–9).[14] As Menton makes clear, the historical leader of the Revolution was not a woodworker, so Carpentier is not referring to the revolutionary leader, Toussaint. Menton's work explains these exaggerations, falsities, and exclusions as part of the genre he defines in his book, a genre that he claims began with Carpentier's novel due in large part to the exaggerations and absences, the reshaping of history that Menton reasons is a "subordination of the mimetic reproduction of a certain historical period to the development of more transcendent concepts. This is probably the single most important trait that distinguishes the New Historical Novel from the traditional historical novel" (184). For Menton the transcendent concept Carpentier tries to communicate is for the reader to question why people struggle for freedom at all in the face of "insurmountable odds" (20). Menton generously decides that the novel is both "pro- and antirevolutionary—that is to say dialogic" (20). But how is this scene mentioning someone by the name of Toussaint, who is not *the* Toussaint "dialogic"? Menton does not explain this. Perhaps it is because it brings to the reader's mind the name of the revolutionary, it is a "wink" that could cause the reader to investigate the story more fully and come to an understanding of what did not fit in Carpentier's story. Similar to the leads and false leads that Borges gives his readers in his stories, here the reader gets one that is both true and false. The reader has to make the determination.

Victor Figueroa does an excellent job of studying Toussaint's absence in Carpentier's text through a comparative study with C. L. R. James' important work on the Haitian Revolution, *The Black Jacobins: Toussaint L'Ouverture and the San Domingo Revolution* (1935 originally). In another attempt to explain the void created by the Pauline/Solimán scene, Figueroa argues that C. L. R. James' work could easily be placed in the exact space where Carpentier offers an erotic interlude rather than focus on historical facts. Figueroa justifies his claim by pointing out that where Carpentier excludes Toussaint's important historical accomplishments, James places overwhelming emphasis on Toussaint's importance to the Revolution to the diminishment of other important figures. Considering Louverture's absence from Carpentier's novel, Figueroa argues that Toussaint's exclusion "must be related to the fact that he does not fit with Carpentier's overall concept of the novel and the events portrayed therein" (59). He concludes that because Louverture was a:

> [D]efender of ideals of the French Revolution, and as a devout catholic who in fact forbids the popular practice of Voodoo, Toussaint does not fit into Carpentier's magical presentation of history and the cosmos of his novel. Carpentier's skepticism of promises and achievements of enlightened rationalism (promises and achievements that, as James convincingly argues, Toussaint incarnates) governs the structure and emphasis of his novel. (62)

Where Paravasini-Gebert wants to use Dessalines to fill the space that Solimán and Pauline occupy, Figueroa wants to do the same with Louverture and C. L. R. James' historical text. Figueroa reasons that Carpentier left Louverture out because the Haitian Revolutionary was "unimaginable" as Rolph-Trouillot would say. The critic agrees with Richard Young that Carpentier wanted to emphasize the "anti-Cartesian" stance of the Haitian Revolution. Following this line of thought, Louverture would also go against a worldview such as that proposed by Spengler that would deny any non-Europeans a philosophical, much less Cartesian, capacity due to the fact that Descartes is a paragon of objective thought that tries to detach itself from the body. Figueroa and Young make a compelling argument, but if accepted it doesn't explain the negative inclusion of Henri Christophe who Carpentier describes as mimicking European values and customs.

To further investigate the "wink" created by Toussaint the *ebanista* in the text it is necessary to look more closely at the description of Toussaint in *El reino de este mundo*. Of course, as Menton argues, there is no direct connection here between the Toussaint represented in the novel and the historical one other than the slim link of his name, but Carpentier constantly undermines the veracity or strength of the connection between representation and history questioning the limits of language. As Carpentier says in *La novela latinoamericano en vísperas de un nuevo siglo y otros ensayos*, he places importance on the ellipsis, the silences and the metaphorical dimension of language. The Toussaint that Carpentier mentions carves a Balthazar who, as is well known, is one of the three Magi and is the one who is most frequently represented as being black. Here, the one that Toussaint carves will not fit within the collection so he must be left out. In the Spanish speaking Caribbean, it is common for people to collect different carvings of the Three Kings or Magi. The assemblage of Magi could be seen as making reference to a community's storehouse of images and representations similar to the literary canon or the historical archive that create what Benedict Anderson would call an "imagined community." But why is this particular Balthazar left out? It could be because of its disproportionate size, though we are not told how big it is, but it is also possible that he is left out because he reminds the owners of the collection of something they would rather forget.

Carpentier tells us that the eyes of this Balthazar "emerge from the night" hauntingly with the accusations of a drowned man. The indictment unsettles and accuses us of something. If this is a "wink" toward the historical Toussaint, then it is yet again a false clue. Louverture was not drowned, but he did face perhaps the most horrible death of any of the Revolutionary leaders. He was imprisoned in a cell high in the French Alps where the cold for him was unbearable so much so that he quickly succumbed to pneumonia and died. Pneumonia is a type of drowning since the lungs fill with fluid until the stricken person is no longer able to process enough oxygen to remain alive. So, this image of a King who will not fit within the archive and drowns creates some links to the historical Toussaint. Another type of drowning is also possible, one that is more metaphoric. Louverture was drowned by the historical archive itself. He and the Revolution he created was and is not visible on the surface of history's text. He is submerged, drowned beneath its surface.

In *The Logic of Fetishism: Alejo Carpentier and the Cuban Tradition*, James Pancrazio argues that absences are in fact constitutive in the formation of the Caribbean. He says that, "This other space (that occupied by Afro-Caribbeans), which participates in the formation of the Caribbean, exists through the disavowal of that absence and lack. Hence it bares the mark of the fetish" (179). Simply put, in psychoanalysis "disavowal" is a translation of the German word used by Freud, *Verwerfung*, to denote a defense mechanism used by the subject to refuse the reality of a traumatic perception. The subject acts as if something were not true, even though it is. Lacan developed this concept saying, "I will thus take *Verwerfung* to be "foreclosure" of the signifier" ("On a Question Prior to Any Possible Treatment of Psychosis," *Ecrits* 465). Here the foreclosure that is undertaken is of the signifier for Afro-Caribbeans in general and for the place of Toussaint Louverture in particular. However, the act of foreclosure does not entirely remove the signified from our consciousness. Lacan relates that it creates a hole in the place of signification. In his later *Seminars*, particularly those dealing with the gaze and *objet petit a*, Lacan will relate this hole to the gaze itself, to the constitutive lack in all signification. The absence is never really entirely absent; there is always something that marks the place where the symbolic order tried to exclude it. This is the place of the *objet petit a* and Louverture's place in Carpentier's novel.

In Carpentier's narrative and in the historical archive in general, Toussaint Louverture as a subject of history as well as the historical events surrounding him are disavowed. However, his erasure from the record is not a complete absence, rather it leaves a traumatic hole in signification that marks the violence of his elimination. Though Louverture does not "fit" in the archive, the spot of his removal creates an anamorphic stain on the historical document itself. This spot, like the eyes of the Balthazar that Louverture the *ebanista* creates, stare out at us, haunting us and unsettling the ideological fantasy that we have been allowed to create by disavowing him and the Haitian Revolution in general. The lack that signals the place of absence becomes an impossible presence. It is present because it is there—even if we disavow it—and it is impossible because, similar to the Magi Louverture sculpts—there is no place for him in the symbolic order. Glaring out at us, the white eyes of Balthazar remind us of this failure on the part of history and globalization's ideological structure itself.

This "non-presence" as Pancrazio labels it, is something like the Real, the *objet petit a*, that remains outside our ability to represent it, nevertheless there is something that reminds us that it is there. It also reminds us of our own lack, the traumatic violence that was necessary for us to become subjects. The question is, now that we are aware of this traumatic event, what do we do? It would be a mistake to argue that this hole could somehow be covered over or overcome by a process of integration. Žižek argues that, "the 'excluded' are, of course, visible, in the precise sense that, paradoxically, *their exclusion itself is the mode of their inclusion*: their 'proper place' in the social body is that of exclusion (from the public sphere)" (*First as Tragedy, Then as Farce* 101). The exclusion of Africans, people of color, and ethnicities that are different from those with roots in traditions of the Global North is constitutive of colonialism and the global world system as described by Mignolo and Wallerstein; a system built on racist hierarchies.

Carpentier in the writing of this presence includes the trace of those who are excluded as a "wink" or something similar to a slip of the tongue. These slips cannot be made a logical part of representation itself for, if they were, they would be domesticated by the very ideology that excludes them. That is to say, their inclusion would result in their normalization by the very ideology that they oppose. Their position, if it is to be truly revolutionary, must remain as a stain within ideological fantasy itself. As Žižek argues:

> This is why Lacan claimed that Marx had already invented the (Freudian) notion of a symptom: for both Marx and Freud, the way to the truth of a system (of society, of the psyche) leads through what necessarily appears as a "pathological" marginal and accidental distortion of the system. (*First* 101)

The distortion that the "slip" reveals is the limits of the ideological fantasy itself. The ethical response to this is not the liberal one of trying to include the excluded, to allow the other to speak and so on, because this would mean that there would be no substantial change in the framework that upholds the ideological fantasy that forms our planetary consciousness. That is to say, the history of the Haitian Revolution cannot be included in the historical archive created by the Global North by means of its colonialist, "imperial gaze." Its inclusion is structurally impossible except through a normative violence that would exoticize it. The exotic and erotic scene of Solimán with Pauline is placed precisely in the vacuum created by so many absences because the historical events going on around them are "unimaginable" to the French and the Global North in general. The inclusion of the events leading to the Haitian defeat of the French as well as the heroic protagonists, is impossible given the current make up of the world system. Carpentier's text, through its distortions, makes those exclusions evident to "any reader" the least bit knowledgeable about Haitian history.

This is not to say that we should be satisfied with the exclusions caused by our own racism. No, what needs to happen is to take the excluded as the basis for any new society (Žižek 102). As Žižek argues, "the general framework has to be surpassed, and everything else should be re-thought, beginning at a zero point" (*First* 87). But the "zero point" would mean a new birth, one that completely eliminates all previous modes, all previous frameworks including language itself since language is the primordial limit. So we need to constantly try to return to this point, realizing that it may be an impossibility. In relation to this struggle Žižek frequently quotes Brecht saying, "Fail again, fail better" (*First* 86).

Near the end of Rolph-Trouillot's *Silencing the Past* he seems to make an argument similar to the one I have been making above. He contends that the crimes committed in the past can never be overcome. He says that white liberals' collective guilt toward "the slave past" or the "colonial past" of Europe can be "both misplaced and inauthentic" (150). He argues that it is "misplaced inasmuch as these individuals are not responsible for the actions of their chosen ancestors. As a self-inflicted wound, it is comfortable inasmuch as it protects *them* from a racist present" (150). His argument is comparable to Carpentier's with regard to the representation of historical events. Rolph-Trouillot maintains that history should not be left in the past, but that it should be "actualized." He states further, "Indeed, none of us today can be true to Afro-American slavery," that is the absences and erasures in the archive will never be filled in by our present efforts. Rolph-Trouillot reasons that we must rather be "true to ongoing practices of discrimination" because "Only in the present can we be true or false to the past we choose to acknowledge" (150–151). This can only be done by not disavowing the constitutive lack in our world, symbolic order and in our confrontation with representation. David Scott argues something similar in *Conscripts of Modernity: The Tragedy of Colonial Enlightenment*, when he says that the various representations of Louverture and the Haitian Revolution in general up until this point have either romanticized or otherwise rendered a dead letter. His study wants to reopen the past, to "actualize it" perhaps, by "changing the questions we ask about the colonial past as a way of beginning the work of imagining new answers for the present" (209). We cannot be satisfied with ourselves and the advancements we have made, rather we must always mark and re-mark the traumatic hole that is constitutive of our own ideological structure. This makes us aware of our own failures so we can attempt to address them rather than allowing us to celebrate our liberal open-mindedness.

V: BIFOCALISM AND LACK

Carpentier presents a dismal view of revolution in general and the Haitian Revolution in particular in *El reino de este mundo*. When taken in the context of his other novels that deal with political revolution and the possibility for change, it is possible to see the struggle to overcome extreme oppression that always fails in some way. He is entirely pessimistic with regard to any proposition of a utopia on Earth when all differences and all social hierarchies would be abolished. Even in novels such as *Los pasos perdidos* that are not concerned with a revolutionary theme, the protagonist searches for the perfect sound, a "threnody," and seems to have found it in the apparent utopia of Santa Monica de los Venados. However, he is never able to return to that place again, the music he wrote there exists only as a troubling memory that he imperfectly tries to recreate endlessly.

At the end of *El reino de este mundo*, Ti Noel assumes powers similar to those of Mackandal and is able to change himself into different animals. He becomes part of different animal communities—ant, goose—and has found that in each one of them there exist social hierarchies, slavery, exclusion and oppression. He arrives at the conclusion that "the greatness of Man is precisely his desire to better what he is" (118).[15] Once we are dead, "in the Kingdom of the heavens there is no greatness to conquer, given that there everything is an established hierarchy" (118–119).[16] So even though he has just witnessed the momentous Haitian Revolution devolve into slavery and oppression and even though it seems that in all social systems, even those of animals, hierarchies and exclusions persist, Ti Noel arrives at the conclusion that what makes humans great is our desire to overcome what is essentially impossible. The narrator concludes that, "Because of that, weighed down by pain and Works, beautiful within his misery, capable of loving in the middle of plagues, man can only find his greatness, his highest measure in the Kingdom of this World" (119).[17] Carpentier, through his narrator and Ti Noel, is arguing that what makes us truly great is engaging in the struggle itself without concern for its outcome, which will always fall short of the mark.

This conclusion, written in 1949 well before the victory of the Cuban Revolution, echoes propositions by many thinkers today such as Slavoj Žižek in his attacks on globalized capitalism. We no longer believe in a dialectic that would result in change. Rather, we feel as if we have come to the "end of history," a time in which there is no true alternative to globalized capitalism. The system, while it may benefit many, also includes large numbers of people who are dissatisfied. As I write this, Brazil, one of the success stories of neo-liberal reforms, is building giant soccer stadiums to welcome the World Cup in 2014 with its eye on also convincing the International Olympic Committee to allow them to host the summer games. As Neymar—the latest pretender to Pelé's throne—dribbles inside the stadiums playing *o jogo bonito* there are huge protests outside the stadium against social and economic inequities that Brazil's "success" has brought. But what is the answer? Žižek and Carpentier argue that it is a mistake to think that history has come to an end, that capitalism as we have it is all there is; that the dialectic of history has come to an end. In fact, the problem with all revolutions, whether they are capitalist or communist, is to think that they have arrived at a moment when all contradictions and all problems are resolved. For Carpentier, striving against our own limits, the end of the dialectic is only possible in *The Kingdom of Heaven* and not in *el reino de este mundo* (the kingdom of this world). It is possible here to see a play on words, as readers we cannot come to a satisfactory reading of his novel that answers all of our questions about it, just like we cannot arrive at a moment in history when all oppositions have been resolved.

One of the major problems regarding the dialectic that recent critics are trying to address is the element of positivistic progress that has always guided its movement. That is the Hegelian dialectic does not, or should no longer be read as, resulting in a final overcoming; one we hope will be brought about by the ideological closure of our choice. In his "Introduction" to *The Sublime Object of Ideology*, Žižek promotes this view when he says:

> [. . .] far from being a story of its progressive overcoming, dialectics is for Hegel a systematic notation of the failure of all such attempts—'absolute knowledge' denotes a subjective position which finally accepts 'contradiction' as an internal condition of every identity. (6)

That is to say there is no final overcoming in the dialectic resulting in an unfragmented identity or a subject that is not barred. At best there is a realization of how distant one is from the perfect unity implied by the imagined synthesis. Returning to Žižek's argument alluded to in the previous section that we must place the excluded as the basis for any social reform, what he is really arguing for is that we no longer disavow the void or lack that is constitutive of our ideological fantasy, but that we continue to encounter it.

The dialectic is a result of the recognized lack at the center of symbolization and the impossibility of ever filling it. Yet, Carpentier's representation causes us as readers to acknowledge that lack in our own presence as readers and to try to come to terms with it in some way. For example, in his novel *El reino de este mundo*, he shows that African culture is more connected to nature (Spengler's culture) especially in the figure of Mackandal and even Solimán who are able to devise cures and venoms using their knowledge of nature. In contrast to this is the Europeanized culture of the slave owners who seem detached from their own surroundings. However, Carpentier shows these two cultures inhabiting the same space, living and developing their own histories in separate spheres punctuated by violent interactions. In this instance, neither culture entirely includes the other; rather each is excluded from the ideological fantasy shaping their worldview. With his concept of *"lo real maravilloso"* he shows how the different cultures in the Caribbean are parallel with different histories and traditions. He is not necessarily saying that one is at an earlier stage of maturation than the other, but that they exist in parallel and dialectic relationship, even if half of the dialectic is unknown to one or the other. The "Kingdom of this World" cannot result in a final overcoming that would successfully integrate all perspectives at once. Rather this world is shaped by the constant interplay or dialectic that is offered between a multiplicity of perspectives.

From the beginning in his "Prólogo" to *El reino de este mundo* he shows how the cultures exist side-by-side and how their encounter produces an "estado límite" in the viewer or participant (15). The effect of the marvelous that is produced by the Real is something that occurs in the viewer or reader as a result of "faith." He says that, "To begin with, the sensation of the marvelous presupposes a faith" (15).[18] But he lists things more associated with Western religion rather than Voodoo; "Those who don't believe in saints can't be cured by their miracles" (15).[19] However, if someone truly believed in the powers of a saint, this would not create an "estado límite" or a disruption in that person's belief system or ideological fantasy. The limit state, the disturbance only arrives as an effect of the overlapping of two belief systems or ideological fantasies. For example, I don't believe in Voodoo, but if suddenly a real zombie appeared at my door, then I might start believing. It would upset my belief system, my ideological fantasy, and force me to accept a different possibility. What is Real to one culture may seem "marvelous" to another; the culture that is not one's own is usually seen as "marvelous" while one's own is seen as Real. Solimán's medicine that protects Pauline and him from the plague is Real even though the practices that produce it may seem "magical" or "closer to nature" to the Western eye. Similarly, the poisons that Mackandal devises come from a real knowledge of nature and have a real effect even if they are surrounded in, again to Western eyes, mysterious and exotic religion of Voodoo.

This is not to say that the parallel cultures do not come in contact forcing an "uncovering" of the other. When this happens in Carpentier's novels, it is usually a scene heralded by or imbued with violence as the decapitated heads in the first chapter portend. Though "lo real maravilloso" is a way of explaining the dialectical differences between cultures that seems to encourage a desire to know the other, knowledge of the other here is almost always violent because it causes a distortion in the ideological fantasy; it makes us see things from a different perspective and thus helps us to question the limits of our reality. Rather than explaining the differences by placing one culture, usually the European, in the realm of "reality" and another, usually Latin American, indigenous, or African, in the realm of "the marvelous," Carpentier shows how the two cultures intersect and how what is marvelous to some is real to others. The "marvelous" labels the event that signals the "limit state" since it is something that shows us the limits of our own ideological framework. Rather than accepting it and using the marvelous to exoticize our others, we should rather move toward it and investigate its reality.

Most critics would agree that the paradigmatic moment of "lo real maravilloso" is "death/ or rebirth of Mackandal" in Carpentier's novel. In that scene the Europeans see him burned at the stake while the Afro-Haitians see him transform and fly away. Even though many critics (see Figueroa for a recent example) seem to side with the version that recounts Mackandal's death, the narration of this event does not take sides; it tries to show the antagonism or impasse between the two ways of seeing the same event showing their dialectical opposition. The way Carpentier presents the event shows that the antagonism between different viewpoints will never be entirely overcome by a synthesis. However, by engaging radically different perspectives and encountering the absence or void in our own ideological fantasy, the dialectic motion is animated, creating the possibility for change. But this "change" should never be thought of as being final or perfect.

The white authorities in Haiti are perfectly happy to let Mackandal run free. Though they chase after him it is only for show since "a slave with one arm less was worth little" (30). But Mackandal, from his position of total absence in the slave order, uses his time to increase his knowledge, to unleash a plague and to start a revolution. For his crimes, the whites capture him and decide to burn him in full view of their slaves to teach them a lesson. Carpentier describes the scene showing how racial differences create social hierarchies. The whites are gathered on the verandas surrounding the square to witness the event, while the slaves mill around on ground level.

What happens during Mackandal's "execution" is uncertain, and the reader is given two possibilities: Either Mackandal is burned at the stake or he transforms himself into a bird and flies away. The two descriptions are given, initially at least, with equal authority. One description of the event relates:

In that moment, Mackandal screamed and moved his stump, which they were unable to tie down, [. . .] screaming unknown conjures and throwing his torso violently forward. The ties fell, and the body of the Black man shot up into the air, flying above the heads, before immersing himself in the black waves of the mass of slaves. A single cry filled the plaza.

—*Mackandal sauvé!* (42)[20]

This explanation is followed by one that is equally objective but that details the death of Mackandal: "And as soon as the racket and the cry and the mob arrived, very few saw that Mackandal, grabbed by ten soldiers, was thrown headfirst into the fire, and that a flame that grew because of his hair drowned out his last cry" (43).[21] The question is which version to believe. It would seem that the last one is more convincing since it comes last and details the death that, because of the confusion, no one saw. However, the first one is equally replete with details and shows Mackandal's escape. The difference, of course, is between the African slaves and the white masters. It is a question of what their differing realities allow them to believe. Those who see Mackandal die are the outnumbered whites watching the execution from their privileged position on the balconies surrounding the plaza. On the other hand, having seen Mackandal fly away, the African slaves begin a revolt. The exclamation that Mackandal is saved is followed by the following description: "And the confusion and roar. The guards threw themselves with the butts of their rifles against the moaning blackness, which seemed like it no longer fit between the houses and was climbing towards the balconies" (42).[22] This great mass of people does not see Mackandal die, just as the white slave owners "los pocos" do not see him fly away. This is one of the most evident examples of how Carpentier resists conclusions in his writing. The scene of Mackandal's death/flight shows the impasse that exists between the two cultures that is perhaps unable to be bridged. The effect of the impasse here, of an inability to understand or even see the possibility of another perspective, is violent revolution. The slaves move to take over the whites that sat in safe position of control and authority in the balconies above the square. In this case, the revolution fails; the army firmly puts down the revolt.

Following Mackandal's execution/escape, the scene immediately shifts from the chaos in the square to an interior space. Lenormand de Mézy, after the event, is in his home discoursing on the "unfeelingness of the blacks before the supplications of their equal—deriving from it certain philosophical considerations regarding the inequalities (differences) between the human races" (43).[23] We see de Mézy's take on the African celebration during Mackandal's execution/escape. He cannot see why they would celebrate such a thing, and this inability leads to confirm his prejudices. As if to confirm his, and perhaps the reader's, thoughts on Africans, we see Ti Noel having sex with the maid in the horse manger. The language used to describe this event at first confirms a de Mézian vision of the universe. As part of the same sentence describing de Mézy's thoughts, we get the conclusion of de Mézy's thoughts on racial difference, "he proposed to develop a speech highlighted with Latin quotes—Ti Noel impregnated one of the kitchen slaves with twins in the horse trough"(42).[24] The verb Carpentier uses here, "trabar," is one that has several connotations. The most immediate in this case is perhaps the most violent, that he tied her up three times to have his way with her. The verb *trabar* also carries with it the notion of impasse, for example a "traba-lenguas" is a tongue twister or a difficult, if not impossible, to speak piece of writing. It can also mean "tartamudear" or to stutter. So this word can convey images of violence and an inability to fully and clearly communicate. On the other hand, in the *Diccionario de la Real Academia Española*, the first meaning of the word is to unite two things to make them stronger. This last meaning would have some bearing on the impasse between two cultures that was just portrayed in the previous scene of Mackandal's execution/ flight. And an impasse that is evident in the description itself since it inserts a stereotypical representation of African sexuality—violent, bestial and prolif-ic—within the "higher" image of Mézy's philosophical musings. However, as readers we also have to take an active role in the creation of meaning. Ti Noel's sexual act shows a violent coming together of opposites that unites them making them stronger. Carpentier creates the image of a violent over-coming of an impasse made by an inability to clearly communicate or "tar-tamudear." The result, however, of this overcoming in a union of opposites is the birth of twins; the outcome then is not a single vision or person, but two new and perhaps different visions. The result of Ti Noel's union with the maid is an overcoming that breeds more antagonisms rather than a satisfying synthesis.

As is the case in much of Carpentier's narratives, the reader has to be attentive to the ellipsis and metaphors that Carpentier emphasizes are of primordial importance to his narratives. The ellipsis and metaphor do not communicate a single truth or possibility. In other novels such as *Los pasos perdidos* and *El siglo de las luces*, the characters look for some unity as they travel to different places and experience different cultures, yet in the end they are left, like Ti Noel, embracing disjunction and antagonism. Carpentier underlines the endless search and travel by mentioning "Ithaca" in either the prologue or epilogue (depending on the edition of the novel you read) of both *Los pasos perdidos* and *El siglo de las luces*. Whether he is picking up on Cavafy or Saint John Perse's poem of the same name is unknown and per-haps irrelevant. Though the unanswered question of source is at the heart of what he is trying to communicate. What is important is that both poems remind the reader of an alternative epic poem to the victorious *Iliad*. Written by Xenophon, *Anabasis* (translated as *The Expedition* or *The March Up the*

Country) tells the story of those who fight their way back home through the Persians. It is also worth noting that Alexander the Great used it as a guide much later when he decided to conquer the Persians and the known world. But the story recounted in the poems based on *Anabasis* is one of loss, of not encountering what you expected, and of enjoying the voyage itself as well as loss or lack rather than a satisfying conclusion. The poem ends by saying:

> And if you find her poor, Ithaca has not defrauded you. With the great wisdom you have gained, with so much experience, you must surely have understood by then what Ithaca means.

Here there is no closure, but rather a desire to return to the novel, to the journey itself in case any wisdom was missed. Like the unnamed "I" in *Los pasos perdidos* or Ti Noel at the end of *El reino de este mundo*, the reader is left lost looking for a resolution. It is one that the reader must provide.

NOTES

1. "Carpentier vivió, y murió por cierto, en París como ambulante ministro de cultuar del gobierno revolucionario. Significativamente, sin embargo, pasaba temporadas en La Habana, alojándose en el Hotel Nacional, o el Habana Libre (antes Hilton), como si Cuba fuese no su patria, sino un lugar que se visita en viaje de turismo o vacaciones."

2. For more on this connection see José Olivio Jiménez's article "Hacia la poesía pura en Cuba."

3. Ortega y Gasset's concept of *poesía pura* was put forth in his essay *La deshumanización del arte*. It influenced the poetics of the Generation of '27, one of the most important poetic movements of the twentieth century in Spain.

4. I will go into greater depth regarding this argument later. For the moment, consult Michael Valdez Moses' article, "Magical Realism at World's End."

5. Vasconcelos' famous essay, "La raza cósmica" could be read as a document that shows how one Latin American thinker tried to apply Spengler's ideas to the Latin American context. Rather than viewing history from a positivistic frame—that would see history as narrating a linear progression similar to the human life of birth, childhood, etc., until death and decay,—Vasconcelos sees Mexico and the world as participating in a cyclic progression. In his essays "La raza cósmica" and "Indología" in particular he claims that Mexico was the place of los Atlantis. The work of Mexican culture now is to return Mexico to the center of history and restore Atlantis to its former glory.

6. "Creyendo que se trataba de una de las camaristas, estuvo a punto de deslizarse hacia ella por una maroma. Pero un gesto de la durmiente, anunciador del pronto despertar, le reveló que contemplaba el cuerpo de Pauline Bonaparte. Ella se frotó los ojos, riendo como un niño."

7. "Cuando se hacía bañar por él, Paulina sentía un placer maligno en rozar, dentro del agua de la piscina, los duros flancos de aquel servidor a quien sabía eternamente atormentado."

8. "[. . .] como sabe todo aficionado a su obra, es muy dado a los paralelismos, el contrapunto y la simetría, algo que se debe no sólo a su erudición en cuanto a la música, sino a la minuciosa atención que presta a la estructura de sus obras."

9. "Carpentier, establece una inquebrantable vincula entre la actualidad histórica y la habilidad que el novelista tiene para capturarla."

10. See for example González Echeverría's *Myth and Archive: A Theory of Latin American Narrative*. Or Hayden White's *Metahistory: The Historical Imagination in 19th Century Europe* for more on how historical events are fictionalized.

11. "[. . .] tipicista, acepta los giros latinoamericanos por lo que tienen a menudo de elípticos, metafóricos, plásticos."

12. Dubois argues that they did so strategically in order to survive and ultimately win the Revolution.

13. "Para Carpentier el lenguaje es un vehículo que sirve para la comunicación de cosas verdaderas y tiene que ser la imagen auténtica de la realidad que representa."

14. "[. . .] había tallado unas reyes magos en madera, demasiado grandes pare el conjunto, que nunca acababan de colocarse, sobre todo a cause de las terribles corneas blancas de Baltasar—particularmente realazado a pincel,—que parecían emerger de la noche del ébano con tremebundas acusaciones de ahogado" (38–9).

15. "[. . .] la grandeza del hombre está precisamente en querer mejorar lo que es."

16. "En el Reino de los Cielos no hay grandeza que conquistar, puesto que allá todo es jerarquía establecida."

17. "Por ello, agobiado de penas y de Tareas, hermoso dentro de su miseria, capaz de amar en medio de las plagas, el hombre sólo puede hallar su grandeza, su máxima medida en el Reino de este mundo."

18. "Para empezar, la sensación de lo maravilloso presupone una fe."

19. "Los que no creen en santos no pueden curarse con milagros de santos."

20. "En ese momento, Mackandal agitó su muñón que no habían podido atar [. . .] aullando conjuros desconocidos y echando violentamente el torso hacia adelante. Sus ataduras cayeron, y el cuerpo del negro se espigó en el aire, volando por sobre las cabezas, antes de hundirse en las ondas negras de la masa de esclavos. Un solo grito llenó la plaza." —*Mackandal sauvé!* (42)

21. "Y a tanto llegó el estrépito y la grita y turbamulta, que muy pocos vieron que Mackandal, agarrado por diez soldados, era metido de cabeza en el fuego, y que una llama crecida por el pelo encendido ahogaba su último grito."

22. "Y fue la confusión y el estruendo. Los guardias se lanzaron, a culetazos, sobre la negrada aullante, que ya no parecía caber entre las casas y trepaba hacía los balcones."

23. "[. . .] insensibilidad de los negros ante el suplicio de un semejante—sacando de ello ciertas consideraciones filosóficas sobre la desigualdad de las razas humanas."

24. "[. . .] se proponía desarrollar en un discurso colmado de citas latinas—Ti Noel embarazó de jimaguas a una de las fámulas de la cocina, trabándola, por tres veces, dentro de uno de los pesebres de la caballeriza."

Chapter Three

The National Symptom in Three Puerto Rican Authors

René Marqués, Ana Lydia Vega, and Judith Ortiz Cofer

In the previous chapter I analyzed how canonical literature and the historical archive have largely excluded or misrepresented the Haitian Revolution and its heroes. My argument in that chapter is that the exclusions or silences are constitutive of coloniality and the world system. I showed how traces of the people and events that have been excluded are visible within the very fabric of the canon or archive. I then showed how they stare out at us through the examples, Toussaint's eyes in *El reino de este mundo* or Christophe's naming of his Sans Souci palace unsettling our attempt to master history and signification in general. While in the previous chapter I analyzed a single, canonical text, here I shift my attention to works by three Puerto Rican authors, René Marqués, Ana Lydia Vega, and Judith Ortiz Cofer. One reason I choose to group these authors together is that as Puerto Ricans they write about history and the formation of the symbolic order from the position of people who are largely excluded from representations in the archive or canon created by the Global North. Whether they live or lived on the Island of Puerto Rico or in the United States—as is the case with Ortiz Cofer—they nevertheless inhabit a colonized space that is largely ignored by the Global North and South alike.

One of the key arguments I made in the last chapter is that in its construction of the ideological fantasy of colonialism and globalization, the Global North casts an imperial gaze that disavows the constitutive trauma. My argument is that rather than acting as if such traumas or such lacks do not exist, it is of the utmost importance to engage them. The conundrum of my assertion is that any effort to speak requires entrance into the symbolic order, which is constituted by lack. If one speaks from the place of this lack, the location of the *objet petit a,* then what is spoken would be unintelligible since it would not resemble language. René Marqués in his play, *La carreta,* engages the trauma created by the colonial condition of Puerto Rico by offering a unitary and unifying image that ignores lack. With narratives by Vega and Ortiz Cofer it is possible to see how they engage the constitutive trauma at the heart of the world system, colonialism, and their own nation. Where Marqués, like writers of his generation and before, offers a clear, transparent response to colonialism, Vega and Ortiz Cofer offer a response that is more elusive, but also more inclusive.

The other reason I have chosen these authors is that Puerto Rico holds a similar position to that of Haiti in the consciousness of the Global North. That is to say, it is another geographical and political place that is largely forgotten in part because the Global North—particularly the United States— has a troubled history with the Island and its people. Puerto Rico is frequently referred to as the oldest colony in the world since, from the time Colón arrived in 1493 until the present day, Puerto Rico has been a dependent colony. First it was under the authority of Spain and then, after the Spanish American War in 1898, Puerto Rico became a colony in all but name of the United States. Most people are aware, if at all, of Puerto Rico as a tourist destination; it is a place of pearly white beaches, turquoise waters, a rainforest, and an interesting Old Town filled with T-Shirt shops. For those U.S. citizens traveling to the Island for the first time it might come as something of a revelation that no passport is needed because Puerto Ricans have U.S. citizenship as members of the "Free Associated State." The moniker used to describe Puerto Rico's political status was decided upon by the United States and Puerto Rican leaders to disguise its colonial status. The United States wanted to have colonies so it could be like other powerful nations, yet its Constitution forbids such a relationship with other countries and its people. In reaction to its colonial relationship with the United States, Puerto Rico erected a strong national identity that was based largely on models of exclusion inherited from the previous colonizer, Spain. In what follows, I will analyze how René Marqués writes against colonialism by recurring to Hispanist models. I will then show how Ana Lydia Vega and Judith Ortiz Cofer engage with the particular constitutive trauma that confronts them as Puerto Rican women.

I: HISTORY AND CULTURE IN THE OLDEST
COLONY IN THE WORLD

To characterize Puerto Rican culture, critics tend to use metaphors or images that connote movement. Critics and artists say that Puerto Rico can be found in *el vaivén*, that it is a nation "on the move," that it is located in *la guagua aérea*, that its identity is in *la brega*; the list could go on. These terms reflect the present episteme informed by postmodernism and post-nationalism. An image that characterizes globalization as being made up of "global flows" also has a concrete referent in the life of Puerto Ricans who travel between the United States and Puerto Rico. With some exceptions these tropes of movement predominate in the literature and criticism of transnational or diasporic Puerto Ricans who have lived long periods off the Island. Nevertheless, said images of movement used by diasporic Puerto Ricans often enter into conflict with national constructions and official images created by writers, politicians, and others who occupy important positions on the island of Puerto Rico. Like any nation that conceptualizes its identity using models rooted in Western modernity, Puerto Rico's official culture uses a framework based on a system of inclusions and exclusions. By analyzing the work of two authors, Ana Lydia Vega and René Marqués, it is possible to see how writers from distinct generations represent transnational Puerto Ricans and Afro-Puerto Ricans. In the following analysis I show how it is possible not only to understand how Puerto Rican culture officially creates its own cultural discourse against the pressures of globalization and colonization, but also I will show how new definitions of citizenship and nation are emerging.

Any project that has as its end another way of imagining the nation in Puerto Rico is always weighed down by problems due to what many have called the "peculiar status." Given that the nation of Puerto Rico employs an official cultural imaginary as a bastion against colonizing influences, any person who criticizes the form in which the current imaginary is constructed runs the risk of being misunderstood or excluded from the nation as such. Juan Gelpí, in his monumental study, *Literatura y paternalismo en Puerto Rico*, makes mention of some of his friends living in Puerto Rico who criticized drafts of his book saying that the approach that he, Gelpí, used was not "Puerto Rican," which thus invalidated his entire project. Gelpí adds that, without intending it, his friends had helped him better define the objective of his study which is "the rhetoric of cultural nationalism" (16).[1] The irony is that his book is now one that everyone interested in Puerto Rican literature must consult and cite; it has become Puerto Rican in spite of or perhaps even because of the negative comments.

Though it is possible to detect differences and criticisms with respect to how the nation is defined and who is allowed to belong, what does not exist is a difference in the desire to belong. Transnational, gay, Afro-Puerto Ricans, and so on all want to belong and to be able to call themselves "Puerto Rican." The difference is in how belonging is defined and by whom. It is possible to see said difference in the point-counterpoint that is initiated between two popular refrains: "Tiene la mancha del plátano" [He or she has the stain of the plantain] or "tiene algo de afuera" [he or she has something undetectable from outside or off island]." The first one comes from popular knowledge that if you peel a plantain incorrectly you will end up with dark stains on your skin that last for quite awhile. The meaning is that one has the indelible mark or stain of Puerto Rican culture. The other saying is less common in written culture and is rarely if ever spoken to the person in question directly. It is something that is said of Puerto Ricans who have spent time off the Island.

Generally the comment "tiene algo de afuera" has to do with speech and is said in reference to something in the accent or word choice that do not form part of typical Puerto Rican discourse. Saying that someone "tiene algo de afuera" is a way of denoting a difference between those who are "from here," that is the Island, and those who "are not from here." Saying that someone contains or displays the mark of an outsider is one of the ways that have been employed to create difference between those who feel like they belong to the culture and the nation as a whole. Even though it is a common experience for transnational Puerto Ricans to be told or hear that they "have something from outside," the othering through language differences is something that is very much connected to the creation of racial difference in Puerto Rico. Depending on the situation, what comes from the outside enters as a phantasm, like an unwelcomed memory of what has been excluded from the nation in the attempt to imagine it. The conflict here is created because on the one hand a group of people want to create a national identity that is "homely" or *heimleich*, but this "homely" place is always created by means of exclusions that the included can name, "lo de afuera" or *unheimleich*.

In part, the limits of nation as constructed within Puerto Rico come as a result of the history of colonization that the Island nation has survived with the resultant imposition of occidental paradigms. The concept of nation that is based on normative unities is perhaps the imposition that has the most consequence. Because its political status has always been determined by colonialism, Puerto Rico's official discourses have always made use of the various cultural spheres in order to articulate an autochthonous, national identity as a response to and a rejection of U.S. colonialism. Nevertheless, the official discourses design their construction of the cultural imaginary by employing the scaffolding inherited by Western modernity. The scaffolding they use to create a separate Puerto Rican identity creates a nation that imitates exclusions common in the Global North. The exclusionary structure implies the creation of a dominant culture that represents the values of the classes in power. The same values that are used to define national identity in colonizing countries are used to construct the cultural imaginary in the colonized location. In such a construct, identity is based on a relation to a well-defined geographic space, on following specific linguistic norms, on being able to interpret common cultural signs and on the participation in ceremonies with other members of the community. This paradigm is one that some call "paternalist" and exclusionary. Paradoxically the paternalist structure is one that is inherited from the same colonizing powers that inhabited the Island for more than five hundred years. The concept of linguistic, racial, cultural and religious "purity" was one that traveled with the Spanish colonizers to Puerto Rico and it was the same ideal of purity that would be used to combat U.S. colonizing practices. [2]

Eleuterio Santiago Díaz has shown in *Escritura afropuertorriqueña y modernidad*, the paternalism, which inscribes Hispanism on the Island after the United States took possession is not a new phenomenon. The roots go as far back as the Spanish colony, which imposed a heavily codified linguistic norm in the Puerto Rican colony based on *La gramática* of Antonio Nebrija first published in 1492 to aid the Catholic Kings in their purifying of Spanish culture following the expulsion of the Moors and the Jews. In Puerto Rico, social status and inclusion or exclusion as a participant in the nation was, and in many cases still is, based on linguistic as well as racial, sexual, gender, and ethnic differences. This has led not only to exclusions of those who live on the Island, but also those in the diaspora who return to the Island. Marisel Moreno, in her article, "Family Matters: Revisiting *La gran familia puertorriqueña*" remarks that, "The exclusion of diaspora literature, mainly written in English or a mixture of Spanish and English, is a product of the strong association that exists between language literature in nation" (79). Noted differences in accent as well as usage or grammar are enough for the Island Puerto Rican to notice that the speaker *tiene algo de afuera* [has something from the outside] and to marginalize or in other ways view the interlocutor as a non participant in the Puerto Rican family. [3] Defined difference takes on a particularly racial tint when, as Santiago Díaz asserts, "the black voice appears frequently codified in literature and other media as a defective zone in the language. The black person is the one who does not know how to speak and does not know what to say" (*Escritura* 86). [4] This characterization of language used by Afro-Puerto Ricans or diasporic Puerto Ricans as deficient creates impediments to their inclusion in the cultural imaginary. Along with being an obstruction to full inclusion, linguistic difference also characterizes how Afro-Puerto Ricans are included as deficient, less than complete beings. If the Afro-Puerto Rican is thought of as a person who does not know how to speak or, worse, does not know what to say because he or she is too ignorant, then Afro-Puerto Rican culture is only included as a representation of what is undesirable or of what is not said. It is seen but not seen. These exclusions based on racial differences extend to gender and sexual differences as well. Those who migrated to the United States or other places and decided to come back are also seen as being Other as having something *de afuera* that distances them from the official image of the ideal Puerto Rican. Particularly in the early years of migration (1930s and 1950s) most migrants from Puerto Rico to the United States were seen as undesirable by the elites due to their race or class. In fact, they were encouraged to leave as a "válvula de escape" to ease the economic and political pressure on the Island. So, those who left the Island were already seen as undesirables by the elites even before they left.

In spite of the exclusion of diasporic Puerto Ricans from the imaginary, migration to the exterior dates since the years of Spanish colonialism—and even before if we include the Taíno migrations and movements between islands. Puerto Rican national heroes such as Eugenio María de Hostos and Emeterio Betances lived in exile as they wrote against Spanish colonialism in the nineteenth century. Hostos went so far as to ask to be buried in the Dominican Republic rather than his home country because he wanted to be interred on free ground. Even though Puerto Rico and its people have always been a nation on the move, the largest migrations occurred during the years of greatest economic and political instability on the Island: the 1930s and 1950s. During these same years, due to the colonialist incursions of the United States and the lack of a political identity many Puerto Ricans, above all the elites, saw the need to establish a national identity through the use of cultural representations. Critics refer to the Generation of 1930 as the beginning and the 1950s as the explosion of the phenomena of employing cultural products to fill the absence of an internationally recognized, political identity separate from the United States.

The Generation of 1930 was the first to live with U.S. colonialism. In the aftermath of the War of 1898, Puerto Ricans had no officially recognized citizenship. It was not until the Jones Act of 1917 that Puerto Ricans were given U.S. citizenship, which allowed them to travel to other countries using a U.S. passport. One reason Congress passed this law was that it included the proviso that Puerto Ricans could be drafted into the military. Given that the United States was at war and in need of troops, this part of the bill convinced many senators to vote in favor. In the 1950s, due to the fact that Puerto Rico had elected its first governor, Luis Muñoz Marín, and due to changes in the Island's status to *Estado Libre Asociado*, which Muñoz Marín initiated, the colonial relation changed slightly. Mostly what these changes meant was that Puerto Rico gained local autonomy and, as a result, the official government started a concerted effort to establish norms that resulted in a definition of the nation.

Muñoz Marín with others in power decided that official culture would take the place of politics in the establishment of identity. To combat extreme poverty and unemployment, Muñoz Marín, in a neo-liberal move, gave incentives to corporations to industrialize Puerto Rico initializing a program called "Operation Bootstrap." The cultural counterpart to the industrial invasion of the Puerto Rican countryside was a program he called "Operation Serenity." This second program used culture as a way of solidifying Puerto Rican identity against colonialist pressure. As the name implied, its purpose was also to calm the rebellious elements in Puerto Rico by giving them a venue in which to express their opposition. During these same years Puerto Rico created official organizations like *El Instituto de Cultura Puertorriqueña* (ICP) that finances cultural events as well as publications. The elite classes, those who before 1950 always had occupied positions of power, officially initiated a concentrated effort to create a definition of culture that reflected their desires and values.

As a precursor to the construction of a national identity founded on culture, and to establish the basis for the creation of the *Estado Libre Asociado*, a gag law had been enacted called *La Ley Mordaza*. This law made it illegal to speak in favor of Puerto Rican independence or against the U.S. government precisely during the years (the late 1940s and the 1950s) when Puerto Rico was debating its future: whether to be independent or how to define its relationship to the United States.[5] This law created a situation in which open debate was impossible. No views that were not in agreement with U.S. control of the Island and Muñoz Marín's position as leader were legal. After consolidating power, Muñoz Marín agreed to the newly defined status (*Estado Libre Asociado*) between Puerto Rico and the United States. As a consequence, the cultural sphere replaced the political as the place where Puerto Rican identity would be defined. René Marqués's *La carreta*, which I will analyze below, is emblematic of how culture was used to construct identity in the absence of political alternatives.

Within the established cultural sphere, perhaps there is no more important, emblematic and preponderant figure than the *jíbaro*. The figure of the *jíbaro* is a constant in Puerto Rican culture since the nineteenth century with the literary works of Manuel Alonso in 1849 and Ramón Frade's famous painting, "El pan nuestro de todos los días." During the years after 1898 the *jíbaro* increasingly gains in importance in the cultural imaginary and eventually occupies the position of cultural icon during the 1940s and 1950s when Muñoz Marín and his *Partido Popular Democrático* (PPD) begin to use the *jíbaro* as the distinctive symbol of its party.[6]

Part of the reason for the *jíbaro*'s appeal as cultural emblem is that he is generally thought of as inhabiting remote locations in the mountains where he would have been free from influences of African culture that might have created a closer, more pure link to Spanish precursors.[7] Because of his association with the land and with the romantic, pre-modern past that, according to cultural myths, existed before the arrival of U.S. influence, the *jíbaro* is a figure used to represent the pure essence of Puerto Rican identity and culture.

Nevertheless, seen from a different angle, the *jíbaro* comes to be representative of the desire on the part of elites who want to establish Puerto Rican identity based on a connection between Puerto Rico and its Spanish and European past while ignoring—or paying lip service to—the importance of African culture as well as other ethnic, gender and sexual differences of the people living on the Island. As Arlene Dávila has noted, in the 1940s and 1950s, the members of elite sectors of society were those who controled the official cultural symbols, demonstrated in the emblems they constructed to represent culture. In the cultural emblems the elites chose, Dávila says it is possible to observe, "Hispanophile and occidentalist (sic) tendencies prevalent among Puerto Rican intellectuals" (62). It is also conceivable to add to Dávila's assertion that the image elites created of Spain as a place of racial and ethnic purity is selective and not based on an understanding of the rich and varied culture of that country. In spite of this, the *jíbaro* forms a metonymy for Puerto Rican culture and illustrates how groups in power during the 1950s imagine culture with an ideal of racial, ethnic, and linguistically pure.

As is well known, the United States is no better in terms of how it has constructed its national identity based on racial and linguistic purity. However, the implications of U.S. racism came as something of a surprise to many Puerto Ricans who saw the results of the War of 1898 as liberation from an oppressive and regressive colonial power. The end of what is called the Spanish American War resulted in Spain handing the Puerto Rican archipelago over to the United States as a *botín de guerra* or "war prize." Because the United States had a history of turning newly acquired lands into states, some Puerto Ricans feared while others hoped that they would soon become another star on the U.S. flag. Previous to its acquisition of Puerto Rico, the United States had won another large extension of land, again by means of war and invasion, resulting in the *Treaty of Guadalupe Hidalgo* (1849). What is now California, Nevada, Arizona, New Mexico, and part of Colorado were ceded by Mexico to the United States to end hostilities. Since these formerly Spanish-speaking lands were now part of the United States, Puerto Ricans had every right to think that they too would become another state. However, there was a barrier that would prevent the inclusion of Puerto Rico. With Mexico and the acquisition of new, previously Mexican lands, the United States had learned how to justify its racism using legal and historic precedent, a lesson it now applied in the case of Puerto Rico. [8]

The United States applied what it called "Teutonic exceptionalism" to the legal cases that determined Puerto Rico's status. [9] Such exceptionalism drew a direct line of precedent from the Teutonic tribes who, U.S. lawyers and statesmen claimed, ruled themselves democratically based on a rule of law that gave rise to our own democratic systems. Even the likes of Henry Adams, son of a founding father, argued that non-Teutonic races were incapable of democratic reforms and therefore should not be admitted into the United

States.[10] This formed a seeming paradox with the ideology espoused by the Monroe Doctrine, which had exerted the United States' right to expand and acquire lands as well as "protect" countries in the hemisphere from external influences. With the "Freedom Ordinance" it was determined that as the United States expanded there would be no "second class territories" and no "colonies except on a temporary basis" (Zimmerman 21). However with the case of Latin American countries, the United States ran up against the limit of racism.

With Haiti in the nineteenth and Puerto Rico, Haiti, Nicaragua, Panamá, Cuba, Chile, and other countries in the twentieth centuries, the United States showed its paternalism in protecting its own interests with regard to those countries. However, the United States refused to consider Puerto Rico for statehood despite its geographic proximity because of a belief in Teutonic exceptionalism.[11] Puerto Rico comes to occupy an often-ignored position in U.S. history. Puerto Rico is a colony in all but name, but, since the United States cannot think of itself as an imperial power complete with colonies, Puerto Rico was saddled with the long and weird moniker of "Free Associated State" occupying a legal position that is labeled "foreign in a domestic sense." In this way Puerto Rico becomes a symptom of the United States' own racist limits and imperialistic tendencies, but since it cannot be fully interpreted within the space defined by the United States' own symbolic order, it remains as a sinthome: it is something that cannot be fully interpreted, cannot acquire a determinant meaning. Yet, through its negative relationship to the U.S. colonial order it provides structure to the symbolic order as a whole. It is the thing that the symbolic order casts out as it defines itself, against which it defines itself, and is, nevertheless, that thing which is in it more than itself.

II: RENÉ MÁRQUES'S *LA CARRETA* AND THE CULTURAL IMAGINARY

René Márques's drama *La carreta* (*The Oxcart*) published in 1953 presents an image of the *jíbaro* that is perhaps one of the most memorable if not long lasting in the Puerto Rican cultural imaginary.[12] In his drama Márqués shows a *jíbaro* family that, because of economic pressure, migrates from their ancestral home in the mountains to San Juan and later to New York.[13] When the drama begins the viewer sees the bankrupted family selling the furnishings of their home as they prepare to move. As the family follows Luis with his dreams of a modernized life and fascination with technological marvels, Márqués shows him as the one who is guilty for the family's decline into poverty. The family's decline increases as it gets farther and farther away from its home in the mountains. Luis's voice in favor of modernity offered by the United States is shown in opposition to Doña Gabriela's discourse in favor of family unity, traditional values, and her dreams of returning to the mountain village they left behind.

As Juan Flores has argued in his essay "The Insular Vision: Pedreira and The Puerto Rican Misére," Marqués's drama expresses a worn out Latin American ideology that asserts that U.S. culture is entirely superficial and only offers technological advancements. Opposing the United States *La carreta* imagines a Latin America and a Puerto Rico that are spiritual and in harmony with nature.[14] Against the colonizing culture that is defined by modernization, technology, and superficiality, Marqués, together with the cultural elite in Puerto Rico, constructs the figure of the *jíbaro*.

In *La carreta* the family follows Luis and his love of technology, as it does so, the family distances itself from the Puerto Rican mountains and an identification with nature. As a result, the family begins to disintegrate. After Luis dies, Doña Gabriela, the matriarch, and her daughter Juanita decide to return to their Puerto Rican mountain home in order to put the family back together. Their return is possible only thanks to a *Deus ex-machina*. Juanita's fiancé, who lives in the small mountain town that the family abandoned, wins the lottery and is able to purchase land in which Juanita and he can begin their own family. What exactly will happen to the family once they return to the Island is left to the viewer's imagination. However, given the positive images of life in the mountains, we are left thinking that things will be much better for them. The total effect of the drama is to criticize those who succumb to the desire to migrate to the United States. Juanita and Doña Gabriela return to the Island beaten but not defeated at the end of the drama to reestablish themselves "tan fuertes como ausubo" (as strong as ausubo) as Juanita says, and not in the *vaivén* between the Island and the United States and much less in the country of the colonizer. Their return is also possible because of Luis's death. He dies literally devoured by a machine, a fitting death perhaps for one so enamored of technology.

III: CENSORSHIP ON AUTOPILOT: ANA LYDIA VEGA AND THE NEXT GENERATION

The generation that follows that of Marqués is marked by the growing influence of U.S. culture on the Island. Things that before might have been associated with the evils of colonialism—technology and other signs of modernity—are now everywhere and are mixed with official culture or they are right next to them. Vega's generation had to live with the *double consciousness* that is the result of the paradoxical strategy employed by the PPD and Muñoz Marín to stabilize the political and economic situation in Puerto Rico. That is, they had to accept U.S. influence while, at the same time, asserting independence in cultural representations. Meanwhile official groups like the ICP, frequently under the control of *independentistas* and the PPD, promote a cultural imaginary that emphasizes a return to an idyllic, premodern past. As Dávila shows, "Muñoz Marín's focus on economic development soon turned the PPD into a party of accommodation rather than one of resistance to colonization" (31). In order to alleviate the economic problems of the Island, Muñoz Marín made concessions to the United States. Together with the conciliatory gestures on one hand, goes the hypocritical use of the *jíbaro* on the part of the ICP and the PPD as a cultural icon on the other. The *jíbaro* comes to be emblematic of the political motives of the elites and their own necessity to connect "symbolically with the popular classes whom they actually shun in practice" (Dávila 103). The majority of writers in the generations after Marqués respond to the fatigue that results from their official labor in the creation of ideal images that do not correspond to reality and which have the effect of excluding a large number of people who would otherwise consider themselves Puerto Rican.

Ana Lydia Vega wrote a now famous article called "Sálvese quien pueda: La censura tiene auto" detailing how writers performed acts of auto-censorship in order to keep producing acceptable images that uphold Puerto Rican identity. Against a return to a mythic past defined by stability and purity, the generations after Marqués create narratives and other texts that are heteroglossic. Against images of Puerto Rico and Puerto Ricans that are transparent and unitary, writers of Vega's generation and after, when they write about such matters, use images that are open to interpretation. By doing this they can avoid exclusionary representations while at the same time articulate a point of opposition against globalizing and colonial pressures. In the process they imagine the nation in a different way; a way that might be characterized as "post-national."[15]

Ana Lydia Vega, one of the better-known authors from the generation that began publishing in the 1980s and 1990s, satirizes the restrictions imposed by official discourses. The laughter that much of her work evokes has a caustic effect on paternalistic structures. Nevertheless, the same time she makes fun of tradition, Vega also participates in the construction of a cultural imaginary. Her employment of popular—non-official—images and her use of colloquial speech in many ways reflects and betters what Marqués tried to do with his famous play. Even though *La carreta* tries to imitate popular language use, it usually ends up being an inaccurate caricature. Using laughter and parody, Vega reinscribes the classical texts and traditional icons using language and images that are popular, not the imaginings of the cultural elite. As a result, her writing has the effect of re-imagining official cultural representations in a way that is more inclusive.

Parody has a subversive quality that frequently breaks with tradition by deriding it through inversions and burlesque humor. However, parody has another side. Parodic writing also re-inscribes the traditional text or image in the present and, in many ways, actualizes it by repeating the old form in a more up-to-date way. As Linda Hutcheon argues in her *A Theory of Parody: The Teachings of Twentieth Century Art Forms*, the term "parody" in classic times referred to two songs sung at the same time. In parody, even as the new song is sung, the people listening to the new song—or reading the new story—remember the older song or story. In this way the two texts and the two periods are interwoven creating a single text or song. At the same time that the parody subverts the older text it actualizes it, brings it alive, in the public's imagination.

Vega's stories frequently re-articulate official cultural norms by situating them "in the earth" at the same time that they subvert this grounding gesture by parodying it. In her use of parody it is possible to see something similar to what Arcadio Díaz Quiñones defines as "el arte de bregar" (the art of "dealing with").[16] Using this phrase to characterize many elements of Puerto Rican culture, Díaz Quiñones concludes that there are many possible forms in which it can be deployed. With respect to the relation between past and present he says that "the images of *bregar* (dealing with) produce the same sensation of being, simultaneously, between something new and something old" (27).[17] In a similar way, parody in Vega is a point-counterpoint created by the art of *bregando* between the new and the old. Díaz Quiñones uses *el arte de bregar* as a metaphor for Puerto Rican identity formulation; it is a definition that is constructed aware of its own lack and inconsistencies. The result is a definition of what it means to be Puerto Rican that is much more open to differences.

In much of her writing, Vega has at least two points of criticism: colonialism and paternalist cultural formations that previous generations had formed to combat the United States. Instead of inserting her writing in the binary constructions of past generations, which at times produce a paternalist construction of culture, Vega constructs a culture *en la brega* by employing parody, irony, and humor. She creates complex texts that have no obvious resolution for the problematic situations that she presents. Her stories offer images and cultural icons that are frequently contradictory, and these are tied together with humor that is at times disconcerting. In two of her stories, "Sobre tumbas y héroes: Folletín de caballería Boricua," (On Tombs and Heroes: Folio of Boricua Gentility) and "Pollito/Chicken," Vega parodies the official cultural imaginary by inventing an alternative one. However, due to the parodic, ironic nature of her writing, her stories make evident the constitutive closure of all such creations. The reader becomes a participant in the text's creation and by extension the cultural imaginary in which it participates. However, her writing—through laughter and parody—also makes evident the lack at the center of all symbolic structures. Such a type of writing avoids paternalistic, exclusionary, and totalitarian closures.

IV: THE PROBLEM OF BEING AN OUTSIDER:
"POLLITO/CHICKEN"

The story "Pollito/Chicken" takes its title from a song used in Puerto Rican schools to teach students English. In the story, Vega creates the protagonist, Suzie Bermiúdez, as a representation that puts in relief the ridiculed figure of transnational, diasporic Puerto Ricans. Suzie does not want to identify herself with Puerto Ricans whether she is in New York—where she lives—or Puerto Rico, where she is from. The narrator of the story tells us that Suzie is a secretary for a "housing project de negros que no eran mejores que los New York Puerto Ricans pero por lo menos no eran New York Puerto Ricans" (75–6).[18] When she decides to go to Puerto Rico she apparently does it for the same reason as many tourists. Like anyone in the middle of a New York winter, Suzie allows herself to be seduced by a poster with vibrant colors and a brilliant sun announcing trips to Puerto Rico. Once on the Island and inspired by a bestseller novel that represents the history of a woman who is raped by, in the words of Vega, "un haitiano negro," Suzie seduces the waiter at the poolside bar in her hotel. At the moment of her orgasm, Suzie screams, "Viva Puerto Rico Libreeeeeeeeee" (79). Haiti makes an appearance here, but only in the most stereotypical, orientalist way. The type Suzie is reading about in her book is transposed onto the body of the waiter, "tres piña colada later y post violación de la protagonista del bestseller, Suzie no tuvo más remedio que comenzar a inspeccionar los native specimens con el rabo del ojo" (78). The stereotype creates a desire in Suzie and she looks for someone with whom she can have sex.

Dissatisfied with the "native specimens" she sees, her eyes finally land on a waiter at the bar who happens to be black; providing her with what she sees as a close match to the figure in the book she read. Back in her room she calls down to the pool asking for the waiter to bring her room-service. Her hand moves almost on its own toward the phone to make the call; "Oh my God, murmuró, sonrojándose como una frozen strawberry al sentir que sus platinum-frosted fingernails buscaban, independientemente de su voluntad, el teléfono" (78). Here she is attracted to precisely what had previously repulsed her. In addition to that, her drive aims at the unrepresentable lack at the center of Puerto Rican culture, Afro-Puerto Rican culture. By aiming at Haiti through an Afro-Puerto Rican, she targets the unrepresentable void at the center of her and Puerto Rico's identity. It is an act that will result in the collapse of the framework that holds up her identity and, by extension, that of Puerto Rico. By having sex with the waiter, she experiences a moment of *jouissance* resulting in a cry of freedom.

It is possible to interpret her move toward the waiter as an iteration of the death drive. This isn't to say that she is trying to kill herself physically, but that she moves toward something that will have a devastating effect on her psyche and the scaffolding she uses to define herself and prop up her identity. As Richard Boothby argues in *Death and Desire*, "the death drive emerges as the crowning discovery of psychoanalysis; it designates the ultimate mystery, the dark engine of transformation that operates at the heart of the human being" (223). What Suzie displays in the story is what we all have, something that is in us more than ourselves, something that drives her to destroy—even if momentarily—the stultifying order that denies its representation. That is to say, she is driven toward the destruction of the social and cultural frameworks that silence and separate African culture from her, and Puerto Rico's, consciousness.

The scream of pleasure at the end of the story during the "little death" of Suzie's orgasm breaks open the idle patter of daily language and the symbolic order that defines her and us. In her encounter with the Afro-Puerto Rican/ Haitian slave/waiter, she faces the irrepresentable lack and "dies" a little bit. Throughout the story Vega shows how Suzie is subject to stereotypical representations and understandings of Puerto Rico and the Caribbean in general. From the vacation poster, to the piña colada, to the Haitian violator and the waiter himself, all are prefabricated images that she unquestioningly assimilates and follows. When she calls the waiter, she can't believe it because she is transgressing the limits established by the United States racism to which she has subscribed. That is, she must avoid all Puerto Ricans, especially black Puerto Ricans. As the story tells us, she is also going against Puerto Rican societal norms that are based on racist hierarchies. Her orgasm allows for the possibility of freedom. By screaming the cry of all *independentistas* and people who are proud of their Puerto Rican heritage, Suzie encounters the possibility for new images and different types of representation. Her experience is one of the characteristic products of the death drive. As Boothby argues, it is not necessary to find new words, what happens with the destructive force of the death drive is that, what is rendered ineffectual by their overuse are "really heard for the first time, thus enabling something other to be registered in the heart of what is most familiar" (213). The familiar cry of "Viva Puerto Rico Libre" is here re-inscribed not just for Suzie, but also for the possible Puerto Rican reader. Having someone like Suzie who so thoroughly rejects—and is rejected by—Puerto Rican culture scream for Puerto Rico's freedom creates an odd and unsettling image in the mind of the reader.

As a result, and as might be imagined, there was a strong negative reaction by transnational or diasporic Puerto Ricans to Vega's representation of Suzie. Island Puerto Ricans can see her as a representation of diasporic Puerto Ricans and so can look to her as conforming to the distorted view they have of those who don't live on the Island. Israel Reyes in his book *Humor and the Eccentric in Puerto Rico* studies Vega's story from both sides of the "charco," that is to say, his study takes into consideration the perspective of diasporic and Island Puerto Ricans. Instead of simply accepting the famous criticism lodged by diasporic Puerto Rican writer Nicolasa Mohr against Suzie, Reyes adds another possibility. Taking as a point of departure the work of Diana Vélez on the same story, Reyes notes that the narrator "speaks as the implied author, who distances herself from Suzie through irony, but the narrator also speaks in the plural to and for the insular Puerto Rican nation"; this is for Reyes the story's "ideal audience" (81). Reyes and Vélez resolve to focus on the way in which the story does not so much make fun of diasporic Puerto Ricans as it derides the negative attitudes that Island Puerto Ricans maintain with regard to those living in the diaspora.

"Pollito/Chicken" is told in a burlesque version of "Spanglish" which, according to Mohr, does not reflect the typical speech of diasporic Puerto Ricans. Instead of imitating the unconscious code switching that takes place in Spanglish, the language that Vega employs is conscious of itself and what it wants to achieve. This observation provides another layer of irony that Reyes wants to describe in his study. By making the code switching "conscious" readers are even more cognizant of the mechanisms that are ordering the story. Added to this is the fact that the "ideal reader" in Reyes' assessment is a reader who lives in Puerto Rico and is capable of interpreting the signs in English and Spanish, signs that indicate Suzie's condition as a subject who is assimilated to U.S. culture. On one level it could be said that an Island writer, Vega, creates this story so that other Island Puerto Ricans can laugh at Suzie and other diasporic Puerto Ricans. In their laughter they distance themselves from her. On another level, in order to laugh at Suzie, the reader has to understand the mixed up language Vega uses to write. Therefore, at some level, the readers have to identify with Suzie, the object of their derisive laughter. That is to say, if the "ideal readers" understand the codes in the story, they have to recognize that their Spanish isn't "pure" and as a result, the nationalistic ideal of linguistic purity that is used to separate them from Suzie and others in the diaspora is beyond their reach.

It can be concluded then that Suzie's struggle is not only shared by Puerto Ricans in the diaspora, but also characteristic of all who live on the Island. As they read of her short stay in Puerto Rico, the Islanders—the "ideal readers"—by laughing at her, deny that part of themselves that comes from outside and which frustrates a cohesive national identity.[19] Reyes argues it is possible for the story to create a location where Island and diasporic Puerto Ricans can find a meeting place. The laughter that runs through the story can unify both groups and allow for the construction of a national ideal that rejects notions of linguistic and cultural purity. Suzie's story unifies Island and diasporic Puerto Ricans when both recognize that they are not pure and, as a result, cannot conform to an ideal definition of citizenship or belonging that government officials and cultural elites have created. The laughter the reader experiences as the story breaks "habitual language" allows for something else to be imagined. The "habitual language" in this case is Spanish, Spanglish and the racial limits placed on the definition of nation.

Though Vega wrote this story in 1977, it is evident that linguistic purity is still a hallmark of official national belonging. As Roberto Ignacio Díaz argues in his *Unhomely Rooms: Foreign Tongues and Spanish American Literature* with regard to "Pollito/Chicken," "[. . .] it is not surprising that writing in English—and, as a corollary, the works of Puerto Rican authors in the United States—should have been viewed not as another form of Puerto Rican writing, but as a foreign development, another tongue that threatens the cultural unity of the nation's literature" (42). Spanish is still considered for many *the* language of Puerto Rican national identity. However, I would argue that Vega's story and others like it are changing that conception and along with it the national imaginary is opening up to accept those from outside as well, those who have "algo de afuera" as those who do not conform to the *jíbaro* ideal proposed by elites.

Without Reyes's important study, the connection between Suzie and Island Puerto Ricans would not be evident except for the fact that she seems to value cultural purity, which leads to self-loathing and racist attitudes. She works in the projects where Puerto Ricans and African-Americans live; groups Suzie says she detests. With this Suzie joins with the "ideal reader" in their disparagement of her as a "New York Puerto Rican" along with her and their disdain for African-Americans who she decides are "no better." Of course, here in my characterization of "Island Puerto Rican" attitudes, I am referring to the attitudes of the cultural elites of the generation prior to Vega's writing and the attitudes promulgated in popular culture. To continue, if, according to Reyes, Vega is creating a connection between Island and disaporic Puerto Ricans through the cultural and linguistic characteristics that they share, then the racism that Suzie expresses at the beginning of the story is demanding that the "ideal readers" attend to other elements of racial difference. Readers need to be aware of the elements within their own cultural edifice that have led to the creation of a paternalistic national ideal, elements that have resulted in the marginalization and erasure of certain groups from the Puerto Rican family.

The narrator of Vega's story tells us that as soon as Suzie arrives to Puerto Rico she is overwhelmed by the colors and the mass of people. As a result, she thinks about going to Lares to visit her maternal grandmother. However, she decides not to do it and instead focuses on the image she sees on the travel agency poster announcing a hospitable paradise. Significantly, the narrator tells us that the reason Suzie resolves not to go to Lares is because her mother was thrown out of her grandmother's home because she had married a man with "pelo kinky" and that the grandmother did not want to see her "ni en pintura"(76). Along with the rejection she feels from her grandmother, it is important to remember that Lares, Suzie's maternal home, occupies a central position in the Puerto Rican collective imaginary. It is the symbolic location of the birth of the nation. Annually people return to Lares to celebrate the revolution against the Spanish colonizers and participate in a ritual commemoration of the nation and its heroes. Vega tells us that Suzie and her family have been exiled from that place and consequently from the nation due to perceived racial differences.

Reyes assures us that in Suzie, both diasporic and Island Puerto Ricans find each other. Vélez and Reyes affirm that this reunion is possible due to the narrative technique that Vega employs, which distances "ideal readers" from Suzie as it provides points of contact and identification between them. Both critics describe the narrator as someone who ridicules Suzie while other times they say that her attitudes show her to be assimilated, "sometimes ("the ideal reader") sees Puerto Rico's problems through Suzie's gaze" (Reyes 82). Until the last paragraph of the story Suzie is quite ambivalent. However, the oscillation ends with her final scream.

Vega uses the waiter's voice to retell the sexual liaison and Suzie's orgasm, thus adding another narrative voice to the story. As Reyes says of Suzie's orgasm, it "mocks phallologocentric nationalism, while at the same time reinscribing the diaspora into a bilingual national family" (85). Along with Reyes's observation, I would like to add that because she first fantasizes with having sex with a black man and later she actually has sex with an Afro-Puerto Rican (the waiter), she and the waiter re-inscribe Afro-Puerto Ricans into a national family that, this time, is multi-racial and based on popular images given to her in the "chick lit" novel she reads poolside. Vega's story, along with parodying the official images of Puerto Rican culture, also parodies commercially popular images in bodice ripper novels.

The irony in this text is not one of binaries where one signifier hides another; rather it is the counterpoint of multiple possibilities. The laughter that Vega evokes with Suzie's orgasm at the end explodes the binary of those who are from here and those who are from *afuera*, those who "don't belong." Instead of going to the maternal house in Lares to find the place of national memory and in this way re-establish her identity as a Puerto Rican, Suzie has a "national" encounter of a different variety. Here the place of national independence is not a place, rather it is found in the orgasmic scream of *jouissance* that unites Suzie and the Puerto Rican readers with their African past. Her orgasm shatters the scaffolding of the cultural imaginary created for her and others by the elite cultural forefathers and makes it possible for a new space to be imagined.

Given the place that this new freedom is found, its definition remains open. Given the relationship between Suzie, her scream and Lares—the place that the failed revolution against Spain began—we as readers are reminded that all revolutions miss their mark. Recalling the words from the previous chapter, we must "fail again" and "fail better." That is to say, we must keep aiming at a decolonial ideal and, at the same time, we must recognize that we will always fall short. Given the context of the story it is possible to interpret the epigraph that Vega places at the beginning by Albert Memmi, "Un homme à cheval sur deux cultures est rarement bien assis" (75). The counterpoint that is initiated in this story between two or more cultures is never going to be comfortable, sure, or complete. One is never well seated or "at home" on a horse of this type, but the journey must continue; or you have to kill one of the horses.

V: HISTORY'S GHOSTS IN ANA LYDIA VEGA'S "SOBRE TUMBAS Y HÉROES: FOLLETÍN DE CABALLERÍA BORICUA"

The *arte de bregar* between memory of the past, particularly Lares, and the present takes shape in Ana Lydia Vega's "Sobre tumbas y héroes: Folletín de caballería Boricua." In this story there are two researchers whose mission is to find the tombs of the participants in the historic event that unifies Puerto Rican cultural identity known as "El Grito de Lares." Appearing as a counterpoint to the figure of Suzie in the story, "Pollito/Chicken," published before this one, Guiomar is described as a "nuyorican" who is also a fervent nationalist trying to find Puerto Rico's forgotten past. Emanuel, the other researcher, is a typical young scholar whom Vega describes as a "Young Researcher Anxious to Contribute to the Rescue of Our History."[20] He takes his work seriously, but he is also attracted to Guiomar, who guides them both on their search. What they find in their journey to the interior of the island is a woman very similar to Doña Gabriela in Marqués's *La carreta* as well as the place where the some of the national heroes were buried.

In her story, Vega parodies her literary ancestors and her own story with Guiomar and Don Virgilio's parrot that imitates Lola Rodríguez Tió singing "La borinqueña," one of the national hymns. When it sings "La borinqueña," the parrot ends the song with "laa liiiii-beeeeer-táaaaaaa" in a way that is reminiscent of Suzie's "scream/cry" at the end of "Pollito/Chicken." An effect of parody is the subversion of the power that the classic and venerated text maintains. Here, Vega puts the almost sacred song "La borinqueña" in the mouth of a parrot. Heightening the parodic power of the scene is that the parrot is the property of a Don Virgilio, reminding readers of the classic epic poems, *The Aeneid* and Dante's *The Inferno*. The laughter that parody induces lowers the respected text from its elevated status. Nevertheless, at the same time, given the way parody functions, Vega also re-inscribes classical figures and texts in the minds of readers in the present. She places Puerto Rican culture alongside classical, European, canonic texts and authors, in this case Virgil and Dante. At the same time as she causes subversive laughter, she reinterprets the classics in a language that the current public can understand. One way she does that here is with a parody of *La carreta*.

Since we never know what happens to the protagonists at the end of *La carreta*, Vega invents a possibility. The two historians get lost in the mountains looking for tombs, and in the process Doña Remedios saves them and gives them directions to their objective. If the readers have not recognized the connection between Doña Remedios and Doña Gabriela from Marqués's play, Vega makes it very clear. She describes Remedios's scream as something that is reminiscent of "Lucy Boscana in the role of Doña Gabriela in *La carreta*" (133). Vega, following postmodern techniques and loyal to the parodic process, describes Remedios as a palimpsest. If Remedios's character makes the reader laugh, it is because he or she recognizes the connection between the past and the present. At the same time that she is making fun of the procedures of literary tradition and the creation of the cultural imaginary, Vega ingrains herself in that same tradition by actualizing the classic figure and by remembering historic texts.

Her story creates layers upon layers of canonical, popular, and marginalized cultural products. Lucy Boscana is the actor most identified with the role of Doña Gabriela, but she is also identified with Toña, an Afro-Puerto Rican character in Francisco Arriví's drama, *Vejigantes*, which she interpreted on numerous occasions. Camilla Stevens says that the role of Toña is not so well remembered because *La carreta* was produced much more frequently including a 1972 televised performance. Though her argument is much more complex, generally Stevens attributes the popularity of *La carreta* to the number of times that it was staged due to the fact that the official culture wanted to exclude Afro-Puerto Rican elements from the imaginary. The other play that Boscana acted in, *Vejigantes*, takes its name from masks worn frequently during the *fiestas patronales* (Saint's day fiesta) in Loiza, a town connected to a history of runaway slaves and a site that would be the polar opposite to the mountains where the *jíbaro* is thought to dwell. So, as the title suggests, *Vejigantes* is more closely related to Afro-Puerto Rican culture than the *jíbaro* culture portrayed in *La carreta*. Here, with the mention of Boscana in her parody of the play, Vega creates a possible relation between her work as well as *Vejigantes* and *La carreta*. By relating the female figures—Gabriela, Remedios, and Boscana—Vega also signals toward a silence inhabited by Toña and Afro-Puerto Rican culture. She does this at the same time as she creates a space from which it is possible to criticize colonial influence on the Island.

In addition to her identification with a symbol that is doubly or triply national—*el jíbaro*, Toña, Doña Gabriela—Doña Reme, as Remedios is called, also expresses her frustration with regard to the fact that a "Míster Klin" is the owner of a large parcel of land containing the tombs of the national heroes that the young researchers are looking for. The figure with his comic name, "Míster Klin," linking him to the cleaning product "Mr. Clean," has a strong and obvious association with U.S. colonialism's incessant presence that impedes the recuperation of Puerto Rico's past and the formation of its national identity. U.S. culture here has not only invaded the metropolitan area of San Juan or the shopping malls like Plaza las Américas, it has also created a beachhead deep within the mountains on the geographic location of the cry for Puerto Rican independence.

The influence of U.S. culture and power on every level of Puerto Rican society threatens the existence of the *jíbaro* icon along with Doña Reme/ Gabriela/Toña. Míster Klin's link to U.S. consumer culture stands in contrast to Doña Reme, who serves the young researchers homemade food cooked in the traditional style: *café ricamente cola'o* along with *asopao de pollo con tostones*. As they eat Reme's food, it seems that the scholars have come in contact with real, live Puerto Rican culture, which is shown in contrast and as a bulwark against the increasing influence and power of Míster Klin.

Along with the other characters and adventures in this story in search of the epic, historical figures of Puerto Rico's past, Vega adds the figure of Don Virgilio, who motivates the young scholars on their journey. He encourages them to go without him since he is too old and infirm to go with them. As already stated, his name reminds the reader of two epics from Western tradition, *The Aeneid* and *The Divine Comedy*. In the first, Virgil begins a journey of return after the battle of Troy. In the second, he guides Dante during part of his journey. Similar to the multiple characters that are compressed into the figure of Doña Reme, Vega gives different possible identities to the Virgilio in her story. As he directs the two young people, he is guided by a silent Taíno Indian.[21] With this, Vega evokes a return to the interior of Puerto Rico and the essence of Puerto Rican culture such as the *jíbaro* and the Taíno, all of which connect Puerto Ricans to each other and to their silent, phantasmatic past.

Similar to Marqués's drama, *La carreta*, where the mountain center of Puerto Rico hosts the essence of Puerto Rican identity, Vega's story resonates with modernist concepts regarding how a nation is defined. True identity is found in the journey to the place of origin that, at least in the case of *La carreta* and "Sobre tumbas y héroes," takes place in the mountainous jungle of the Island. In order to find the nation's true essence, it is necessary to travel to the center of the Island and not to the exterior or margins because in those areas, on the border what is found is contaminated by the foreign and African culture. Such a contamination is thought to pose a threat to the stability of the nation. Significantly, Arlene Torres notes that the construction of the official image of the *jíbaro* as a racially pure icon coincides with its imagined location in the center of the Island and not on the coasts or margins where, supposedly Afro-Puerto Ricans lived.

Contrary to a conceptualization of the Island center as a location of pure essence, in Vega's story it is the place of defeat and adulteration. Instead of finding the place where the new nation was or could be born, as Virgil did when he founded Rome, Emanuel and Guiomar end up in a place called "Villa Troya." That is to say, they find themselves in a place of defeat. The "place" and the "defeat" again offer multiple interpretations. The young historians are defeated because they don't find what they were looking for, the place where the defeated Puerto Rican revolution began. On top of those defeats is the fact that they are in a place, "Villa Troya," named after another place of conquest and loss, Troy. Like the place the historians are looking for, Troy was a place that was covered over by years and which was thought to be mythical until Henrich Schliemann discovered evidence of its existence in 1868. It was discovered because the Austrian archaeologist believed that *The Iliad* was more than just a good story. With this and other tenuous connections between history and her stories, Vega seems to encourage us to look for connections to history and reality in her stories while at the same time cautioning us, demanding that we question everything. Truth here consists in multiple layers that are at times contradictory. Along with the multiple layers of possibilities that exist in counterpoint to each other is the fact that the colonial presence impedes access to information that could be included in the historical archive.

The presence of Míster Klin in the exact location where they had hoped to find the heroes' tombs makes painfully evident that the place of origin is less than pure. It also makes evident that access to history and its archives is interrupted by the colonial presence of the United States. Klin's presence—also as a specter since he never appears in the story—as absentee owner of property defeats the young researchers in their quest more than anything else. The defeat of Puerto Rican culture seems even more complete when influence of non-Puerto Rican, U.S. culture is evident in the *jíbaro* the young researchers find. This is manifest in the language of Doña Remedios' son when it is evident that English forms part of his active vocabulary. He calls Doña Reme "model," a Spanish inflected version of "mother," rather than the Spanish *mamá* or *madre*. In addition to this, Emanuel and Guiomar find out that her son was the one who had stolen their clothes when they bathed, leaving them totally naked. Like Míster Klin, he impedes their progress and causes them to deviate from their paths. In this story/history, the return—whether it is to the place of origin, the historical past or the location of cultural essence or purity—is always corrupted or interrupted by another influence or possibility. The return like the history they search for is haunted by the spirit or phantasm of what is left out in its telling. That or the "original culture" is seen through the optics created by a palimpsest, which presents multiple interpretations of the text as in the case of Doña Remedios/Gabriela/Toña.

Surprisingly perhaps, Vega takes a position against the influence of Míster Klin and what he represents similar to the position that Marqués held against U.S. influence. However, unlike Marqués, for Vega, Guiomar, and Emanuel, no transparent, unambiguous answer is found. In spite of their apparent failure, they have not found nothing. Like the absence over which the symbolic order is constructed, it is not "nothing" that is there. Rather, it is a something that resists representation. The history that Vega tells parodies paternalist models at the same time that it creates a concept of belonging that is different to that of her precursors. In recent years critics like Carlos Pabón, Rubén Ríos Ávila, and Arlene Dávila, as well as writers like Ana Lydia Vega, have begun a critical questioning of the traditional model of nation that still persists in Puerto Rico. For example, Pabón in his book, *Nación post-mortem: Enasyos sobre los tiempos de insoportable ambiguedad*, asserts that the nation as it was imagined by Marqués and his generation is one that still exists for the majority of Puerto Ricans in 2003, the year Pabón's book was published. He says that the political arguments and many of the accepted cultural representations are not trying to imagine a departure from the "unsupportable ambiguity" that Puerto Ricans must live with due to their peculiar political status. Rather, Pabón claims, most representations keep looking toward the past, using a very particular understanding of history to limit who belongs to the nation to those who "fulfill ethnic and cultural criteria" (386). Dávila, in a similar way, shows how the three political groups, the PPD, the PIP, and the PNP, use cultural icons that have an effect equal to that of the PPD's *jíbaro* in terms of unifying and limiting representation to a select group. The consistency of images across political spectrums shows a desire for cultural and racial purity combined with an exclusion of transnational or diasporic Puerto Ricans. The accepted symbols demonstrate a desire and a connection to the past that does not recognize a reality composed of a heterogeneous mix of differences. A conception of what it means to be Puerto Rican that is unaccepting of differences leads to the exclusion of those who represent the "impure," those who have something "de afuera." The idea, then, of the nation must be reconfigured. It is necessary to rethink how the nation and its people imagine themselves as belonging to the nation in order to create models that are more inclusive and which can be more representative of the majority of the people.

Vega's stories are not an argument in favor of colonialism or one that would cede to globalizing pressures. It should be recognized that the way that the concept of the nation is imagined in Puerto Rico and elsewhere is based on a model given by occidental modernity. What is needed then is a cultural imaginary similar to the one that Vega creates, one that does not abandon the anti-colonial posture of previous generations and which, at the same time, accepts differences. What Vega proposes along with others is an amplification of the representative models used by those who occupy official positions in order to construct a more inclusive cultural imaginary (Dávila 18). As Pabón says, it is necessary to imagine "new forms of postnational communities that are not founded on the fact of being native to a territory, nor in filiation to or coherence of a particular ethnicity, nor should it be founded on the act of belonging to a particular State" (386).

VI: THE PUERTO RICAN SINTHOME IN THE TWO NOVELS BY JUDITH ORTIZ COFER

Like many authors of the Puerto Rican diaspora, Judith Ortiz Cofer's novels, *The Line of the Sun* (1989) and *The Meaning of Consuelo* (2003), portray young, female protagonists who both are and are not at home in the United States and Puerto Rico. From this position they are able to form part of the community that surrounds them even as they adopt a critical distance from it. The main character in each novel notices how society functions through a system of signs that gives basis to a code of values upheld by the local community. Ortiz Cofer often shows more empathy for outcasts than for other characters. Those who are unable to conform to society's symbolic order in her novels are often sensitive artists, homosexuals, and women who do not live up to society's code of sexual purity and motherhood, as well as those who represent Afro-Puerto Rican culture. However, far from arguing for inclusion of the outcasts or marginalized—an act that would require domestication of the outcast elements and elimination of differences—Ortiz Cofer shows that there is something in them and in her main characters that is inassimilable by the larger order that governs society. It is this protruding, inassimilable kernel that represents a possibility for a disturbance in society's established order that may cause disruptive events in its narrative fabric. Only by remaining outside the order can it maintain its energy as a disruptive force. Because of this Ortiz Cofer's protagonists resist assimilation even as they learn to survive within the social order. In addition, Ortiz Cofer shows the dangers of living in a position that is entirely beyond the constraints of society. Her novels are filled with marginalized characters who disappear entirely and often tragically; the sensitive uncle, Carmelo, in *The Line of the Sun* is blown up in the Korean War into so many pieces there is nothing left to ship back home, Mili in *The Meaning of Consuelo* disappears when her aunt takes her eye off her for a minute at the beach. While her female protagonists do not fully assimilate to either United States, Puerto Rican, or even diasporic culture, neither do they operate from the position of the complete outcast; a position that would result in annihilation. The result is that Ortiz Cofer's writing, and her protagonists, offer a response to the doubly colonized situation confronting Puerto Ricans that allows for a type of resistance that does not domesticate or completely silence the oppositional force.

Ortiz Cofer and others show how it is necessary to encounter the thing, the sinthome of colonialism, which cannot be articulated or understood. I argue that it is a sinthome and not a symptom since the sinthome remains beyond all efforts to assimilate it.

The sinthome unlike the symptom, is an inassimilable, constitutive kernel in the symbolic order that cannot be incorporated through a curing process. The relationship between symptom and sinthome in the construction of identity is evident in Puerto Rico as well. If Puerto Rico is a sinthome of the United States, since it constitutes U.S. imperialism and will never be able to be fully assimilated to it, then Afro-Puerto Ricans, women, gays, lesbians, transgender, and diasporic Puerto Ricans are sinthomes of Puerto Rico. In other words, in the construction of its own response to the racist imperialism of the United States, Puerto Rico enacted similar exclusions, in a sense doubling the repressions of the master. On a linguistic level, these exclusions resulted in the exiling of voices that do not speak Spanish with a particular accent or in a way that measures up to an idea of grammatical, linguistic purity based on colonial and exclusionary models. On a cultural level, exclusionary practices meant the affirmation of a heteronormative, paternalistic, Hispanophilic identity to the elimination of all else. This symptomatic reaction to U.S. imperialism created a number of sinthomes: gestures, sounds, and acts that cannot be fully articulated within the newly found, paternalistic order.

Patricia Gherovici works as a psychoanalyst in the Puerto Rican community of Philadelphia. In her book, *The Puerto Rican Syndrome*, she has shown how many Puerto Ricans experience *ataques* or *ataques de nervios* (attacks or nervous attacks) in reaction to the social exclusion they feel. Gherovici characterizes *ataques* as hysteric responses to extreme poverty experienced by many Puerto Ricans. Though it is tempting to me to apply her work, I would argue that the sinthome is a more appropriate label for what Ortiz Cofer portrays in her novels. As Gherovici says, "the hysteric shows what the physician wants to see, while at the same time revealing the limits of his gaze" (52). The hysteric always shapes his or her discourse to the desire of the Other that is lacking. The sinthome, on the other hand, is a radical departure, an eruption in the symbolic order without concern for the desire imposed by the gaze of the Other. One usual response to exclusion is to argue that the marginalized voice be included, resulting in a series of maneuvers that have the consequence of domesticating that voice. The act of domestication and homogenization sees the sinthome as a symptom, something that can be cured and made better by a series of acts that conforms it to the symbolic order.

The other typical response is for the sinthomatic to form a separate community with others who are equally sinthomatic. This, of course, is impossible since the sinthome is something that cannot be interpreted. It resists all efforts to arrive at symbolization, yet it forms an intimate part of all identity whether at the personal, local, national, or global level. As Slavoj Žižek relates regarding the difference between symptom and sinthome, "in contrast to symptom which is a cipher of some repressed meaning, sinthome has no determinate meaning; it just gives body, in its repetitive pattern, to some elementary matrix of *jouissance*, of excessive enjoyment" (*Tarrying* 226). Although it has no meaning, the sinthome does, nevertheless, appear within the fabric of symbolization. However, the sinthome is an eruption that resists interpretation, which we, nevertheless, feel the need to interpret. Our effort to do so reduces or domesticates the sinthome as symptom or as some other marker such as shame. The sensed presence of the sinthome fills us with the anxiety for meaning. The mistake is to think that in our attempts to interpret or make sense of it that we arrive at full enclosure of the sinthome within the symbolic universe.

VII: *THE MEANING OF CONSUELO*: MILI AS SINTHOME

In Ortiz Cofer's *The Meaning of Consuelo* for example, the title character, Consuelo, seems to be surrounded by characters that exist within the social network, but because of some inassimilable aspect of themselves, they are not allowed to participate fully. Their lack of complete assimilation, or their inability to completely hide their difference, makes everyone around them feel uneasy. The novel opens with the two sisters, Consuelo and Milagros (called Mili), observing María Sereno strut around the neighborhood. We soon learn, through the shifting personal article, that María is transgender. Because of her/his location as a transgender subject in 1950s Puerto Rico, María is unable to find work and is ostracized from the community. However, because she is so adept at manicures, and she does them for a good price, she is permitted into the households of the *casas decentes* (good/decent homes) through the backdoor when no one is watching. As the narrator says, "In public we were to pretend that we didn't know him. But Mili sometimes forgot" (5). When María comes to Consuelo's house to paint her mother's nails, Consuelo is signaled to serve him water and food in the plate and glass "with the tiny black dot on the bottom. [. . .] It was the one she [her mother] had marked for his use only" (11). The horrifying treatment of María as well as that of other outcasts, Consuelo's sister, Mili, and Patricio, bears the marks of the abjectification; the abject is a subject that is treated like the undesirable waste that might cause illness or infection and so must be served on a separate plate, exiled and flushed away. Their relationship to the abhorred smelly stuff that we want to wash away also links the characters to the sinthome. The unrestrained *jouissance* of the sinthome, when seen from the position of the symbolic order, is something that we want to exclude even though it is part of who we are.

In keeping with the sinthomatic characters in her novels, María and others are banished from the page. Though María has a job in one of the tourist hotels, she no longer lives in the local community. After her appearance at the beginning of the novel, she all but disappears until we see her in a fabricated underwater world where she does manicures. Patricio, Consuelo's sensitive, gay neighbor and cousin, who learns how to change the colors of the flowers growing in his yard by injecting them with dye, is forced to leave to New York from where he sends Consuelo postcards detailing his liberation. Mili slowly retreats from the family and social life, chanting apparently non-sensical phrases or repeating rhymes with the color "azul, azul, azul." Through colors, her relationship to the sea and her impenetrable language, Mili is related to Afro-Puerto Rican culture and *santería*. The color blue and Mili's connection to water draws a connection between her and Yemayá, the Orisha closely associated with the sea. Making this connection even more evident, in an effort to find a cure, the mother goes against the father's wishes and looks for help in *santería*. The mother then takes a "promesa" to wear the colors of the Orisha in the hopes that a cure is found. The father upholds an assimilationist view of culture putting his faith in U.S. technology when it comes to every matter including his daughter's cure. The mother, who lives under the thumb of the father's repressive regime as *la sufrida*, the long suffering wife, acts in desperation by turning to more traditional methods to cure her daughter, but is denied to seek a cure by following Afro-Puerto Rican traditions through the violent assertion of power by the father. In the end, nothing works and Mili disappears one day at the beach when her aunt, charged with watching her, is distracted for a few moments. It could be assumed that she is called back to the sea by Yemayá as are many of the adherents to that Orisha or that she is kidnapped or drowned.

The Line of the Sun, Ortiz Cofer's first novel, has a similar dynamic to the later *The Meaning of Consuelo*. Again set in the 1950s, the protagonist's family travels back and forth from the Island to Patterson, New Jersey, and "El building" where they live.[22] Guzmán is similar to the Mili character in the later novel since he has a connection to the Afro-Puerto Rican past and is increasingly marginalized from the family. Where Mili is related to Yemayá, Guzmán is associated with Changó. Due to an injury his body takes the shape of a lightning bolt—Changó is associated with lightning and fire—and he walks with a limp, similar to Changó. He is said to have dark skin and has a "fuzzy head," aspects that show Afro-Puerto Rican blood in a family that lives in the middle of the Island where whiteness is prized. Similar to *Consuelo* where the mother and Consuelo seek out help from the abject María in his faux underwater nail salon at a local tourist hotel, Mamá Cielo in *The Line of the Sun* seeks help from Rosa, a person who lives on the outskirts of town, practices *santería* rituals and has, in the eyes of the strict Catholic town, questionable morals. Even her *santería* is questionable since she reveals that the person who taught her what she knows was a con-man. Though Rosa's cure seems to help Guzmán for a time, it does not appropriately adjust him to dominant society. Guzmán eventually must leave town due to a brush with the law and from then on appears and disappears in the narrative. Similar to the Patricio character is Guzmán's brother, Carmelo, who spends time locked up in a room in the church's rectory reading poetry with the handsome, young priest "El padrecito César." Because Carmelo does not respond to the advances of a pretty girl, she reveals that there is more to Carmelo and César's relationship than poetry and both men are forced to leave the town. Carmelo joins the army and is blown to so many pieces that they cannot ship his body home.

The treatment of the apparently gay and transgender characters in Ortiz Cofer's novels mirrors that of the Island novelist Magali García Ramis' *Felices días tío Sergio* in which the eponymous Sergio poses a threat to the family unit, a microcosm of *la gran familia puertorriqueña*. However, since it isn't until the final lines of the novel that we learn from the narrator—who similar to Ortiz Cofer's protagonist narrators is a young woman—that he might be gay. The chief threat Sergio poses is that he teaches the children Puerto Rican history and culture and in the process adds to what they learn in school in ways that complicate and contradict the official education they are given. Even though he is an outsider at the beginning, he seems fit to serve the role of family leader since he knows more about Puerto Rican history and culture than the teachers who instruct at the school attended by the family children including the narrator. However for the matriarchs he is a questionable *pater familias* due to his *independentista*, nationalist, and anti-colonial leanings. As Juan Gelpí notes, García Ramis situates her novel in the 1950s, a time of political and social upheaval, when Pedro Albizu Campos with other *independentistas* were jailed. As the voice of opposition is silenced publicly, so is Sergio's in the family. Soon he is forced back into exile in New York. The narrator tells us that he was "a man almost at the margins of society" (160)[23] and that on more than one occasion he "had spent six months in the New York county prison on more than one occasion for participating in a protest. According to what we are told, he was "a pariah, an nonconformist and, probably, a homosexual" (160).[24] These fictional exiles in the novels by Ortiz Cofer and García Ramis underline the real exile of the Puerto Rican gay writer Manuel Ramos Otero as well as many others.[25]

The same pivotal time period of the 1950s forms the background for both of Ortiz Cofer's novels discussed here. It was during the 1950s that Puerto Rico had invoked *la ley de mordaza* or a gag law that, as I mentioned in the introduction to this chapter, prohibited anyone to say anything against the United States or in favor of Puerto Rican independence. Even expressions of patriotism were considered against the law. During this time, the leader of opposition to U.S. colonialism, Pedro Albizu Campos, along with the poet Francisco Matos Paoli were jailed. Albizu Campos suffered years of torture called "radiological experiments," eventually dying from his injuries. Matos Paoli spent the rest of his life dealing with the diagnosed mental illness that resulted from his long imprisonment. The point is that precisely when Puerto Rico was deciding its status, whether to accept the moniker of *Estado Libre Asociado* or not, whether to submit to U.S. colonialism or not, a law was invoked that abrogated free speech in favor of any oppositional ideas. As the nation defined itself in the 1950s, it also showed what would happen to anyone who did not conform, they were either expulsed entirely—as in the case of Albizu—or they would be deemed mad as in the case of Matos Paoli. It was also the time when, as Gherovici relates, the so-called "Puerto Rican syndrome" was identified and catalogued.

Though many Puerto Ricans left and continue to leave the Island, exile is not always physical. Those who do not conform to the popular image are also exiled from it. As Rubén Ríos Ávila argues, it is more a "a notion of exile as an intermediate state, like a mediated purgatory, always open, always unfinished and always frustrated" (*Raza* 228).[26] Noticing how the gay Puerto Rican writer Ramos Otero's literary production made even José Luis González uncomfortable, Ríos Ávila says that he wants to see González' mortification and discomfort with Ramos as "a symptom to read the exile of these writers. It is there, in the mortification of discomfort, that the precise zone of this particular expatriation is marked" (*Raza* 232).[27] It is interesting that Ríos Ávila would pick up this incident between González and Ramos Otero especially since González himself lived in self-exile in Mexico and wrote the important essay *El país de cuatro pisos*. In his essay González criticizes the class hierarchies of the island that he argues are largely based on racial differences. It would seem that he would be more empathetic to other exiles, other members of the abject community. Though González was something of an outsider due to his self-imposed exile, his work is foundational for much of the work being done today. He could be called a canonical writer, accepted even in his difference or perhaps because of it. In the encounter between González and Ramos Otero, Ríos Ávila focuses on the sinthome that makes González, and perhaps many others, uncomfortable, the thing that expatriates Ramos Otero and that, in many respects, is inassimilable. Ríos Ávila wants to leave it there, "unfinished and frustrated" since from that position, it maintains its potential to create "the mortification of discomfort" in the symbolic order. A discomfort that the ruling order has to deal with, or in the words of Arcadio Díaz Quiñones, it will have to *bregar* with this problem even if it never finds a solution to it.

An important element in Ríos Ávila's argument is that what is thought of as an outside threat is really also an internal one. González as well as Ramos

Otero are not U.S. imperialists by any stretch of the imagination. In García Ramis' *Felices días Tío Sergio* the threat is from someone who knows more about Puerto Rican history and culture than the schoolteachers, Guzmán in *The Line of the Sun* is an unwelcomed reminder of the Afro-Puerto Rican past, supposedly an essential part of the triumvirate that makes up Puerto Rican identity along with indigenous Taíno culture and white, Spanish culture. However, Guzmán, Sergio, Mili, and María Serreno, like Ramos Otero, are all figures that represent an unbearable thing that has been cast out of the national order. As Ríos Ávila argues in his article "Queer Nation," " the fear the causes nations to erect its protective walls in reality refers to an enemy that all nations carry within itself" (1135).[28] For Ríos Ávila it is lesbians and gays who have been left out. For others like Ilia Rodríguez and Eleuterio Santiago Díaz, it is the Afro-Puerto Rican.

Ilia Rodríguez and Eleuterio Santiago Díaz underscore language's insufficiency to capture or represent the Afro-Puerto Rican experience when they remark that any literature or discursive project will be reduced to the limits of an order, no matter what the order. They say that delimitation of representation "[it] seems to us an inevitable reduction regardless of how flexible the limits of the institution in question might have become" ("Desde las fronteras" 1217).[29] Showing how the Afro-Puerto Rican, diasporic writer Piri Thomas' work *Down These Mean Streets* is expulsed from the Puerto Rican Island cannon because it makes evident "the racial conflict at the margins of the Puerto Rican and Hispanic *gran familia*" (1215).[30] Here the critics use "Hispanic" to refer to all Latino/a cultures whether in the United States or Puerto Rico. This conflict comes in part because the subject must undergo a violent transition in order to speak. Describing the subject's entry into the symbolic order Rodríguez and Santiago Díaz say that this violence erases the specific difference of the Afro-Latina/o subject, "for the Afro-Puerto Rican writer, to incur into the question of race and personal identity implies activating the dictates of the grammar [by Nebrija] as a norm of exclusion. For this writer [Santiago Díaz or Rodríguez], the practice of signification in the racial attack—and perhaps outside of it—always will remit to the historical processes that suppress African voices and which result in the loss of languages" (1212).[31] What is read here as an inevitable loss when entering into the symbolic order as dictated by the colony is read from the perspective of queer studies as the granting of a position of antagonism in relation to any closure that might be affected by the symbolic order, whether on the level of nation, local community, or family.

Any ideological structure casts out that which is "in itself more than itself." The thing it fears most is the thing it exiles, precisely because it is a constitutive part that the ideological fantasy does not want to recognize. Its exile is symptomatic of the closure created by nation, but the symptom marks the place of the sinthomatic eruption; the place where an inassimilable kernel that is, nevertheless, part of the organizational structure broke through the symbolic fabric. The symptom is the way that the inarticulable sinthome is spoken about within the symbolic order. The sinthome would not exist if not for the closure created by the structure itself, and it cannot be included in that structure or removed from it without causing either its own or the structure's downfall. The question is what to do with this thing that is in us more than ourselves. Antonio Viego argues in his *Dead Subjects: Toward a Politics of Loss in Latino Studies* that Latino studies have been shaped by an erroneous understanding of Freud that led to sociological criticism that sees assimilation or conformity as the ultimate goal for a well-adjusted subject. Viego corrects the translation of Freud and shows how it is necessary to understand that each subject contains within him or herself a thing that cannot be translated or assimilated into a community no matter how large or welcoming. There is always something that is going to keep us from identifying entirely with any group; it is impossible to wholly assimilate to any order since we always must amputate part of ourselves in order to enter. Every community will create an order that will split or divide the subject no matter how open, welcoming, or politically correct it might be. If I like country and western music, for example, this might cause me to be exiled from the group of friends who are jazz enthusiasts and vice versa.

In an effort to create an "imagined community" that is not limited to the strict definitions of geography and Hispanic purity that have traditionally formed Puerto Rican identity, Carlos Pabón, in his *Nación postmortem* argues that, "So, it isn't about, like Duany proposes, an issue of making the limits of the nation more permeable or elastic. In my way of seeing things, what can be proposed is something more radical; abandon the concept of nation and imagine new forms of postnational communities that are not founded on the fact of being native to a territory, nor in the ethnic filiation or coherency, nor in the belonging to a State" (386).[32] However, a community without limits is impossible. No matter how radically fragmented or postnational his proposed model, Pabón admits that some sort of community, some sort of limits, must be formed. Even the smallest micro-community would result in exclusions, exiles, and amputations.

Efforts have been made to read marginalized groups as forming a single community. For example, Yolanda Martínez-San Miguel in her *Caribe Two Ways: Cultura de la migración en el caribe insular hispánico*, says she is looking for ways that national identities "are forged in collaboration with proper and outside mobile populations, and based on which the coordinates of identification processes are postulated that are simultaneously local and transnational" (33).[33] Equally, Agustin Laó-Montes tries to bring Afro-Latinidades together to form an "Afroamerica (that) can be represented as a creolized diaspora space, a translocal crossroads, a black borderland" (128). However, he is not arguing for total inclusion. Rather the space becomes queered by bringing together diverse, dispersed elements of the diaspora, into one big family. However the family is not entirely "happy" if happiness means complete satisfaction and unity. What happens is that each member is forced to encounter the uncomfortable difference that Ríos Ávila notices between González and Ramos Otero. As Laó further argues, if in order to come together differences are erased, it would produce a "false sense of sameness and a superficial notion of community" (132). Instead he sees the Afro-American—using this term to refer to all of America not just the United States—community as one that should be represented "in its diversity and complexity" (132) that also recognizes the conflicts. Laó and Martínez-San Miguel seem to adopt an attitude toward culture similar to Juan Flores' when he calls Puerto Rican culture "este revolú que nos identifica" [this mess that identifies us]. The *revolú* is a mess that is difficult to make sense of. Even though you may arrive at one understanding of it, because it is such a *revolú*, other interpretations are possible. Like Laó, Flores' *revolú* notices the "conflicts" that would arise in the bringing together of any group of people would come out of the need to exclude or purge differences in the search for commonality. What these present day theorists are arguing for is a Hegelian synthesis of opposites, something that is entirely impossible. As Žižek argues regarding the Hegelian dialectic; "The underlying premise is that *the Whole is never truly whole*: every notion of the Whole leaves something out, and the dialectical effort is precisely the effort to include this excess, to account for it. Symptoms are never just secondary failures or distortions of a basically sound System—they are indicators that there is something 'rotten' [antagonistic, inconsistent] in the very heart of the System" (*Less than Nothing* 523). There are two things to bring out with regard to Žižek's statement. First of all, the idea that the dialectic is ever finished, that it ever reaches a state of satisfactory overcoming, is impossible. There is always something left out that the system will try to include via the dialectical process. Secondly, what is left out, the thing that we interpret as a symptom, is a sign referring to the antagonistic inconsistency at the very heart of the System or symbolic order itself. To live an ethical life, we should constantly engage the inconsistency, the thing left out, of our system. By doing so, perhaps, we can correct the dysfunctions of our own order. Though to ever be satisfied with whatever corrections we make would be to assume that we have arrived at an impossible wholeness or completeness. The latter is a sign of totalitarianism of the worst sort.

For Žižek and Viego conflicts are necessary and we should not ignore them in our efforts to form a community. Following Viego's argument, the Latina/o subject has been rendered dead precisely because the nagging something that prevents complete assimilation into any community has been theorized out of the equation as undesirable. In order for the subject to come alive again, she or he must once again encounter the sinthome. Viego says that "a Lacanian psychoanalytic model that understands all of us as necessarily divided seems crucial for the simple fact of effecting something new and *keeping it moving*" (241). What unites queers with Afro-Puerto Ricans, women and others who find themselves living in the borderlands is that the symbolic order designates a very important part of their selves as shameful or outcast, a sinthome of the nation.[34] It often uses an even more extreme term "shameless" or *sinvergüenza*, words that tell the person they must have no shame, or no sense of morality or decency, if they can allow themselves to engage in certain shameful or unacceptable behavior. One way of understanding shame is as a symptom, the mark of the sintome's eruption. It shows the point where the inexplicable breaks through the symbolic order only to disappear. As we try to make sense of it, we bring it into symbolization. Doing this, we elide the force of the sinthome even as we mark the place of its rupture. But there is no choice but to try and make sense of the sinthome. Vega's work analyzed above is an attempt to do just that. The work of the elites in 1950s Puerto Rico attempted to create a unified and unquestioned image of Puerto Rican identity tried to ignore or eliminate the presence of the sinthome. A primary cultural example is the image of the *jíbaro* as portrayed in René Marqués's *La carreta*. Marqués's stance with regard to the sinthomatic elements in society is all the more problematic or interesting due to the fact that he was a closeted homosexual—a fact unknown by many until recently—showing how successfully he ignored that part of himself, and that part of Puerto Rican culture, that was deemed unacceptable.

What unites queers with Afro-Puerto Ricans, women and others who find themselves living in the borderlands is that the symbolic order feels discomfort by their presence and designates this unsettled feeling as shameful or outcast, a sinthome of the nation. In Ortiz Cofer's novels the young protagonist often describes not just moments of shame in her own life, but also the shameful actions of others in her family or community. In her novels, there is extreme pressure to be thought *gente decente* or decent people and eliminate *sinvergüenza* tendencies. It is interesting, though not surprising, that Consuelo, in *The Meaning of Consuelo*, and the protagonist, Marisol, in Ortiz Cofer's earlier novel, *The Line of the Sun*, find refuge in language by reading and writing. Marisol always finds a place to hide and be with books. She hides on the fire escape in El Building to read and, when they move, in her new house, she loves the enclosure created by the dormers where she places her desk and writes. In *The Meaning of Consuelo*, Consuelo learns to use language to reverse *el chisme* or gossip, and she hides from the ever-vigilant eyes by escaping to her grandfather's library. Where her mother's proverbs "only warned [her] about life" and have a panoptic effect, she says, "I looked to books for hope" (154). She also says that, "I began to understand that words were the key to power and freedom" (155). Her *abuelo*'s library is "a secret source of wealth" (155). She is able to reshape her exile by taking refuge in it. From this space, if we can read the novel as a *bildungsroman*, the young artist as a young woman learns to tell the stories of others who have been exiled from the cultural imaginary.

Lisa Sánchez González, in her interpretation of the ending of *The Line of the Sun* says, "Marisol takes up residence in an attic room where she can finally read and be at peace with herself and her imagination. Marisol's alienation thus ultimately fulfills the formula of American success and assimilation" (152). Though she does find solace in domestic places, Marisol, along with Consuelo, also identify with the exiles, the outcasts from society. In *The Line of the Sun* for example, she identifies with Guzmán when he shows up at El Building and tells her stories. After listening to him she says that he makes her realize that "I was being counseled in humble acceptance of a destiny I had not chosen for myself: exile or, worse, homelessness. I was already very much aware of the fact that I fit into neither the white middle-class world of my classmates [. . .] nor the exclusive club of El Building's expatriates" (*Line* 177). Consuelo is similarly exiled from her family, her classmates, and everyone else. Her only friends are Patricio, María, and a classmate who lives in extreme poverty. Near the end of *The Meaning of Consuelo*, the young protagonist refuses to listen as the women indoctrinate her mother back into acceptable society by giving "back her old vocabulary." Consuelo refuses to listen saying that "I did not need to hear those old stories again" (181). By now she realizes that she has created her own stories, "how you tell a story to yourself, makes *you* up. You tell yourself as you live your life" (181). She refuses to be cured by her family's story, and denies herself entrance into its welcoming confines. Instead, she decides to make up her own story. Since she is writing and using language, her decision allows her to be visible in language. However, in language she finds a place to hide a secret. She realizes that though her family loves her, "they did not, or perhaps could not see me for who I became" (180).

Though she does not feel completely part of the community, she is nevertheless part of it. The exiled Patricio assures her that, "You may leave the island, niña, but it will never leave you. We all carry the plantain stain with us, *la mancha*, inside or out, wherever we go" (174). Encountering the inassimilable kernel that separates her from the community she says that people see her, but they do not see all of her. By engaging with the sinthome—or its visible apparition, the shameful—Consuelo sees the symbolic order thrown out of balance and realizes that the law upon which her community is based is an ideological fantasy. It no longer holds the secret to her happiness, that secret is within the self. However, even there, she will encounter dissatisfaction caused by the sinthomatic something that can never be interpreted or resolved satisfactorily into a narrative structure. However painful or however much anxiety this causes her and us, according to Viego, we will remain alive, as opposed to dead subjects if we remain dissatisfied. It is how, in

Viego's words, we "keep it moving," how we resist conforming to dead, pregiven definitions of who we are. Marisol ends *The Line of the Sun* saying "I would always carry my island heritage on my back like a snail" (273). Her home is one that is portable and in constant movement, *en el vaivén.*

Communities are united by a mutual relationship to the visible—the symbolic order—that forms a shared tradition. But since entrance into any community also requires an amputation of certain aspects of the individual that do not conform to the shared symbolic order, communities are also founded upon a violent, traumatic event of mutilation. It would be a mistake to assume that the visible is not haunted by the traumatic event; that the invisible excess does not or cannot return to trouble the visible.[35] Subjects, as well as communities, are founded upon this double relation between the visible and the invisible. Between what can be known and understood and what forever resists our ability to understand it. Members of all communities are therefore marked by their relation to what is unacceptable to the community at large, by what must remain hidden in order to be allowed to participate in the communal. The hidden something is sometimes interpreted as shame. Though we hide what we are ashamed of, we are also what we hide, the shameless thing that cannot be articulated into the social order. We are all *sinvergüenzas*; whether we want to admit it or not, we all have something to hide. The creation of another community—whether feminist, ethnic, gay, and so on—founded upon what must remain hidden to a larger community, does not result in a utopia where everyone is welcome "as they are" without sacrificing some part of themselves before entering the community. One need look no farther than Gloria Anzaldúa's work to see that as a lesbian she was not entirely welcomed into the Chicano community, similarly Francés Negrón Mutaner, Lawrence La Fountain-Stokes, and others, write of their exclusions on both sides of the *charco* between Puerto Rico and the United States because of their sexuality. Likewise, Ortiz Cofer's work shows that resistance to colonial power has resulted in a symbolic order, a law that has excluded gays, lesbians, and Afro-Puerto Ricans and severely limited the roles of women.

What an encounter with the sinthome allows is an encounter with the veil that hides our shame: an examination of the scar where the amputation was performed. As Rubén Ríos Ávila says, since shame is a singular experience enacted on the individual it is impossible to form a community around a common experience of this singular event, so "its actual capacity to become a truly productive engagement of differences would have to stem from the shared respect of each other's veil, from the empowering, transformational energy of their respective shame" ("Bite" 25). For what is behind the veil is, in Ríos Ávila's words, "a void," and therefore it is unable to enter into the symbolic order. The veil marks the place of the sinthome. The presence of the veil, of the encounter with shame and our other, reveal the limits of our own community, our language and symbols that unite us, and the traumas upon which they are founded. This engagement with the sinthome throws our ideological fantasy out of balance, but it also allows us a certain freedom. In Vega with Suzie we can see how the engagement with the sintomatic elements of her character created the space for an enlarged definition of the Puerto Rican cultural imaginary. In Vega's "Sobre tumbas y héroes," it as possible to see how what defines the nation also includes, through exclusion, elements that can never be fully found, encountered, or articulated within the larger structure of nation. In Marqués we saw an attempt to eliminate all undesirable elements and to elide the sinthome at the heart of the nation. In Ortiz Cofer and Vega we see an effort to engage the sinthome.

By engaging the sinthome it is possible to realize that the law is not all there is. It is up to critics and writers to encounter the shameless ghosts, the sinthomes that haunt our communities, to keep moving. Juan Duchesne Winter describes the dialectical nature of Puerto Rico's situation when, in the opening lines of his introduction to an issue devoted to Puerto Rico published by *Revista Iberoamericana*, he says in words reminiscent of Hegel himself that, "Every nation is also the others that subvert and, more than anything else, seduce its precarious sameness" (933).[36] Assimilation to sameness that would remove or short-circuit the dialectic renders subjectivity inert if not, in Viego's words, dead paints the image of a prison that most would want to escape. Engagement, with the anxiety caused by the sinthome, whose most evident mark is shame, vivifies the dialectic and the possibility for movement and change.

We have the choice to either engage the sinthome or to disavow its presence. Marqués disavows the sinthome and contests U.S. colonialism by affirming a well-defined, oppositional identity that creates an enclosure around the icon of the *jíbaro*. With his enclosure he participates in decolonial nationalistic gestures, which themselves have their roots in exclusionary, colonial practices. They imitate exclusionary models handed down to them by the colonial paradigm. So by creating the nationalistic, defensive enclosure Marqués and others are still fighting colonialism on its own terms and with its own weapons. This makes it an interminable, losing battle.

Vega and Ortiz Cofer's fiction offers perhaps the most radical response to the colonial situation. They make readers aware of the subjects left out of the nationalist, decolonial enclosure created by Marqués and others of his generation. Rather than engaging colonialism on an epistemological ground from within a framework articulated by the colonial reason, they instead put at risk the very integrity of the framework itself. In this gesture they pass beyond the limits of colonialism and of nation. Like Carlos Pabón, the definition of community they imagine is so broad that it runs the risk of fragmenting the nation itself.[37] This would mean that the nation and colonialism would no longer form a limit to how people who identify themselves as Puerto Rican

can imagine themselves or their connections to others. In the more recent fictional creations of Mayra Santos Febres, Eduardo Lalo, Pedro Cabiya, and many others, it is possible to see how this new imagined community is taking shape.

NOTES

1. "[. . .] la retórica del nacionalismo cultural."
2. It should be recognized that even though the ideal of linguistic and racial purity was first imposed in Spain in the aftermath of the "reconquista" in 1492, it was an ideal that was never achieved.
3. The term commonly used to denote Puerto Ricans who left the Island and came back, *nuyorican*, was originally a derrogatory term and one I will avoid throughout this article choosing to follow Lisa Sánchez-González use of the more inclusive Boricua or Diaspora to refer to writers who live off the Island or who migrant between the Island and some other place.
4. "[. . .] la voz negra aparece frecuentemente codificada en la literatura y en otros medios como una zona defectuosa del idioma. El negro es aquél que no sabe decir y en otras instancias, aquél que no sabe qué decir."
5. For more information on this see Ronald Fernandez and Ivonne Acosta.
6. Much of what I am saying here is based on Nathaniel Córdova's study as well as that by Torres and Dávila.
7. Torres demonstrates that the *jíbaro* was, in fact, not as racially or ethnically pure as the cultural elites might have hoped.
8. Lázaro Lima argues that the United States' war with Mexico and its aftermath with the Treaty of Guadalupe Hidalgo set a precedent for how U.S. hegemonic culture would perceive Mexicans and other people from Spanish Speaking countries in America as racially inferior. My addition to his argument is the point I make in the following paragraph regarding Teutonic exceptionalism.
9. These are known as The Insular Cases for more on them and how the United States resolved them see *Foreign in a Domestic Sense*.
10. For more on this see the essays contained in the book *Foreign in a Domestic Sense* as well as Fredrich Katz's book.
11. It could also be argued that Teutonic exceptionalism became a self-fulfilling prophecy that justified the United States in propping up dictators and destabilizing democratically elected governments.
12. In addition to the work of Maneul Alonso and Frade already mentioned other works that include the *jíbaro* is Luis Lloréns Torres' *El grito de Lares* (1917) and countless others. As Camilla Stevens has noted, Lucia Boscana acted in stage performances of *La carreta* more than eight hundred times.
13. The representation of this particular migration is also seen in the popular song "El lamento borincano," and forms an enduring part of the cultural imaginary.
14. As Flores says, the ideas and the ideological opposition between the United States and Latin America expressed by Marqués were developed by José Enrique Rodó in his essay *Ariel* (1900). What Rodó says in his essay influenced the formation of Latin American culture at the beginning of the twentieth century. For example, it is possible to see traces of his thought in José Vasconcelos and the Puerto Rican Antonio Pedreira writer of the essay *Insularismo*, which had an important impact in the Generation of 1930 and Marqués.
15. The ideas presented by Carlos Pabón and others that I discuss later in this chapter will clarify this term.
16. The word *bregar* is impossible to define with one word in English. Indeed, Díaz Quiñones takes an entire book to define its many uses and possibilities. One definition is "dealing with." I will use *bregar* in Spanish in order to remain open to the various possibilities the word can connote.

17. "[. . .] las imágenes de *bregar* producen la sensación de estar, simultaneamente, ante algo nuevo y antiguo."

18. Since Vega's language in this story goes between English and Spanish I will not translate the text since doing so would be near impossible.

19. In spite of what Reyes and Vélez say, I still find something problematic with the representation of Suzie above all because it represents a woman who fantasizes about being raped.

20. "Joven Investigador Ansioso por Contribuir al Rescate de Nuestra Historia."

21. The Taínos inhabited Puerto Rico and other Caribbean islands when Colón arrived. It is thought that they were exterminated due to disease and over work in Spanish servitude. However, recent DNA studies have revealed that many Puerto Ricans have a high level of indicators that would connect them to Taíno ancestors.

22. Usually U.S. Puerto Rican culture is more commonly associated with New York. By placing the family in New Jersey, Ortiz Cofer changes our typical conceptualization of U.S. Puerto Rican culture to some extent. Although it is also true that she and her family lived in New Jersey and that currently she lives in Georgia.

23. "[. . .] un hombre casi al margen de la sociedad."

24. "[. . .] pasó seis meses en la cárcel del condado de Nueva York por participar en una protesta. Según nos fuimos enterando, él fue un paria, un inconforme y, probablemente, un homosexual."

25. In Francés Negrón Mutaner's autobiographical film *Brincando el charco*, she obsesses about how her father, living in Puerto Rico, will accept or not her now that she has come out of the closet. The film closes with the plane taking off from the Philadelphia airport leaving the question suspended.

26. "[. . .] noción del exilio como estado intermedio, como purgatorio mediático, siempre abierto, siempre inacabado y siempre frustrado."

27. "[. . .] una síntoma para leer el exilio de estos escritores. Es allí, en la mortificación de la incomodidad, que se marca la zona precisa de esta particular expatricación."

28. "[. . .] el miedo que impulsa a las naciones a edificar sus muros protectivos en realidad se refiere a un enemigo que todas las naciones llevan adentro."

29. "[. . .] nos parece, es una reducción inevitable, no importa cuánto se hayan flexibilizado los límites de la institución en cuestión"

30. "[. . .] el conflicto racial en los márgenes de la 'gran familia' puertorriqueña e hispana."

31. "[. . .] para el escritor afropuertorriqueño incidir en la cuestión racial y la identidad propia implica activar el dictado de la gramática (de Nebrija) como norma de exclusión. Para este escritor, la práctica de signifiación en el abordaje de la raza—y quizás fuera de él—siempre remitiría a los procesos históricos en los que se suprimen las voces africanas y se pierden las lenguas."

32. "No se trata entonces, como propone Duany, de hacer más permeables y elásticos los límites de la nación. A mi modo de ver lo que puede plantearse es algo más radical; abandonar el concepto de la nación e imaginar nuevas formas de comunidades posnacionales que no se funden ni en el hecho de ser nativo de un territorio, ni en la filiación o coherencia étnica, ni a la pertenencia de un Estado."

33. "[. . .] se forjan en colaboración con poblaciones móviles propias y ajenas, y a partir de las cuales se postulan las coordenadas de procesos de identificación simultáneamente locales y transnacionales."

34. Here I use the term "borderlands" in the same sense as Gloria Anzaldúa as a place of transition in some ways on the outside of the ontological and geographical border defined by the symbolic order. It is a place where the perverse dwell.

35. Indeed an entire issue of the prestigious *Revista Iberoamericana* was devoted to Puerto Rico and Trauma, edited by Juan Duchesne Winter it is called *Puerto Rico Caribe: Zonas poéticas del trama* 75 Oct-Dec (2009).

36. "Toda nación es también las otras que subvierten y, más que nada, seducen su precaria mismidad."

37. Similarly, Jorge Duany in his *The Puerto Rican Nation on the Move: Identities on the Island and in the United States*, shows how migrations to and from the Island of Puerto Rico

from the Dominican Republic, Cuba, and elsewhere threaten the imagined identity of what it means to be Puerto Rican.

Chapter Four

An Interlude

Magical Realism and Failed Incorporation

In the previous chapters I have analyzed the way different writers imagine the place where the Global North and the Global South join. The meeting of the two groups results in colonizing violence with one, the Global North, exerting its control over the other. Of great concern is how authors and thinkers respond to the imbalanced overlapping of the two systems. In each instance, the writers of the Global South are at a disadvantage due in part to the asymmetrical power relation that exists in the transnational, global interchanges occurring between them. Specifically I am looking at moments in the processes of transculturation that transpire during the epoch of colonization and its new, sped up iteration, globalization. Angel Rama described transculturation as "the incorporation of new elements [. . .] through the total rearticulation of the regional cultural structure" (208). What particularly concerns me in this chapter is the process of incorporation. How is it that a more powerful body takes in another as part of its own corpus? What happens to the body that is consumed by the larger one and what happens to the larger body itself? It is my contention that, even though the more powerful body tries to remove those parts of the other body that are unsavory to it, a process of trimming or elimination is impossible. As a result, the practice of incorporation is never complete and what the Global North thought it had removed as it incorporated its other can produce violent disturbances in the colonizing or globalizing machine. This meeting place produces odd effects, I argue that magical realism is one of those effects that narrate, or try to narrate, the violent exclusions caused in the process of incorporation. Magical realism is one way of narrating the meeting place of two or more systems and the failure of the symbolic order to fully register the event.

An example of how the removal of unwanted bodies or body parts can cause disruptions would be Mackandal in *El reino de este mundo*. As Carpentier relates, the slave's arm was crushed in the mill that squeezes the juice out of sugarcane so it can be processed into molasses and refined into sugar. As a result of losing his arm, Mackandal was unable to do the heavy work required of most slaves on the plantation; he was given minor tasks and considered worthless. When he runs away Lenormand de Mezy is almost relieved since it means one less unproductive mouth to feed. It is possible to understand Mackandal's lost arm and what happens after his escape as a metaphor for the colonialist structure and the way it deals with non-incorporable bodies.

As Antonio Benítez Rojo relates in his *La isla que se repite*, the machine of the plantation is the continuation of the colonizing machine. Therefore it is possible to read the mill that crushes Mackandal's arm as a metonymy of colonization and its practices. When it crushes and removes the arm of the revolutionary leader, it is emblematic of the process of incorporation that transpires between the colonizing Global North and the African slave of the Global South. The mill, which in the end creates a product that is sold globally to generate capital for the French, incorporates Mackandal's arm into the machine an act that renders him apparently less powerful. However, the mill is unable to incorporate his entire body, in fact, it takes only his arm. The process of failed incorporation, the way that the slave's body is taken partially into the colonizing body of global capitalism, can be read as an allegorical image of the interrelations between globalizing capitalism and those it uses to create its own wealth.

Following Deleuze and Guatarri in their *One Thousand Plateaus*, Benítez Rojo says that the colonizing machine forms "a coupled chain—the machine, the machine, the machine." Though the machine is connected in an unending chain, each subsequent machine "interrupts the flow that the previous one provides." The continuity of the colonialist "war machine," as Deleuze and Guatarri call it, is a continuity of interruptions and flows: Benítez Rojo concludes that, "It could be said rightfully that the same machine can be seen as much in terms of flow as in interruptions" (viii). It is credible to see the colonial, globalizing machine equally as one of unending continuous flow and as interruptions: as a coupled flow of interruptions. It is possible then to draw a connection from the localized sugar mill on the Mezy plantation to the global flow of sugar, products, slavery, and capital that it was a part of. One of the defining terms of globalization is the flow of goods, capital, culture, people, and so on throughout the planet. Within the flows defined by globalized capitalism, we must look for or create connections between interruptions in order to form a chain of disruptions. If we look at globalization in "a different sort of way" as Benítez Rojo asks, then it is possible to see interruptions in the narrative of continuity, assimilation, and accord that globalization wants to present. By focusing on the interruptions we create a critical narrative of what globalization and colonization have left out.

From a perspective that looks for connections between interruptions we might read the painful and violent event that Mackandal suffers as the colonial "machine" incorporating his body. However, the fact that the machine can only incorporate part of him creates the possibility for disruption. With the free time afforded to him after Mezy reduces his workload, Mackandal studies and learns about herbs as well as how to make elixirs and poisons. He escapes from the plantation, poisons plantation owners, and initiates a rebellion. When he is captured we see in the staged event of his execution another meeting place between the Global North and the Global South. In this meeting place Carpentier gives us one of the definitive moments in magical realism. As I discussed previously, the description of the moment results in an impasse, an unresolvable opposition. The representational practices of French, colonial ideology are incapable of fully incorporating Mackandal into its structure. Therefore the colonizer can only witness their victory over the Haitian rebel and the rebellious slaves. Carpentier tries to capture his escape from execution through the artistic device of magical realism, but the representational apparatus he uses has its limitations. The Cuban writer and others who employ magical realism attempt to make legible what is illegible within the limits of their ideological framework.

As Carpentier says when talking about "*lo real maravilloso*" in his "Prólogo" to *El reino de este mundo*, it brings about a "limit state." That is, "marvelous realism" brings the reader to the edge of the capacity of representation. But here it is necessary to understand whose representation and whose capacity we are talking about. At the limit state we begin to spy apparitions that look to us like ghosts. As Stephan Palmié says, these ghosts appear as part of the Western modernizing process in which the Global North attempts to "elide as anomalous" the disruptions that upset its ideal of a complete body. Coloniality engages in the process of ignoring disruptions "to safeguard their own conceptual foundations: the absences, silences and, yes, ghostly revenants from disavowed pasts that are no less constitutive of modernity" (18). The ghosts, the apparitions, the partial beings are constitutive of the ideological framework. It is what colonialism and the processes of globalization seek to ignore or leave out in the construction of their own ideal, unitary identity. In Carpentier's novel and in magical realism in general, we see an attempt by authors to bring into the symbolic order the ghosts and other markers of something that is unable to be symbolized.

I: NON-INCORPORATED MAGICAL REALISM:
NARRATING THE IMPOSSIBLE

In his essay, "The End of Magical Realism: José María Arguedas's Passionate Signifier," Alberto Moreiras conjectures that "magical realism is an impossible scene of emancipatory representation staged from the colonizing perspective" (206). That is to say the apparitions that appear to the colonizer are unable to be included within his ideological structure and are, therefore, impossible. The colonizer therefore stages the emancipatory acts as magical realism, underlining their impossibility within the colonial order. Mackandal's escape is unthinkable to the French colonist for whom control was, and needed to be, total in order for him to maintain his place in the world. In addition, since Carpentier and all other authors writing in Spanish, English, French, and so on, including Arguedas, write from within the limits of the colonial symbolic order, a way to bring the "scenes of emancipation" into representation and into the ideological fantasy constituted by the symbolic order is through the use of something like magical realism.

Mackandal's death, like other narrated moments of magical realism, marks the location of an event within the symbolic order. An event according to Alain Badiou is when the subject or the symbolic "touches the real." The structure or situation in which the event occurs cannot provide us "anything other than repetition" because every event is unprecedented and unexpected (Conditions 189). Only the event creates the possibility for "novelty in being" (Being and Event). It represents the possibility for a new beginning and for a complete and total rupture of the symbolic order. Speaking of Arguedas' last novel, *El zorro de arriba, el zorro de abajo* and his subsequent suicide, Moreiras speculates that the novel "opens transculturation theory to the presence of a silent and unreadable event" (206). Transculturation usually implies the absorption of one culture by another through a process of assimilation with the less powerful culture on the losing side. However, magical realism in its illegibility takes colonial reason to its very limit. It marks the location of the passage of an event, the place where assimilation fails.

Because it would be illegible from a position within the symbolic order, any "language event" that would accurately depict something like Mackandal's escape from certain death would be impossible. Talking about the event and magical realism, Moreiras says, "Perhaps then an event is more of an event, the more illegible it is" (206). If something is illegible, then how does it become part of a novel? Moreiras begins to address this question by saying, "As one opens one's self to the event, the event becomes more and more difficult to inscribe in a process of signification. An event, a language event, is an excess whose sense is only given in its recess, its withdrawal" (206). Similar to the anamorphic marks that I have analyzed in previous chapters, the magical real marks the place of an event in the symbolic order. However, as Carpentier says, and as Moreiras concludes in his essay, the magical real brings the reader to the limits of representation. Magical realism is an attempt to communicate the failure of the symbolic order and the ideology it props up from a place within the symbolic order itself. In the process of taking the reader to the limit state, magical realism risks destroying the very means of its own communication. Magical realism is written at the point of the symptom I spoke about in the last chapter. As it investigates the constitutive symptom, the sinthome—the thing that cannot be included in the symbolic order, but which is nevertheless constitutive of it—threatens the order established by the ideological fantasy. Since it is a "limit state" as Carpentier calls it, the more we investigate the limit, the more we question the definitions that give order and reason to our world. As Moreiras concludes, the accomplishment or fulfillment of magical realism is that magical realism itself "breaks magical realism; it brings it to the end of its narrative and opens it, in all the strength of paradox, onto the possibility of an actual critique of empire" (207). Magical realism is not the place of conciliation between two distinct cultures through a process of transculturation; rather it is the place of impasse, of radical difference from the imperial project. It marks the place where the ideological machine used to incorporate the people and cultures of the Global South breaks down. However, the event of its own wreckage must be communicated within language for us to know about it. Because of this communication is partial, elliptical, metaphorical and filled with inconsistencies. This type of communication is similar to what I have been discussing in previous chapters. It is a type of order that recognizes its own limits and the impossibility of totality—of ever being able to fully incorporate all elements, of the necessity of leaving something out—and yet it reaches for totality even though it knows it will fail. This is why Carpentier's narratives as well as Arguedas's are histories of failure; fail again, fail better.

II: THE CRITIC'S ROLE IN UN-INCORPORATED MAGICAL REALISM

Magical realism was employed by Latin American authors as a way of avoiding the limitations and stereotypes of the folkloric, realist novel and *novela de la tierra*. As I argue above, it is a technique that can be used to launch an analysis of globalization. However, it is also a technique that is criticized. Many critics, such as Michael Moses Valdez and Franco Moretti, view magical realism as a literary style that normalizes Latin American culture within the globalizing paradigm. It reifies the nostalgia that the Global North has for a past it never had even as it engages in a process similar to what Edward Said called *Orientalism*. As Elzbieta Sklodowska says in her article, "Viajes sin salvoconducto: Haití en Carpentier y Benítez Rojo," "[. . .] to read today another magical real or testimonial text is like participating in a wake" (224).[1] In spite of its death or lack of any real critical vitality the term seems to be everywhere. Indeed, usually if anything from Latin America has any fantastic elements or dream sequences it will be labeled "magical real" in an effort to attract audiences. Removed of its critical function, magical realism becomes like Kafka's Hunger Artist, left in a cage to starve on its own, a laughable, misunderstood sideshow that spectators and participants in the global circus hardly notice or understand. With magical realism we have witnessed or are witnessing yet another way that the globalizing machine attempts to incorporate cultures, people, and traditions that are contradictory and in opposition to its own functions.

As documented by Seymour Menton, Wendy Faris and Lois Parkinson Zamora among others, magical realism was one of the many avant-garde movements in Europe during the early part of the twentieth century. Its translation from Europe to Latin America via the pens of Alejo Carpentier and José María Arguedas and others was more than just yet another artistic movement coming to Latin America from Europe. Along with the fact that it seems more adept at explaining the complex realities and multiple belief systems in Latin America and the Caribbean, it also responds to the early scientific, Linnaean systems described by Pratt. It unsettles scientific belief by juxtaposing it with another paradigm. The important point here that is often missed as the term moves from country to country in the global market is that scientific objectivity that creates a sense of progress and technological advancement is one belief system among many. What appears fantastic or magical to a European or North American schooled in the objective gathering and categorization of knowledge is real to others. Similarly, technology with its wonders and science with its theories are seen as magical or fantastic to the outsider. Therefore when critics elide fantastic with magical realism, they are doing so from a position given to them by their own belief system that makes them categorize certain events as magical. For those readers and view-ers, the choice has clearly been made on the side of Western reason and science. From this critical position it is difficult to maintain the destabilizing *contrapunteo* offered in the magical real text.

Menton, in his analysis in *Historia verdadera del realismo mágico*, fol-lows a strict definition of the term given by Franz Roh, who first coined it in 1925 as *Magischer Realismus* in reference to a movement in German paint-ing. Menton emphasizes the type of focus made available in the magical real text, which "makes the observer feel a certain strangeness" (23). He contrasts magical real strangeness with realist painters who "in general reduce the precision of the focus for far away objects" (23). On the contrary, magical realist painters "tend to paint all the objects in the painting with the same precision" (23). In its earliest understanding then, magical realism is a term used to reference a bifocal, stereoscopic, coldly objective perspective that causes all elements to remain very clear. The effect of the objective clarity communicated is to impart a sense of strangeness to the viewer or reader rather than creating a sense of profundity or perspective. No special importance is given to events, what is apparently minor is brought into sharp relief. Perspective, which would otherwise establish a hierarchy of visible elements in the frame, is warped in an effort to bring all elements into view equally. Magical realism attempts what might be the impossible; it tries to keep all elements in view at the same time and to eliminate the sense of mastery the viewer might have over the viewed object by eliminating the use of traditional perspective and the vanishing point.

Magical realism, as Menton defines it, is another way of dealing with the multiple points of origin that come into contact in the Caribbean and even other parts of the globe. It is a de-hierarchical way of viewing culture and the diverse reality presented to the viewer or traveler of or in Latin America and the Caribbean. Where before the Caribbean was mapped through a colonial matrix using "imperial eyes"—to use Mary Louis Pratt's formulation—magical realism is a way of looking at and representing culture that presents the multiple in a way that destabilizes hierarchical singularity. However, since the mind seeks closure, meaning or a satisfactory ending, the reader or viewer of a magical real text is somewhat unsettled by the open-ended, irresolvable type of representation that characterizes magical realism. Wendy Faris talks about the effect of magical realism on the reader or viewer in her book on magical realism, *Ordinary Enchantments: Magical Realism and the Remystification of Narrative*. There she says that:

> [T]he reader may hesitate between two contradictory understandings of events, and hence experience some unsettling doubts. The question of belief is central here, this hesitation frequently stemming from the implicit clash of cultural systems within narrative, which moves toward belief in extrasensory phenomena but narrates from the post-Enlightenment perspective and in the realistic mode that traditionally exclude them. (17)

This type of representational practice is a long way from the Bartolomé de las Casas's translation of Colón's voyages. As I showed in chapter 1, in order to maintain the hierarchy of the Great Chain of Being and to fit it in the "new" understanding of the world as round, he came to the ridiculous conclusion that the world is shaped like a pear. Not satisfied with that image, he eventually said the earth was the breast of a reclining woman. In part he did this to maintain and justify an ordering of the world based on a racial hierarchy. But the act of writing of the encounter with the Indigenous people of America and Africa the way he did also shows how he tried to exert his mastery over a situation that left him feeling full of "unsettling doubts," as Faris describes it. In order to read magical realism, the critic or reader has to try and take a position with regard to the text that leaves him or her "unsettled." Rather than pointing out aesthetic qualities, the critic looks for instability. Instead of looking for elements that are easily marketed and consumed in the global bazaar, the critic looks for what is, in a sense, indigestible and unsettling to the system.

IV: MAGICAL REALISM AND THE DIALECTIC

The hesitancy, contradiction, and sensation of being "unsettled" all point to a dialectical relationship with the Other, made possible in the magical real text that is not resolved in an overcoming and the predominance of a single term over the others. While it has long been thought that the Hegelian dialectic is one that always progresses toward a resolution of opposites in a synthesis, recently theoreticians like Slavoj Žižek have revealed a different understanding. Žižek says,

> We can now see how meaningless is [sic] the usual reproach according to which Hegelian dialectics 'sublates' all the inert objective leftover, including it in the circle of the dialectical mediation: the very moment of dialectics implies, on the contrary, that there is always a certain remnant, a certain leftover escaping the circle of subjectivation. (*The Sublime Object* 208–209)

The hesitancy initiated by our inability to fully control the other whether by our look or additional means in this case points to a certain deficiency in our own ordering structure or symbolic order. This insufficiency or lack is one that points to an insufficiency in ourselves and is in fact the lack upon which the subject is founded. We notice that the things we use to represent the world, such as language, are insufficient to the thing being represented and, in fact, "The leftover which resists 'subjectivation' embodies the impossibility which 'is' the subject: in other words, the subject is strictly correlative to its own impossibility; its limit is a positive condition" (Žižek *The Sublime Object* 209). As with the argument following Viego in the previous chapter, the subject is only a subject when he or she recognizes his or her own impossibility. If I were completely satisfied with who I am, I would not attempt to do anything else. I wouldn't go to the gym to try and lose weight and get in better shape, I wouldn't read the paper to find out about the world, I wouldn't listen to social clues in conversations to avoid things that might be embarrassing to my interlocutor. In short, as Viego says, I would be a dead subject. It is in the recognition of my own imperfections that I try and fail to become better. These attempts make me a subject. The thing that resists our efforts to subject it—and here I am playing with both the verb "to subject" and the noun "subject"—is the subject itself. It is that bit of the subject that cannot and has not entered into the symbolic order by agreeing to the contract of castration. It is what is left over after castration; it is the sinthome that appears as a symptom within the symbolic order. It is the recognition of lack, or the insufficiency of the symbolic order, that the magical real encounter can make evident to the reader. As magical realism takes us to the limit state and threatens the ordering of our universe, it makes evident to us the inconsistencies that are at the heart of our own identification.

Of course, it goes without saying that the relationship to what is left out, an excrescence, must be resolved at some point even if temporarily. The viewer must choose a meaning, a route to take, in order to make sense of the text and his or her own position as the subject. However, the annoying excrescence that magical realism makes the viewer aware of also forces the reader or viewer to remain open to other possibilities. For example, in the case of Mackandal's death/escape, the colonizer would have to remain open to the possibility of his escape, however unsettling that might be. The insufficiency that we see in the Other initiates our desire to move toward the Other and create a closure or to control in some other way and bind up this gaping hole where we see our own lack reflected back to us.[2] For example, as I speak or look out at the world, I am also made aware that there is more that needs to be said; there is some stuff that escapes my ability to say or see it. Magical realism tries to make us aware of our limitations. It is a type of writing or painting that has a truly subversive effect on the viewer since his or her mastery over the artistic object is severely and permanently destabilized. Yet the point that has to be underlined here is that, unlike other formulations of the abject or border identity that articulate the subject as differed— engaged in an unending slipping of *différance* and hence a displacement of meaning—the argument I am using is not one that proclaims that the subject exists without the Other and is able to somehow establish a community in a "borderland" place avoiding castration. In order to speak, the subject must take up a position in language, and in order to interpret the magical real text, the reader must decide on a meaning all the while knowing that there are more possibilities. While we are made to see what is there, even if it is a specter of some sort, our understanding is unsettled by the feeling that there is more to the image than what we are able to see. The ethical position is to adopt a position that remains open to our own insufficiencies as readers and viewers while at the same time bearing witness to the event.

V: INCORPORATED MAGICAL REALISM IN THE MATRIX OF GLOBALIZED CAPITALISM

As the global marketing system uses the term in the publicity for books or films produced outside of United States and Europe or by minority groups within those places, the term loses its critical force. When used as a blurb to sell books or movies, magical realism is not understood so much as a de-hierarchical representation of a given reality, but as a term signaling exotic difference born, perhaps, from nostalgia for a mythic past. In marketing, the emphasis is not on the unsettling that occurs when two or more worldviews are brought together. Rather, magical realism as a sales pitch becomes a way of looking at the other with an imperialist, Orientalist gaze that exoticizes the other. Noticing this shift, Michael Moses Valdez argues that magical realism is a product of the current cultural logic of globalism creating "compensatory sentimental fictions that allow, indeed encourage, their readers to indulge in a nostalgic longing for and an imaginary return to a world that is past, or passing away" (106). Valdez goes so far as to argue that no one believes in the oppositional fantasies, that they always exist as a nostalgic yearning for some impossible-to-reach, pre-modern past.[3] No longer seen as something that brings readers to a "limit state," magical realism loses its capacity to unsettle our sense of reality and our ideology; rather, it is now a tool that global capitalism uses to confirm its ideology and place in the world. This conversion of the term through appropriation by the global market establishes a hierarchical way of seeing and representing by performing a maneuver similar to Pratt's "imperial gaze." In this way it ends the dialectic by short-circuiting it, by disavowing the lack at the heart of the representational structure. As a result, the colonial ideological framework employed by globalizing capitalism is left intact.

The shift that occurs with regard to magical realism, from one of an unsettling dialectic of *contrapunteo* to a mechanism used to sell products and reify the desires and fantasies of Western viewers, reaffirms a hierarchical ordering based on patterns emanating from Western ideological fantasy. The shift that Michael Moses Valdez notices is one that is difficult to argue against since it is so easy to find examples supporting his argument. For the majority of readers in places where Western modernity forms the basis for the ideological fantasy in which they live, magical realism is a way of assuaging the disconnection they feel in the modern world by dreaming of some pre-modern Edenic past. One example of this in the present would be New Age movements that appropriate practices from Native American, Eastern, or any other "pre-modern" religious practice. Without going too much into it, they erase the rigor from the practices conforming them to Western desires and regurgitate them in a way that is palatable for the modern, globalized consumer willing and able to pay a high price for them. The appropriation of Buddhist meditation by the self-help industry is another similar sign of the way cultural practices that seem exotic to the West are sanitized for consumption by a wealthy public. If our lives become too stressful due to the long hours we work, we can go to meditation retreats and calm ourselves down so that we can return to our jobs and become more productive. Meditation becomes completely delinked from its original purpose and now, in the hands of globalized capitalism, becomes a tool for increasing productivity.[4]

The problem is the way globalized capitalism appropriates images and other cultural products, not the product itself. In other words, the problem is the cultural logic of globalized capitalism, not magical realism. Valdez says: "What we need is a more critically astute explanation of how our leading literary magicians have captivated their audiences and a more penetrating analysis of the cultural logic that informs magical realist fiction" (119). For Valdez the magical real text is one that plays on the sentimentalities of a reader trapped and alienated by capitalism and globalization and as such it plays a similar function to the historical novels written by Walter Scott. According to Valdez, the readers of magical realism "are free to escape the past" unlike the Buendía family in *Cien años de soledad*, and are able to "inhabit a modern world, which they may attempt to refashion as they see fit" (133). And it is "only by facing the challenges of a new global reality, only by relinquishing the burdens of the past, only by ultimately forgoing the immobilizing pleasures of nostalgia can they avoid the fate of the Buendías" (133). Valdez's objective here is obviously to awaken readers in the thrall of the magical real text from what he sees as the nostalgic slumber that upholds rather than criticizes globalized capitalism. Rather than allowing ourselves to be rendered impotent by magical realism, we must engage it critically.

Valdez offers a possible way of understanding magical realism that is not entirely beholden to the cultural logic of capitalist globalization or some notion of progress based on Western values and assumptions grounded in a positivistic modernism. Though he argues that no one believes in the "magical" elements in the magical real text, particularly not the authors who write them, it is evident, particularly in the examples he uses, that someone surely does. For example, the *fatwah* issued against Rushdie is an extreme example, as are the events of 9/11, that there is a rather large group of people who hold to belief structures that allow for things we in the West would characterize as "magical" elements in Rushdie's novel. Against a belief structure characterized here by fundamentalist Islam, Valdez argues that Rushdie, like other writers who employ magical realism, occupies a position of disbelief with respect the "archaic," "pre-modern" cultures and their belief systems. This lack of belief places Rushdie and others outside the ideological fantasy of India, Latin America, or whatever the place might be that they write about. Along with this Valdez also notes that the magical real author "serves as a cultural mediator between dominant—perhaps the preeminent modern Western literary form—and the vestigial, residual, or latent cultural traditions that vary from once society and community to another" (112). From this position the author of the magical real text can observe the overlapping of two or more belief systems, that of Western modernity and the "archaic" society, creating a sense of what I have been calling bifocality. In this way, the author and critic perform the function of mediator between two or more worldview or belief systems.

VI: THE CRITICAL POSITION: THE VANISHING MEDIATOR AND MAGICAL REALISM

In order to occupy the position of mediator between two cultures, the author has to place him or herself in a similar position with regard to all of the cultures he or she represents. That is to say, the magical real writer is not just outside the "pre-modern" culture and its ideological fantasy, he or she is also outside the modern one. In this way he or she is able to function as a "vanishing mediator" between the two opposing ideas.

The vanishing mediator is a concept that comes up in Hegel's *Phenomenology of Spirit* and *The Logic*. It is a term whose etymology goes back as far as Aristotle. The vanishing mediator for Aristotle is the middle term of the syllogism. The middle term is silent or of lesser importance since the emphasis is placed on the first term and the conclusion. For Hegel the vanishing mediator has the function of bringing two opposites together in the dialectic and then "vanishing" once they unite. Similarly, the narrator of a magical real text or moment serves as the silent middle term that brings together conflicting understandings of reality. The position of "vanishing mediator" that the writer is able to occupy is a crucial point for any of us wanting to break out of the deadlock created by the ideological fantasy of global capitalism and the fantasy it has created. That is, the vanishing mediator posits a position located beyond the grasp of the symbolic order and the fantasy it creates.

While the concept of the vanishing mediator is a nice idea, it is also one that brings with it a lot of problems. If, as I have been arguing with psychoanalysis, the subject does not exist except as a product of a contractual obligation he or she has made with the symbolic order, how then is it possible for something to exist beyond or outside of this relationship? In fact the vanishing mediator can only exist as a type of madness. Žižek speaks of the vanishing mediator as "between the two is a 'mad' gesture of radical withdrawal from reality which opens up the space for its symbolic (re)constitution" (*Ticklish Subject* 37). The vanishing mediator then holds a place similar to that of the event as discussed above via Moreiras and Badiou. We can see traces of its passing, but we are unable to see anything more. The vanishing mediator serves the role of destroying the existing order by bringing together two previously antithetical propositions. Once the mediating function is complete, it vanishes.

Using psychoanalytical terminology Žižek locates the "vanishing mediator" with the death drive because of its destructive relationship with regard to the subject and the symbolic order. In this position Žižek also locates the vanishing mediator with the "unconscious" and its forceful ignorance of the social, historical reality that constitute the ideological fantasy. That is to say the "unconscious," which according to Lacan is structured in a way "something like a language," is beholden to and driven by a set of values that have nothing to do with the ideological fantasy the reigns over our lives. The unconscious is rather "the disembodied rational machine that follows its path irrespective of the demands of the subject's life world" (*Ticklish Subject* 73). With the connection to the unconscious and dreams, it is possible to see the link between vanishing mediator and magical realism with its dreamlike, unsettling fantasies that come as "slips of the tongue" to unsettle the symbolic order. The unconscious is a "rational machine" that functions against the globalized colonial machine. Interestingly, the "vanishing mediator" arises out of the tension created between nature (the animalistic death drive and the rational machine of the unconscious) and culture (its opposite, the symbolic order). The result of such tension is the imaginative text, the dream, the novel or other artistic product of the imagination. These dreams are understood from a position within the symbolic order as a type of madness. I would argue that similarly the tensions created in the magical real text allow for the possibility of such a madness by the instability created in its stereoscopic bifocality.

The madness I am arguing in favor of here is one that requires that the subject, in this case the critic and the writer of magical real texts, to recoil from the ideological fantasy that structures his or her reality in order to engage in the disruptive power of the imagination. Before doing this it is also necessary to "traverse the fantasy," that is to go through what Lacan calls the *fantome* and reveal that the gaping abyss that is behind the fantasy (*The Sublime Object* 194–196). In its simplest form traversing the fantasy is the work of the literary critic as he or she reveals the inadequacies of language and its metaphorical structure or relationship to the thing. That is to say it is not a return to a hermeneutics that believes there is a necessary meaning communicated by the literary or artistic text. For Lacan, "interpretation is to be opposed to hermeneutics, since it involves the reduction of meaning to the signifier's nonsense, not the unearthing of secret meaning" (Žižek, "Hermeneutic Delirium" 140). By realizing the limits of language, we are also made aware of what language cannot say, from that position it is possible to be made aware of "the abyss" that language hides. This abyss of the Real leads to an unsettling of our ideological fantasy and to a type of madness or delirium. To do otherwise would be to engage in a more "productive" reading of the magical real text as a reflection of a certain cultural logic created by the global market place. As such, the magical real text fulfills a sense of nostalgia created by the cultural logic of globalized capitalism, the latest iteration of Western modernity.

Seen from another perspective, modernity and its "progress" is a type of madness in and of itself. Bartolomé de las Casas's effort to ignore what science told him, that the globe is round, to force it into a structure that made him and those in power feel more comfortable can be read, from our perspective hundreds of years later, as a type of madness. From within the frame-work or general structure of the order in which we function, what we do and how we perceive the world around us seems "normal." However, the struc-turing itself and the adherence to its totalitarian order can become an obses-sion that leads to madness. De las Casas, for example, and those of his time, were consumed by an ideation of the globe and society that led them to commit acts that are entirely mad. What is more unreasonable, more insane than the enslavement of millions of people? Yet slavery was an act that was logically argued for and rigorously supported from within the logic of global-ized capitalism. Perhaps one reason for the proliferation of self-help gurus as well as things like yoga in our current day and age is not really because we are looking for something more spiritual, but because we are being forced into an order which, in its mechanization of the body and mind, has as its by-product a type of madness. As Lennard J. Davis argues, "Madness, in the old sense, is singular and rare; mental illness, in the new sense, is plural and common. In that manner, it is as democratic as death and taxes" (48). With an increase in progress and the modernizing project, we also have an increase in "madness." But madness now is associated more with the fact that we are not functional parts of the machine. As Davis points out,

> The by-now standard midcentury explanation of neurasthenia is presented here with the familiar analogy of a modern machine being overworked or depleted of energy. Indeed, the word "break-down," according to the *OED* was first used for machinery in 1838, followed in twenty years for mental or physical health. (88)

Madness in this scenario is a term that signals a bit of machinery that does not function correctly within the confines created by instrumental reason, globalized capitalism. From this perspective, the vanishing mediator—and magical realism—denotes a type of madness because it is something that throws a wrench into the machine.[5]

VII: THE NEO-BAROQUE AND THE "MAD VISION" OF MAGICAL REALISM

In the magical real text, as well as the neo-baroque, hypervisuality creates a situation where it is possible to recoil into an imaginary madness that desta-bilizes the ideological fantasy that structures our reality. The hypervisual element of magical realism is related to the baroque or the neo-baroque and now what Lois Parkinson Zamora is calling the "neo-neo-baroque" as it appears in the twentieth- and twenty-first century Latin America. As such magical realism, like the neo-baroque, becomes a strategy used by Latin American and Caribbean writers to represent their complex reality in a way that avoids the monocular, panoptic practice used by Europeans in the categorization of the new flora, fauna and civilizations of the Americas. The emphasis should remain on the fact that it is an effort to represent what is real and not to arrive at some mystical realm beyond reality itself. The instability in the magical real text is a result of the overlapping realities, not some elusive, ineffable mysticism. Surely it does result or come out of a type of madness, but this madness is the result of the limits of one reality when confronted with another, as well as the limits of representation when someone has contacted a new reality, a new object, thought and so on. In this way, the neo-baroque engages two or more cultures at the limits of their own understanding and therefore with a type of madness.

Understanding magical realism as a type of unsettling madness is also different from the way it has been appropriated by globalized, mass-markets to commoditize and sell products. Appropriated magical realism seems to mean anything that is fantastic or strange while for Latin American writers and critics it is a way of representing a diverse reality. In her analysis of Alejo Carpentier's work, Lois Parkinson Zamora underlines the relation between magical realism and the baroque when she says that Carpentier "needed the baroque for its realism. In interviews and essays, Carpentier repeatedly insists upon the realistic character of baroque representation, and on the importance of baroque realism to Latin American writers' attempt to depict Latin America's histories and people" ("Swords and Silver Rings" 41). Parkinson Zamora points out the relationship between the baroque and its realist qualities in her study on Carpentier and other writers such as García Márquez and even the Spanish philosopher José Ortega y Gasset. Rather than understand the baroque as an overabundant ornamentation that might be an escape or an obfuscation of reality, Parkinson Zamora through Carpentier and others categorizes the baroque style, similar to magical realism, as an attempt at realism. Citing Carpentier, Parkinson Zamora says that what he most desired from a work of art was an "object; make it with your words so that I can *touch it, value it, feel its weight.* [. . .] The object lives, is seen, lets its weight be felt. But the prose that gives life and substance, weight and measure [to the object] is baroque" ("Swords and Silver Rings" 41). Parkinson Zamora goes on to say that Carpentier was a student of the baroque and knew full well that: "Baroque realism aims not only to replicate the world but also [more importantly] to reveal an invisible realm beyond the real" (41). The neo-baroque usage of magical realism then seeks to bring into our understanding a reality that is at the limits of the capacities of the ideological framework in which we live. In the following chapter I will analyze two works in an effort to show how magical realism can work to upset the status quo.

NOTES

1. "[. . .] leer hoy en día algún que otro texto mágico-realista o testimonial es como participar en un velorio."

2. This lack in the Other that signals a lack in ourselves is what psychoanalysis refers to as *le objet petit a.*

3. I have my doubts as to whether it is truly the case that what Valdez calls "pre-modern" beliefs can only exist as a nostalgia for a past that is already lost. This is especially the case if you consider his argument that no one believes in the "pre-modern" belief systems and the example he uses of Salman Rushdie. If nothing else, 9/11 and subsequent similar events show the world that there are indeed a large group of people who have different beliefs that Valdez might characterize as "pre-modern." His characterization of modernity emanates from a point of view that is entirely grounded in European values and designs.

4. The day I wrote this an article appeared in the *New York Times* concerning efforts to make "competitive yoga" an Olympic event. Of course the idea of competition in yoga counters the concepts and precepts of yogic discipline. Yoga as we know it in the United States is increasingly western. Practitioners have gone so far as to copyright asana (or pose) sequences as with the case of Anasura and Bikram yoga. Competitions and copyrighting age old practices point to the capitalist habit of not leaving well enough alone, everything becomes a marketing strategy and everything has to be new and improved. All of this creates another space that the next "yoga" must cure/fill, somewhat like endless waves of fashion in criticism.

5. It would be possible to go further into this point of the relation of the machine to the body by exploring the possibilities presented in Foucault and Agamben's conceptualization of biopower. I fear that it would be too much of a digression here. Though it would take the argument into interesting places, the relation of the vanishing mediator, magical realism and biopower is something I have to leave for another day.

Chapter Five

The Vanishing Real

*Magical Realism's Political Swerve in García Márquez's
"La increíble y triste historia de la cándida Eréndira y su
abuela desalmada"*

To uncover the disruptive potential available in a magical real text at least two things are required. First of all the text itself has to contain magical real elements. Secondly, the reader must be critically aware of the text's functioning. That is, the critic has to adopt a position with regard to the text that allows her or him the ability to see the hyper-reality of the text or its extreme bifocality and then be able to relate that particular occurrence in the text to a broader concern. The reader has to avoid the seduction of nostalgia and other pitfalls that Moses Valdez and others warn us about with regard to magical realism. In this chapter I will attempt to show how it is possible to avoid the nostalgic reading by engaging García Márquez's short novel or long short story, "La increíble y triste historia de la cándida Eréndira y su abuela desalmada," ("Eréndira"). I will show how that novel contains a critique of the colonialist past in Latin America as well as how that past weighs down the present and the future. The weight of the past and the apparent inability to escape it and dream of something new renders Latin Americans "dead subjects," as Antonio Viego would say.

Put simply, García Márquez's novella "Eréndira" is about a grandmother who sells her granddaughter into prostitution to pay off a debt. One night the fourteen-year-old Eréndira goes to sleep so exhausted from her daily chores caring for the abuela and the house that she leaves a candle burning. The "wind of her disgrace" blows the candle causing a conflagration that destroys the house. True to magical realist form where the absurd or the unbelievable

is presented in a very matter of fact way, the abuela coolly decides to prostitute the young Eréndira in order to pay off the cost of the house and the other
possessions. The value the abuela places on the burned-down house and its
ruined contents seems insurmountable. But even as high as the cost might
seem, Eréndira comes close to paying it off. Nevertheless, as Eréndira gets
closer to paying off her debt, the abuela inevitably adds more to the amount.
Through a series of adventures, she finally frees herself from the abuela and
all authority in a stunning way.

As curious as it may sound especially given the subject matter of García
Márquez's "Eréndira," most criticism has focused on a discussion of the
magical real elements in the novella leaving Eréndira's fate as a prostitute
who services hundreds of men a day mostly unexamined. That is rather than
connecting this novel to any Real historical events, most critics focus on the
aesthetic, magical quality of the story. Those critics who do discuss the more
troubling aspects of the novella, such as Diana Marting in her article "The
End of Eréndira's Prostitution," unfold how García Márquez's representation
of Eréndira's plight is rather common in Colombia and other places in the
world.

Marting shows how García Márquez was inspired to write the story when
he saw an fourteen-year-old girl working as a prostitute with an older woman
as her pimp. Indeed it seems as though the Colombian writer is haunted by
this image since he first saw the pair when he was sixteen (Marting 176). The
image of a young prostitute also appears in several of his works not the least
of which is *Cien años de soledad* (1969) along with *El otoño del patriarca*
(1975) and *El amor en los tiempos del cólera* (1985). Along with the reap-
pearance of Eréndira or an Eréndira-like figure in his narratives, Molyn C.
Mills relates in his, "Magic Realism, García Márquez and Eréndira," that it
seems as though García Márquez was obsessed with bringing the image of
the young prostitute and her abuela/pimp to film. The Colombian writer first
composed the screenplay and then, after failing several times to develop it
into a film, wrote the novella. Though criticism seems to be able to focus
either on the reality represented in the text or on its magical realism as an
aesthetic quality, García Márquez uses the magical real technique to represent what for him was a real event that haunted him. Using magical realism
allows García Márquez to represent not only the reality of the sex industry
and the prostitution of young girls, but it allows him also to communicate the
real horror that eludes our ability to comprehend it.

The relationship of magical realism to the Real here is an important one
especially for the purposes of representing the subject matter that concerns
García Márquez with "Eréndira." By choosing the magical real technique
over realism and fantasy, García Márquez presents the real events but in a
way that haunts the reader similar to the way they affect the author. Though
he does fictionalize her story, there is nothing fantastic or imagined about the

plight of the millions of young girls and women who work in the globalized sex industry, yet its reality is too horrifying to be contained within the symbolic codes of representation. By employing a magical real technique, García Márquez presents not only the horror of what he witnessed, but also its inexplicable character. Of course, as with all horrific events, we attempt to explain them or make sense of them. In doing that, we bring the horrific event into symbolization and, as is sometimes the case, the horrific is domesticated in such a way as to justify our own beliefs and ideological fantasy. Some immediate examples would be the "sense" that some preachers on the religious right made of 9/11 or by the earthquake in Haiti as being the result of what they think of as a sinful culture. What happens as a result of the domestication of the real event is that it risks being rendered "dead," that we no longer engage it in an attempt to come to terms with it, we disavow its existence. With magical realism, García Márquez creates discomfort in the reader with regard to the reality he depicts. It is possible that the feeling of uneasiness will lead to real action.

Magical realism emerged as a reaction against the folkloric realism evident in novels or tales prevalent in Latin American narrative prior to the 1950s. Even though many now consider magical realism to play into the nostalgia of the Global North for a past it never had, it reacted against the folklorist qualities of realism that seemed to play into similar desires. For magical real writers, realism rendered reality "dead." Magical realism, on the other hand, represents real events while at the same time exploring the limits of representation itself and it risks its own destruction in that exploration as I concluded in the last chapter. While the realist text informs the reader about an event or aspect of a particular culture, magical realism risks destroying the framework in which the horrifying real events take place. An example of how magical realism could be used to relate horrifying, real events in a way that is possibly more efficacious than brutal realism could be seen with the representation of the banana strike and massacre of 1928. As Gerald Martin relates in his biography of García Márquez, "there is no definitive history of this event and no consensus as to the number of civilians killed by the army" (42n32). In fact, before García Márquez and Alvaro Cepeda Samudio relate the story in their novels, García Márquez in *Cien años de soledad* and Cepeda Samudio in *La casa grande*, the massacre was not part of the official story.

The risk in reading magical realism is to interpret the events in a way that reaffirms the phantasmatic frame rather than attempting to maintain a critical angle that requires an engagement with the specters and unendurable loss. Especially with a text like Marques' short novel "Eréndira" where the theme is extreme violence against women, it is necessary to avoid the domestication of the brutality and yet still be able to talk about it in some way. Capitalist driven culture is expert at domesticating the horrific and profiting from it.

Perhaps the most extreme example of how real horrors are made profitable is evident in some efforts to represent the femicides of Juárez. I am referring to the innumerable "Ranchera" movies as well as others concerning the horrific historical reality of the thousands of femicides. The extreme example of "Ranchera" movies concerning the topic of the femicides is an example of how real concern over horrific events can become prurient representational techniques used to sell films by playing to the basest, most horrific desires of the viewing public.

While the intent of directors and writers may be to communicate the horrifying reality of violence against women, often the line between the realism used to portray the events and pornography is very tenuous. The pornographic film tricks the viewer into believing that there is nothing left outside the representational frame, that everything is being shown and that there is no lack. In realism and especially in pornographic realism, the gaze of the author is projected into the space of the big Other. Typically, in the non-pornographic text, the subject's own lack is revealed to him/her by the gaze of the big Other. So, when we look at a painting, movie, or other artwork, the work itself gazes back at us revealing our own lack and, most important for my argument here, our own insufficiency with regard to representation.

In pornographic realism our place as spectators is shifted to that of the big Other. Again, in a typical relation, we have our lack revealed to us by the gaze of the big Other. In the typical relationship our composition as a non-all subject becomes evident and we try to fill out the lack albeit unsuccessfully. In the pornographic relation, we take up the place of the big Other and what we see on the screen is there to fulfill our own desires. The apparent removal of the obscure object of desire, the *objet petit a,* creates a sense that representation has become transparent. The perverse reversal of subject positions results in what is known as "obscene enjoyment." Rather than the horrific event offering the potential for some disruption in our ideological framework we become, as Todd McGowan relates, "desiring subjects looking at a visual field created specifically for our desire" (*The Real Gaze* McGowan 56). As discussed in early chapters, typically the object held in the frame literally looks out at us revealing to us our own insufficiencies; our own lack of mastery with respect to the thing we think is contained within the frame.

The magical real text not only leaves this blot in the frame, but it draws our attention to it at the risk of destroying the frame itself. On the other hand, the horrific realism of obscene enjoyment that I have been describing here tries to ignore the lack or insufficiency in the representational text and acts as if it can expose everything; that it can satisfy our every desire. In this way realism gives way and perhaps even leads to the pornographic, since the claim of the pornographic text is that everything will be shown up close and in excruciating detail. The result is a culture similar to the one we have now where everything is public and the "reality" of whatever we watch or read is emphasized. The result of our every desire being addressed in three dimensional, high-definition detail is excruciating anxiety in the viewer precisely because the image presents itself as complete, as without lack. It is there to satisfy us and yet we want more. An example of how this works would be my own experience with cable television. Even though the cable company does what it can to provide endless entertainment, it never really is enough. The cable company does everything to hide its constitutive lack making it appear complete. It is this completeness that is overwhelming, since there is so much to choose from, I end up choosing nothing or trying to watch everything at once by using my DVR and channel surfing; both are attempts to satisfy myself that end in failure. With magical realism, the ghosts or other strange, unsettling events that appear are there as a result of an ideological framework that wants to show itself as complete. They are there to show us that the totalizing system is not all there is.

By employing magical realism to relate such a horrifically real story, García Márquez maintains the "real effect" in his story allowing for the possibility that "Eréndira" not only communicates real events, but that it also leaves us haunted just as García Márquez himself was haunted by its horror and injustice. We have some of the answers, but it is also possible that we remain haunted by the images themselves.

García Márquez's story begins with Eréndira preparing the abuela for bed as the "the wind of [Eréndira's] disgrace" (95)[1] begins to blow. After a long day of labor, Eréndira passes out on her bed without undressing and leaves a candle burning. The wind blows the flame from the candle, catching the house on fire and destroying it in a conflagration from which very little is saved. The abuela calculates that the value of the goods lost is a ridiculously high sum; nevertheless it is an amount that Eréndira must pay. It is the abuela who decides that the way she will pay the debt is by prostituting the young, fourteen-year-old girl. In this act the abuela repeats her own past in the present. We later find out that the abuela was herself a prostitute until she was rescued by her husband, Amadís.

As she calculates how much she can get for Eréndira, how many men she can service per day along with how much she owes, the abuela admits that the debt is essentially insurmountable since it will take two hundred years for Eréndira to pay it off. Eréndira who, in the opening scene of the novel, responds with automatic "Sí, abuela" to any command the old woman issues, goes along with the abuela's outrageous idea without even a word. The relationship between the two of them is one that is trapped in a deadlock that repeats the past in the present. The young girl, knowing no other way of being, and being locked in a relationship with her abuela, has little choice but to follow the incessant and outrageous demands of the grandmother. The grandmother, having known no other life outside the family home, can think of no better way to get money than to prostitute her granddaughter.

From the opening pages of the novella until its final paragraph, Eréndira as much as the abuela are presented as beings who are half conscious and trapped in a slavish existence. In this story, unlike *Cien años de soledad*, there is no patriarchal figure. In fact, García Márquez goes out of his way to demonstrate that the patriarch is dead by showing us the graves of not one but two of them, both with the same name of Amadís. If it is true that you kill a monster twice because you first kill the monster and then the idea that it represents, then here it would seem that the idea of patriarchy along with the figures who embody it are laid to rest. There is, in fact, nothing to keep the two women trapped in their house that is in the middle of nowhere enslaved to the daily routines of maintaining it. Yet, both women are still beholden to a law that enslaves them. This is a perfect example of ideology, the women are presented as performing daily rituals that consume all of their time and yet neither they nor the reader know why they are doing it.

What is the ideology that creates the boundaries of their existence entrapping and rendering both Eréndira and her abuela dead? Trying to find historical markers to make even the most tenuous of historical connections is difficult. The story occurs in something of a timeless, placeless wasteland. Though a large portion of Eréndira's day is spent winding the innumerable clocks in the house, both she and the abuela seem trapped in a space and time that is incapable of actual change. The emphasis on the cyclical motion of time with the clocks and the ritualistic chores punctuated by the repeated "Sí abuela," creates the sense that they are trapped in some sort of atemporal space that history and progress have left behind.

Atemporality here could be thought of as forming an anachronism in this story, which would allow the reader to interpret the story through the lens of nostalgia. Following the Michael Moses Valdez argument I presented in the previous chapter, nostalgia in magical realism confirms the Global North as a place of progress with the Global South as a quaint location where Northern readers can encounter the past they never had. However, the anachronistic atemporality in "Eréndira" creates more than just a satisfying nostalgia. Due to the magical real techniques employed—extreme attention to detail, precision, and cold objectivity on the part of the narrator—the reader also feels a certain strangeness when reading the story that undermines any sense of mastery. If it is a story imbued with nostalgia, the fuzzy dream replaced with an unsettling nightmare. Here, the anachronic as it is presented in the story has the potential to unsettle the reader. With regard to anachronisms in García Márquez's work, Daniel Erickson says in his book, *Ghosts Metaphor and History in Toni Morrison's* Beloved *and Gabriel García Márquez's* One Hundred Years of Solitude, that the wars for independence from Spain did not result in a fundamental rupture with colonialism, "but in some ways intensified the social relations that existed under colonialism" (162). In other words, the wars for independence did not free Latin America from colonialism; rather what happened was that the colonialist models of governing and imagining social bonds remained in place. In addition, anachronism can also be read as, "Latin America's continuing history of economic and political dependence on Europe and, later, the United States" (162). While in the North it is possible to paint the world with a veneer that proclaims progress, Latin America in many places still relates to the North as it did during colonialism. Putting the two worlds side-by-side creates an unsettling sense of time. Along with this it should be added that Northern "progress" is the direct result of ensuring that certain vestiges of colonialism remain in place in the Global South and elsewhere.

The time that Eréndira and the abuela live in is a remnant of the colonial past in the present. Eréndira and her abuela are both trapped by time, they are unable to escape its repetitions and are, therefore, unable to change. They are both left to reproduce the patriarchal ideology given to them even though the patriarchs are long dead. Though there are no powerful male figures in the story, the abuela takes on all of the habits and shapes that would link her symbolically to patriarchal, colonial authority. His description in this story of the abuela is reminiscent of García Márquez's earlier story, "Los funerales de Mamá Grande" (1962). The abuela in "Eréndira," like Mamá Grande, is extraordinarily large, "the abuela, naked and large, looked like a beautiful, enormous white whale in the marble pool" ("Eréndira" 95).[2] Similar to García Márquez's early story, the house is filled with myriad useless objects. And like the earlier story, the abuela, Mamá Grande, and their respective houses are in need of constant upkeep. It takes Eréndira two hours to wind and set the clocks in the house (97) just as it takes her two hours to prepare the abuela for bed. All the rooms are stuffed with the detritus of decades, perhaps centuries, of accumulation and overconsumption.

The relationship between past and present—the old and the young—and the burden of consumerism is made visually by García Márquez as he describes the relationship between the adolescent, slight Eréndira and the enormous, aging grandmother. Eréndira has to bathe her and take her to bed, "she was so fat that she could only walk by supporting herself on her grandaughter's shoulder, or with what seemed like a bishop's crosier" (96).[3] Even though she falls into a deep sleep, the abuela still gives orders. Eréndira continues to respond as if responding to a litany in church with the repeated "Sí abuela," as she sets about finishing up her chores for the day before she passes out without undressing.

There are several ways the relationship between Eréndira and the abuela can be interpreted in light of Latin American history and culture. One way to see their relationship is as a metaphor for Latin America's history of colonialism and how that history shapes its present relationships both internally and with the rest of the world. The two things that support the abuela's girth are Eréndira's youthful vigor and the Church symbolized by the bishop's crosier or "báculo" that the abuela uses to walk. The Church not only formed an important part of Spain's colonizing effort in the Americas, but throughout its history it has frequently formed an impediment to change or revolution by tying it to the past.[4] García Márquez shows how the symbols of authority help the abuela maintain her power, but he also shows how power is a manufactured ideological fantasy that everyone, even its victims, works hard to prop up. It is a fantasy that holds both the abuela and Eréndira in its grip. Each character is able to carry out their functions even as they are asleep, showing how each of them have unquestioningly and unthinkingly entered perhaps without conscious reflection into an agreement to maintain the ideological fantasy that structures their world even as it enslaves them. García Márquez shows how their reality is structured on an agreed upon fiction by relating their past to fiction itself. Since there is no substantial, real presence that makes the abuela and Eréndira maintain a relationship that imitates colonial structures, the only thing that sustains their relationship and the hierarchy it implies is an unspoken agreement based on tradition, based on an unquestioned past. The history given to them forms the ideological framework that they inhabit. Like characters in other works by García Márquez, it is not their own history, in which they purposefully act, but is, in a concrete sense determined from afar" (Erickson 174). They are subjects of history, but they are dead subjects.

Eréndira is so exhausted from the daily routine that she goes to sleep leaving a candle burning. The *viento de su desgracia* blows the candle and creates a conflagration that burns the house to the ground. From here, the abuela and Eréndira set out on their travels that will occupy the rest of the story. Of the few things they take with them are the bones of the long-dead patriarchs, both of whom are called Amadís. García Márquez gives a brief history of how the patriarchs came to America as traffickers in contraband. Even more important than their past as contrabandists are their names. The name Amadís, passed on from father to son, can be read as a reference to the ancient Spanish *novela de caballería*, *Amadís de Gaula*. The novel, *Amadís de Gaula*, is not only one of the first novels written in the Spanish language, but it has been argued that the form of the novel itself structured the way conquistadors wrote about their conquest in the Americas as well as even how they viewed the Americas.[5] Not only did *Amadís de Gaula* and novels of that genre influence how Cortés among others viewed themselves and wrote about their conquests, it also shaped the imagination of perhaps the most important novel written by a Spanish author, *El ingenioso hidalgo Don Quijote de la Mancha*.[6] The reference in "Eréndira" to the one of the first novels written in Spanish creates a symbolic connection between the present of the story and the long-ago past. The repetition of their names—even though it is common to repeat names in families particularly in García Márquez's stories and novels—creates a sense again of repetitive, cyclical time that is inescapable.

Similar to the abuela's weight that Eréndira must support, the patriarchs' bones bear down on the abuela and Eréndira. When the house burns to the ground, Eréndira has to exhume the bones of her forefathers and put them in a box so they can be carried from place to place. The boxes containing the bones are not light as would be expected since the bodies have long since decayed. They are so heavy that one unnamed character in the story comments that the boxes do not contain bones, but rather ivory statues saying, "I bet they are ivory statues" (105).[7] The character's remark shows the connection not only with the revered past, improbable statues of old and long-dead heroes, but also its weight and relationship to fantasy. Statues are made to revere heroes of the past, but they are also creations of fantasy. They are images that a specific culture creates to revere its interpretation of the past in the present. Though they are grounded in historical events, García Márquez wants to underline the connection to fiction. They are "made up," they are inventions that nevertheless control the present of Eréndira and the abuela.

The patriarchs are further related to fiction during an interchange between the abuela and a man with a gun. To save herself, the abuela claims that she is the "dama" or lady of "Amadís el grande" to which the man replies: "Then you are not from this world" (122).[8] Similar to Cervantes' *The Quijote*, a book that questioned the relationship between language and reality and showed how language itself shaped our interactions with each other and the world, the abuela's belief in her own importance based on her relationship to the past—the Amadíses—is also revealed as being "not of this world." That is to say, it is a fantasy that both she and Eréndira believe in, similar to the fantasy Don Quijote believes when he allows the books he reads—mostly novels about knights errant such as *Amadís de Gaula*—to shape his reality and see evil giants instead of windmills. Here, García Márquez performs something of a reversal, the agreed upon belief in the fantasy that structures the abuela and Eréndira's existence makes them blind to evil giants. Rather than tilting at windmills or giants in an effort to destroy them, both Eréndira and Abuela prop them up. The fictional power has real effects. The magical or fantastic form the reality we have constructed for ourselves. They weigh us down as the bones of the Amadíses and the abuela do Eréndira. When García Márquez has a character tell the abuela that she is not "of this world" due to her relationship with Amadís el grande, he causes a distortion in the ideological framework structuring her and Eréndira's reality. The distortion reveals that their reality is built upon an agreed upon fantasy presenting itself as history.

Though her power is revealed as an agreed upon fantasy it nevertheless remains in place; the abuela is still able to control Eréndira and other people she encounters in the novel. The abuela adopts the images of authority and this seems to be enough for her to maintain control throughout the narrative. In one instance García Márquez makes the abuela seem to be one of the "Reyes Católicos"; the so-called "Catholic Kings" like Fernando and Isabel who combined the authority of the Church with that of the state in the conquest of Latin America. García Márquez says: "Supported in the episcopal crosier, the abuela abandoned the stall and sat on the throne to await the passage of the mules" (107).[9] This humorous vision of the abuela as queen overseeing a procession of her mule subjects could have been written by Cervantes himself, it shows the absurdity of allowing such a ridiculous figure to control the lives of others; and yet they still let her have power over them. The abuela commands everyone in her presence throughout the story, and everyone trembles at her word. Similar to Don Quijote in Cervantes' novel, the abuela is unable to see the limits of her own fiction; she oversees the mules as if they were actual subjects even though she and everyone knows they are not.

The fact that everyone knows one thing—that the mules are not subjects—and yet function as if they did not have this knowledge is a perfect example of how the ideological fantasy is constructed by an agreed upon, unstated contract among participants in a community. We all know what the truth is, they are mules, and yet we are acting as if something else is true. As Žižek so humorously puts it, we know what it is and yet we are doing it anyway. But it is even more than this, because it requires a repression of the decision to overlook the illusion that is structuring reality, "and this overlooked unconscious illusion is what may be called the *ideological fantasy*" (*The Sublime Object of Ideology* 33). This image of the abuela as queen sitting in review of her mules/subjects, along with other moments in the book, point toward her fictional authority as well as creating an apt characterization of her subjects as mulish followers and believers. They all know what the real relationship is, and yet they still agree to uphold the ideological fantasy allowing her to maintain control even if it means their subjugation to a ridiculous figure.

Unconscious mulishness is an aspect that characterizes both the abuela as well as Eréndira, they seem locked in a master/slave dialectic from which there is no exit. García Márquez describes the characters as sleeping with their eyes open ("dormía con los ojos abiertos") and that Eréndira had inherited the "virtue of remaining alive in her dreams" (99).[10] This intermediate state of sleepwalking takes on an element of being "undead" when the abuela prepares Eréndira to meet customers she paints her face "in the style of sepulchral beauty that had been all the rage during her [the abuela's] youth" (106–107).[11] The main characters wander through the novel as undead, giving the narrative a strange feel to it in true magical real fashion. Unlike everyone around them they are on the border between two existences, they are neither alive nor dead to the ideological fantasy that they, and everyone else, are propping up. The fact that this border state that they are in also puts them, especially Eréndira, in a special position; one that may allow her to awake to a different type of existence. The relationship described here can also be a way of characterizing the relationship in Latin America between the present and the past, between Latin America and its colonialist past and between Latin America and its globalized presence.

The abuela and Eréndira, like other characters in the novel, seem trapped in time and entirely unaffected by each other. Perhaps one of the more startling moments of the novel comes when the narrator says that from one of their stopping places, "it was possible to see glass buildings that made up an illuminated city" (148).[12] This discreet line in the novel is the only indication that the historical time in which the novel takes place is much different from what we might have been led to believe. Up until this point, although there are certainly other minor indications—the use of motorized vehicles would be a dead giveaway—it would have been difficult to pin this story down to the twentieth century or some more modern time. That is to say, I as a reader was living entirely within the fantasy structure created by the novel and the relationship between Eréndira and the abuela and was able to ignore the motorcycles and trucks. And this made me at best uncertain of the time or to think of it as some time well before the modern age. But the modern, illuminated city disrupts this illusion created by the novel. The city exists in the distance and is a reminder that Eréndira and the abuela are trapped in a time that does not seem to move forward and which is entirely unaffected by the changes of modernity. The description that follows the one about the city is telling: "Eréndira was asleep, chained to the crossbar, and in the same position as the drowned man set adrift from where she called for Ulises" (148).[13] With the modern city of glass forming the backdrop, Eréndira is chained, asleep, and half-dead unable to break free from her abuela or the ideological fantasy created by their master/slave relationship. Her only recourse is to call from her dream to another fictional, fantastic character to come and save her: this time in the form of the young, and handsome Ulises.

The wind of her so-called "desgracia" or disgrace that seems to howl through the novel provides the catalyst at the beginning and near the end, causing a radical change in her circumstances by burning the house down. It is difficult then to understand how the wind can be interpreted as her "disgrace" when it is the wind that first burns down the house and then blows when she and Ulises kill the abuela. The wind leads to and allows her freedom from the stultifying past. It can only be seen as a disgrace from a position within the ideological framework that structures the world that Eréndira and the other characters inhabit. From that position, she becomes a disgrace and a *sinvergüenza*, or shameless person, when she becomes free. García Márquez refuses to leave Eréndira enslaved in the half-dead state we see her in throughout the story. Though breaking free from the abuela's grip and waking out of her undead state also is not that easy.

Several times it is possible for her to free herself from her relationship with the abuela, but she refuses the freedom as offered and returns to familiar patterns. At one point, the abuela and Eréndira run into a group of a religious order that are wandering the lunar landscape of this novel. They force Eréndira out of abuela's hands and make her live in a convent. Though this breaks her out of the deadlocked relationship with the abuela, life in the convent is anything but easy. In fact, she seems to be burdened with the same mindless drudgery that characterized her life with the abuela. In spite of this she says "estoy feliz" when she has time to think about her new situation. To the reader her life in the convent is not perfect since she is still doing hard, physical labor; however I felt relieved when I knew she was sleeping in a clean bed and not one soaked with the sweat and liquids of the hundreds of men she slept with the day and night before. In spite of her proclaimed happiness, Eréndira aids the abuela's plot to free her from the convent. As much as both the reader and García Márquez would like to see her freed, Eréndira seems unable to escape from an existence as a sleepwalking, undead, unconsciousness sex slave. Eréndira and the abuela have sacrificed whatever is human in them, their consciousness, their dreams, and their desires, in order to maintain the ideological fantasy that traps them. By characterizing them as "undead" or half awake, García Márquez shows that to engage in such a contract with the ideological fantasy is to be emptied of life itself.

The one hope for Eréndira seems to be Ulises, the boy with the golden skin who the abuela says seems like an angel without wings. When the abuela makes that comment, he says matter-of-factly that the angel was his grandfather (114) creating yet more resonances, in typical García Márquez fashion, between this and other stories, in this case "Un hombre muy viejo con alas enormes." Ulises is the mestizo offspring of a Dutch father and a Guajira mother. His father and he traffic contraband oranges they grow in their orchards that, fantastically, have a diamond in their center. The relationship here between Ulises and the angel who falls to Earth in his short story, "Un hombre muy viejo," is not just some piece of neat intertextuality. In the short story an old, tired angel falls to Earth and is immediately incarcerated in a chicken coop. The family that holds him charges villagers to come and see him. Soon the venture is so profitable that all of the rooms of the house are stuffed with money. In "Un hombre muy viejo con unas alas enormes," most readers might think of an angel falling to Earth as being an expression of magical realism. However, what is truly magical real in this story is the reaction of the people to the angel falling to Earth. Rather than treating the angel with awe, he is put in a coop and is soon covered with chicken manure. Since the priest cannot understand him since the angel speaks Aramaic—the language Jesus probably spoke—and not Latin, the priest declares that the angel could be a devil's minion. Because the angel does not perform as they expect—he performs strange miracles like causing flowers to spring from a leper's wounds—the people soon lose interest and turn away from him. In *Eréndira*, the effectiveness of the angel is turned on its head. Here, Ulises is an angel who in every way is able to affect the world—for example, he has the magical oranges that are worth a lot of money—though maybe not in a way that is entirely agreeable to him.

The oranges with diamonds inside are another image that García Márquez employs to create connections between Latin America and globalized, neo-liberal exchange. The father is Dutch creating resonances with the history of Dutch trade and the West Indies Trading Company that brought slaves to the Americas as part of the "golden triangle." The triangle was golden because of its economic efficiency. Dutch ships dropped slaves in the Americas, largely Curaçao and other possessions, where they were beaten into the molds of slavery so they could be sold. After dropping off the Africans who survived the Middle Passage, the ships filled their holds with slaves who "were ready for market." They then transferred the slaves to what is now the United States or other parts in Latin America or the Caribbean where they were sold. After dropping off the slaves to be sold, the ships were filled with whatever the place in question produced—sugar, gold, coffee, tobacco, henna, and so on—and returned to Europe. It was a very profitable enterprise for the Dutch and established them as one of the wealthiest and most "progressive" countries in the world.

In the novel, the Dutch father ships the oranges as contraband. This means that the wealth that he generates completely bypasses the local governments. He would not be subject to taxes or other tariffs meaning that none of the wealth he generates would be used to build the local economy, much less schools, hospitals, or other things that would improve the lives of people in the area. Wealth is generated, but it is transferred in ways that are similar to the old colonial system. That is, wealth is produced and extracted from Latin America and it is left in the hands of the few elites. It does not positively affect or change the lives of workers. Again, García Márquez creates a relationship between the present and the past. The contraband that they are smuggling resembles other raw goods that are shipped out of Latin America, the result of "free trade" that continues the relationship of dependency developed during colonial times. The anachronistic feel that he gives the descriptions, the Dutch father seems to live on an old-style plantation, he reads an old Bible in Dutch, and he creates a sense of a time that does not move forward. The fact that the father is unable to communicate to the Guajira mother also exemplifies the relationship between Europe, or the Global North, and Latin America. Though the Dutch man has lived in Latin America and with a Latin American wife for decades at least, he has no desire to know more about the place or his wife than what is necessary for him to fulfill his own wants. The boy, Ulises, speaks both languages, and represents a possibility for a time in the future when things might change.

Ulises steals some oranges from his father with the idea of using the proceeds to free Eréndira and spend his life with her. But even with his help, Eréndira seems unable to break free of the abuela. Significantly, the oranges and the wealth they represent, are incapable of freeing Eréndira from her slavery. Money or capital is not enough to free her. The abuela keeps adding to her debt, so that no matter how many millions of men she might be forced to have sex with, she will never be able to pay off her debt and be free. Similarly, the oranges cannot offer her freedom from the ideological framework she is confined in since the capital they bring is part of the very foundation of the structure that traps her. After Eréndira and Ulises run away and are caught, they try to kill the abuela. Ulises puts enough rat poison in the abuela's food to kill all the rats on the planet Earth along with a couple of elephants. Miraculously, the only effect of the poison is that she has a really good night's sleep. Later, Ulises eventually kills the abuela with a knife. Much to Ulises' and the reader's relief, the abuela finally dies after having survived two previous attempts on her life.

Much to Ulises' chagrin, Eréndira takes the golden vest—yet another reference to classical literature—he brought with him and escapes running in the opposite direction of the city. She breaks free from all holds on her and her life with the death of the abuela. The narrator says, "she went against the wind, faster than a deer, and no voice of this world could stop her" (158).[14] In the story, Eréndira disappears from the page because no voice can stop her. By running away from the dead abuela and the desiring Ulises, she also removes herself from the fantasies each of them had constructed for her. It is easy to imagine what life with Ulises could be like; the pattern is already set. After a few months or perhaps years of wedded bliss, Eréndira would be trapped once again in the marital relationship. This time, rather than being part of the Amadís narrative, she would be Penelope to this new, mestizo Ulises. With the abuela's death, Eréndira has reached a point of freedom that is entirely beyond representation and all it implies; the patriarchal order, limitations, castration, and subservience to the law. She is no longer subjected to language, but neither is she a subject.

She also runs in the opposite direction of the big, shiny, and modern city of mirrors. The image of a mirrored city is another that often appears in García Márquez's fiction. In his discussion of *Cien años de soledad*, Erickson says that "the 'mirror walls' signify Latin America's dependent 'reflection of the foreign metropolis'" (179). The mirrors show how Latin America, in its "progress," tries to reflect or imitate Europe and the rest of the Global North. The mirrored walls also make the buildings an impenetrable presence. Similar to the relationship between the Dutch contrabandist and his Guajira

wife who are unable to communicate since they don't speak the same language, the buildings sit there impassively one cannot peer into them to see
what is going on inside. Placed as it is in the desolate landscape of the novel
the mirrored city also creates a sense of anachronism. The abuela and Eréndira have been living in a tent, yet on the horizon is the modern city of wealth
and progress. Rather than escape to the city, which would have been no
escape at all since it would have resulted in a mere repetition of Northern
modes and values, Eréndira runs like a deer leaving no trace.

The film, *Eréndira* (1983), for which García Márquez wrote the script,
concludes with the Eréndira character providing a voiceover which creates a
sense of an ending to the narrative. Where the story ends with Eréndira's
disappearance from the symbolic order, the film leaves her as a subject of
language. In the novel García Márquez shows only the bloody devastation
caused by Ulises's regicide and how the boy is left not only with a big mess
on his hands, but also with the burden of guilt for having single-handedly
killed a human being. In the film, rather than disappearing from representation, though she does appear visually from the frame, Eréndira seems to have
become a subject of language. Rather than simply responding "yes" to all of
Abuela's commands, she is now able to speak for herself. Though due to the
absence of her body, it could be said that she hovers off camera haunting the
images on the screen; the voiceover does more to place her in a dominant,
albeit disembodied, position giving her the narrative voice that concludes the
film. In the film her presence continues to haunt the filmic screen of representation. In the novel García Márquez is careful to emphasize her complete
disappearance through repetition. The last paragraph is devoted to her erasure and the final words attempt to complete her entry into complete absence,
"and no one ever had the slightest news from her and the smallest vestige of
her disgrace was never found" (158).[15] This, of course, is another narrative
trick or technique that García Márquez employs in his narrative, most notably *Cien años de soledad* where at the end of the novel, the very novel we
are reading falls apart. The book containing the history of the Buendía family, now being read by the two remaining patriarchs, is destroyed and carried
away with the wind. But here rather than having the story refer back to itself
giving the effect of a closed, cyclical time within the narrative, in "Eréndira"
there is only devastation. Rather than enclosure, there is complete fragmenta-
tion and rupture.

Though García Márquez inserts himself in *Cien años de soledad* and
other stories as well as "Eréndira," he does it little bit differently here. In
"Eréndira," the narrative "I" inserts itself when he says "Las conocí" [I met
them] (141) near the middle of the novel. But this "I" never really asserts its
presence beyond this short interjection. However, it could also be said that
the "I" here is the voice of the author who exerts authority over the narrative
by recuperating Eréndira's story and putting it on the page for us. Because of

the ending's total erasure of Eréndira and anything dealing with her "disgrace," the only trace that the readers have of her is the writing produced by the "I" or García Márquez himself. The act of erasing his own writing creates an ironic tension at the end of his famous novel, *Cien años de soledad*, and the short novel "Eréndira" that the film removes by providing the voiceover. The tension emanates from the conundrum caused in the reader's mind by the story. Similar to the book falling apart at the end of *Cien años de soledad*, where the question is, if the book has fallen apart how can I be reading it? With "Eréndira" the question becomes, if every trace of Eréndira has been removed then what have we just read? I would assert that, at least in the case of the short novel "Eréndira," what we see as readers is the trace of what Badiou would call an "event." The event is the rupture of a "truth event" in the symbolic order that might result in political change. Badiou argues that the Maoist revolution was an "event," but such events are only known in retrospect since when they happen they resist symbolization. In the case of Eréndira, her revolt against the abuela and the order the two of them were enslaved to can be categorized as an event. Eréndira emerges from that revolution as a "true subject" in Badiou's terms, but she is so "true," and is so closely related to the Real, that she cannot enter into symbolization.

García Márquez shows the undead relationship between the abuela and Eréndira in a way that allows the reader to create links between their relationship and Latin American history and colonialism. By imagining the death of the abuela and the absolute freedom of Eréndira, García Márquez imagines a truly revolutionary event. That is it is an event that opens the possibility for radical change not only in the political systems, but also in language and representation. But like all such events, once it has achieved its effect at the moment of the event, it then disappears. The disappearance however is never total; rather it remains as a haunting absence reminding the reader of its potential. The possibility of a powerful, transformative eruption is kept in reserve by the erasure of the event itself. If the event—in this case the murder of the abuela and the transformation of Eréndira into something or someone else beyond her grasp—were able to be entirely rendered into representation, then it would lose its transformative potential.

To understand how García Márquez is representing the possibility of change in "Eréndira," it is necessary to understand the abuela figure as the classic archetype of the authoritarian who becomes monstrous in its demands and its hold over us. The abuela here is similar to Freddy Kruger or any other monster just as she also represents any dictator in Latin America or elsewhere. Unbelievably she survives attempts on her life and in effect must be killed three times. This is typical not only for monsters but also for Kings or other authoritarian figures. The monster must always be killed more than once. First they must be killed physically and then the idea of them—their authoritarian position or hold over us in the ideological fantasy—must be killed. It is never enough to kill a dictator; she or he must always be killed twice. In addition to this, the revolutionary act of overthrowing the dictator or the ideological limit represented by any authoritarian structure, as is true for the importance of any historical event, is known only in retrospect. The failures to overthrow the abuela/dictator will only be "redeemed" when at some point in their future the revolution finally arrives.

The revolutionary importance of her death will only be known in the future once the change has truly been enacted, or once the effects of the change can be understood. Then, from the point of revolutionary change, it will be possible to look back on the so-called failures of the past. It is only then that they will be understood and be able to come into language and understood. Until then, Eréndira will remain a trace that haunts history and representation. Žižek says that revolution happens,

> [. . .] when the texture of previous history, that of the winners, is annihilated, and when, retroactively, through the success of revolution, each abortive act, each slip, each past failed attempt which functioned in the reigning Text as an empty and meaningless trace will be 'redeemed', will receive its signification. (*Sublime Object* 143)

In this way, García Márquez's erasure at the end of the story shows how his text is not yet ready to be read, that it will be interpreted and receive its signification only at some point in the future, a future that may never come. Until then it haunts the present.

The haunting that comes as a result of the swerve in signification caused by Eréndira's revolution can be seen as creating a sense of the magical real in the story. That is to say that the symbolic order creates what appears to be a closed structure made by a chain of signification. Though it allows us to speak and become subjects, it also causes us to castrate that part of ourselves that cannot enter into signification. García Márquez shows how Eréndira and even the abuela are trapped in an ideological fantasy that is sustained by the symbolic order. Rather than leave them there, something comes along to disrupt that order, the abuela's death. However, rather than occupying a role already made for her she escapes without a trace. That is, rather than taking the place of matriarch now that the abuela is dead or marrying Ulises and having children with him, committing herself to yet another pre-established pattern within the order, she escapes the scene leaving no trace. The tension created by her disappearance within writing itself brings the story to what Carpentier called a "limit state," when he characterized "*lo real maravilloso.*" At the limits of the symbolic order the reader can potentially think of other possible futures for Eréndira and what she represents: women, Latin America, people of color, all and any marginalized group. Her escape and disappearance cannot be related in the present since we are still bound by our own forms of signification.

The magical real moment at the end of the story creates a sense of a reading yet to come. The tension created by the disappearance that is, nevertheless, apparent in signification is magical real since it creates a sense of haunting in the reader. The story is magical real not because of the fantastical images such as a boy who is the grandson of an angel and who traffics in oranges that have a diamond in their center. Those are all "fantastic" elements. At the end of the story, we are haunted by the future that will come, rather than the past that imprisons and deadens subjectivity. The haunting is magical real since it postulates another perspective from which the real might be viewed, but it is a perspective from a point similar to the second, obscure center in Sarduy's ellipsis, a point that for the moment is hidden in darkness. It is the relationship of the visible to the invisible here that creates a sense of heightened reality or that there is something in this reality that escapes our ability to contain it.

The other way that this story is magically real is that it presents something that seems entirely outrageous to us in a way that is matter of fact or objective as if the unbelievable real events were normal everyday occurrences. The number of men Eréndira is forced to have sex with by her grandmother no less, is told with an almost cold objectivity with no comment by the narrator, as if it were a real event because, unfortunately, it is a reality for far too many young girls. We are shown how she is initially measured and weighed by the older man who "buys virgins" and for whom she is neither old enough or weighs enough. In the objective distance and detail that García Márquez uses to describe this scene, he is drawing attention to his own narrative distance from the subject at hand. The objectivity used to describe something so horrific creates another tension within the novel. As readers we are almost allowed to ignore it and focus on other events until we are shown the effects of the innumerable times Eréndira is forced to have sex. The unfortunate truth of García Márquez's representation is that Eréndira's fate is perhaps an understatement of a horrifying reality in Colombia and elsewhere in the world.

As Diane E. Marting notes in her article, "The End of Eréndira's Prostitution," in the film *Eréndira* the young protagonist's fate portrayed in the fictional frame bears a striking and horrible proximity to real events. Marting says that the unbelievable number of men Eréndira is forced to service in order to pay off her debt to the abuela is not really far from an all too common reality for many young women. As Marting says, the fact that Eréndira will have to service "around a hundred men a night once her tour has gotten into full swing" (182) is horrifying. Nevertheless Marting adds, "[h]owever exaggerated the number may appear, and however frequently hyperbole may be a technique in this and other García Márquez's works, this number of tricks is not out of the range of possibility for certain kinds of sex workers in documented studies" (182). Marting completes some more calculations and reveals that with travel, time for dinner, and so on, that Eréndira is probably "only" servicing about seven men per night. However, García Márquez makes that number appear much more since men are always waiting in endless lines to spend a few moments in the tent with her. As stated before García Márquez is haunted by the image of the prostitute and especially the child prostitute. It was an image that he saw when he was an adolescent. As Marting relates, "[a]ccording to published interviews with the author, 'La increíble historia' ['Eréndira'] is based on an experience when, as a sixteen-year-old, García Márquez saw an fourteen-year-old girl working as a prostitute. She was accompanied by a woman he presumed to be her relative" (176). It might be hypothesized that the reason it is a recurring image in his work and why he worked for over a decade on the film script and novella *Eréndira* is precisely because he needs to capture the haunting nature of the relationship successfully. In effect, numbers or statistics are not enough here. Yes, the numbers are staggering and reveal the truth of a horrible reality, but for García Márquez, the only way to relate the true horror of the event is through fiction. And the only way to imagine a way out of it is in the fictional realm. Sociology, for all the good it tries to effect, can only study reality; fiction brings us closer to the event by working on our imaginations and emotions. In fiction it also is able to imagine a possible way out of the horror, a way of reconfiguring the fantasmatic structure and the symbolic order.

García Márquez is not just trying to master the ability to relate the real event, but even more, he is trying to represent a real event that is too real to be completely understood even though it really happened and continues to happen. In order to represent the horrific reality of violence against women, realism whether in the form of documentary, testimonial, or some other Real form is incapable of relating what García Márquez wants. The Colombian writer's magical realism is, however, capable of providing the possibility for an encounter within the text of a Real event. In "Eréndira" the element of magical realism that García Márquez uses is not so much the fantastical events of diamonds appearing in oranges or other similar things. Rather, he presents the horrifying real as objectively as possible and in a way that causes us repulsion precisely because of the rationality used in the narrative voice. The cold, scientific objectivity in the narrative voice to represent the horrific reality of child prostitution creates a sense of hyper-reality, of the more real than real in the narrative. However, as can be noted by the bibliography on the novella, because the writer does not do more to draw our attention to the horrible events, it is quite easy perhaps to ignore them and to focus on the more fantastic elements, reading Eréndira as a sleeping beauty who wakes from her nightmare at the end of the story. In many ways this is similar to another work of fantasy that includes the horrific; Brueghel's' *The*

Fall of Icarus. As the poem by William Carlos Williams "Landscape with the Fall of Icarus" and W. H. Auden's "Musee des Beaux Arts" make evident, the tragic, mythical event of Icarus' fall is hidden in the painting. Due to the objective, distant perspective of the painter, the viewer's attention is drawn to the landscape filled with the riotous spring. Auden notes "how everything turns away" from the important moment of Icarus' fall. Similarly, García Márquez surrounds Eréndira's horrific story with other fantastic events. In the magical real painting classical perspective is shifted or perhaps even flattened out so attention is given to all objects in the frame. In García Márquez's story, elements that should be in the background or perhaps even excluded are brought to the foreground and vie for the reader's attention with other events. While this narrative technique can allow the reader's eye to wander and become more focused on less horrifying details—hence the number of articles that study the more fantastic and less real events in this story— the reader will, perhaps, be haunted by his or her inability to fully contain the events in the novella similar to the way García Márquez felt with regard to his subject. That is, the reader as much as the author are haunted by Eréndira's fate.

NOTES

1. "[. . .] viento de su [Eréndira's] desgracia."
2. "[. . .] la abuela, desnuda y grande, parecía una hermosa ballena blanca en la alberca de mármol."
3. "[. . .] [e]ra tan gorda que sólo podía caminar apoyada en el hombro de la nieta, o con un báculo que parecía de obispo."
4. Of course the exception to this would be the liberation theology movements. However, those who espoused liberation theology often had a troubled relationship with the Church hierarchy not to mention the *caudillo* who controlled the country at the time.
5. The novel was first published in 1508, but earlier versions existed. García Rodríguez de Montalvo, who published the first Spanish version of *Amadís*, admitted to "enmending" or copying the first three books but authoring the final one himself. *Amadís de Gaula* is one of the novels found in Don Quijote's library in the first book when his library is purged by authorities.
6. See for example, Mary Malcom Gaylord's "Don Quixote's New World of Language." *Cervantes: Bulletin of the Cervantes Society of America.* 2007 Spring; 27 (1): 71–94.
7. "[. . .] apuesto que son estátuas de marfil."
8. "Entonces no es de este mundo."
9. "Apoyada en el báculo episcopal, la abuela abandonó el tenderete y se sentó en el trono a esperar el paso de las mulas."
10. "[. . .] virtud de continuar viviendo en el sueño."
11. "[. . .] de un estilo de belleza sepulcral que había estado de moda en su juventud."
12. "[. . .] se veían edificios de vidrio, de una ciudad iluminada."
13. "Eréndira estaba dormida, encadenada al travesaño, y en la misma posición de ahogado a la deriva en que lo había llamado (a Ulises)."
14. "[. . .] [i]ba corriendo contra el viento, más veloz que un venado, y ninguna voz de este mundo la podía detener."
15. "[. . .] y jamás se volvió a tener la menor noticia de ella ni se encontró el vestigio más ínfimo de su desgracia."

Chapter Six

Engaging the Darkness in Mayra Montero's *Tú, la oscuridad*

The baroque and the neo-baroque employ artistic techniques that take representation to its very limit, risking the sign's ability to communicate. In previous chapters I have argued that the neo-baroque risks the capacity of representation because its engagement with the *objet petit a* through anamorphism, magical realism, bifocality and other techniques. Another way the baroque or neo-baroque takes representation to its limit is by using techniques such as *claro oscuro*, which emphasize or at least allow for darkness or what cannot be fully seen or known to enter the frame. The Cuban writer Severo Sarduy characterized the Latin American baroque—and Latin American art in general—as the obscure point in an elliptical structure around which the world constructed by coloniality revolved. Where the Global North was satisfied to conceive of its cultural imaginary based on the seen, Sarduy destabilizes the surety of the seen by interjecting a second unseen, unknown, and unknowable element. The structure is no longer a circle with one clearly visible axis but rather an ellipsis with an additional, unseen point around which the world circulates. The act of reminding viewers, readers and thinkers that something is out there that they cannot fully see and therefore cannot satisfactorily know upsets the Cartesian "clear and distinct perception" that Western science has used to construct and maintain its authority. As Mary Louis Pratt argues, scientific surety created a certain arrogance among Western scientists that allowed them to believe they could know and categorize all phenomena within a predetermined structure. They believed that if anything exists, it can be seen, understood and categorized within their system. The thing that exists, no matter what it is, must fit within the framework devised by Carl Linnaeus. This led to what Pratt characterizes as "the imperial gaze." Against this gaze, the baroque and neo-baroque postulate darkness, lack and, therefore, a loss of mastery. There is something within the field of vision itself, within the representational text, that stares out at us. We are not able to look at this "thing," the *objet petit a*, head-on. We can only see it through some trick of anamorphism or as some sort of haunting that appears as a distortion in our field of vision. The proper place for this "thing" that cannot be seen is darkness, it exists in the obscure pole in the binary, *claro oscuro*. In the following analysis of Mayra Montero's *Tú, la oscuridad* (1995), I will analyze how a particular scientist in her novel, Victor Grieg, confronts and interacts with the darkness he encounters in Haiti in his quest to find the last remaining blood frog on Earth.

Mayra Montero is a Cuban exile who lives in Puerto Rico. She has worked as a journalist and contributes frequently to the Puerto Rican daily newspaper, *El Nuevo Día*. She is a prolific novelist. Her second novel, *La úlitma noche que pasé contigo* (1991), was a runner up for the *Sonrisa Vertical* prize for erotic literature awarded by Tusquets press. Her novels cover a wide variety of topics. At times she writes intimate, erotic novels like *La última noche que pasé contigo* or *Púrpura profundo* (2000). Others like *Tú, la oscuridad* or *La trenza de la hermosa luna* (1987) deal with relationships that take place within a turbulent historical backdrop. The majority of her work, whether fiction or non-fiction, treats the relationships that cross some sort of divide—sexual, social, racial, class are among many other divisions she explores—that separates characters or, as in the case with her essays published in *Aguaceros dispersos* (1996)—between herself and others. The novel that will occupy my analysis in this chapter, *Tú, la oscuridad*, is as much about the relationship between Victor Grieg and his Haitian guide, Thierry, as it is about his obsessive search for the blood frog and the apocalyptic setting of the Duvalier's last years.

As the mysterious, provocative title of the novel implies, darkness is a central theme that the reader tries to explore as he or she follows Victor Grieg in his relentless pursuit of the blood frog. Haiti forms the backdrop to his pursuit and, as presented, it forms one aspect of the mystery. Her novel, in many ways, could be read beside Carpentier's *El reino de este mundo* as something of a bookend to what he presents there. Carpentier showed the Haitian Revolution, which brought Haiti freedom and thrust it into a troubled modernity.[1] Montero shows what has happened to Haiti nearly a century after its first revolutionary uprising. In her novel she shows a Haiti that has suffered centuries of environmental and sociopolitical devastation at the hands of U.S. intervention and the tyrannical dictators like Papa Doc and Baby Doc Duvalier the United States props up. We see the grinding poverty that Thierry and other Haitians live in as well as the fear they have of Baby Doc's secret police force, the *ton ton macoute*. Though Montero makes the reader conscious of the historical events in the novel, the reader must also try to piece together clues to arrive at a specific time and places. The *macoute* and the horrors they inflict on the people of Haiti, such as necklacing (a practice whereby the *macoute* placed a tire around the body of a victim and lit it on fire), are described often in vivid detail. But if the reader has little knowledge of Haiti during the time of the Duvaliers the references might be lost.

Due to her focus on the precise, intimate details with little mention of the larger, historical events that surround them, the reader is left trying to make the connection to the historical events and the unnamed and unmentioned tyrant leading the country. Once the reader makes some of the connections between the images and history he or she finds that those who run the country in this novel, at least on the local level, are the drug traffickers and their gangs. Montero employs the magical real technique of close, precise description of detail that orients the reader by showing the horrors. At the same time, her precision leaves out—or leaves the reader in the dark—with regard to other, important historical details. This is not a criticism, it is merely an observation of the way she employs the magical real technique of cold, precise observation. Her extreme focus on events is similar to Carpentier, García Márquez, and other paragons of magical realism. True to her other novels that focus more on the personal relationships, here she emphasizes the relationship between the obsessed scientist, Grieg, and Thierry, his guide.

In what follows, I will attempt to analyze the mysterious darkness of this novel even though I know from the outset such a task is impossible, since no one can see in the dark. Of particular importance to my analysis is Montero's representation of Grieg's scientific objectivity in relation to the other knowledge systems that Thierry and Emile Boukaka present to him. Grieg has a firm belief in his ability to know, and it is his belief that Montero makes fun of and tries to undermine with other types of "local" knowledge. Grieg's adherence to science prevents him from really knowing his wife, along with Thierry and others since he believes he already knows them. Though it is possible that he changes over the course of the novel, his arrogance leads to a tragic blindness causing his ultimate fall into the abyss at the end. Along with discussing Grieg's blindness, I will also show how Montero reworks magical realism by, in a sense, inverting it. We see through the eyes of Thierry how our world, the world of the Global North, can be seen as something "magical" to an outsider. In the first section I will talk about how darkness or the "obscure" has formed an important part in Latin American letters and the baroque or neo-baroque.

I: DARKNESS IN LATIN AMERICA'S BAROQUE
AND NEO-BAROQUE

The emphasis on darkness in this novel connects it and Montero to a long tradition of poets and other Latin American writers. The emphasis on the unseen and the unknowable characterizes some of the most revolutionary texts in Latin American representation. The use of masks in the baroque or neo-baroque can be understood as a type of obscuring of meaning. Sor Juana Inés de la Cruz is perhaps one of the first, if not the first, Latin American artist to use masks to undermine our sense of mastery and to question representational capacity.

Hernán Vidal in his article, "Aesthetic Categories as Empire Administration Imperatives: The Case of the Baroque," situates the baroque within its socio-historical context showing how much of what went on during that period is a reflection of the instability in the Court. With his historical edifice fully in place Vidal analyzes the use of *persona* in the baroque to create identities that allow subjects to negotiate power hierarchies. *Persona* refers to a type of mask used in classical theater to hide the identity of actors so they could take on the personalities of the characters in the play. Vidal's criticism seeks to remove the mask from the baroque drama in order to reveal the truth. In particular, he focuses on cross-dressing such as that employed by Sor Juana Inés de la Cruz, a tactic that allowed her to enter into the male only university for a time. He shows the continuity of such a tactic by creating a comparison between Sor Juana and the twentieth-century Cuban writer Severo Sarduy who wrote about characters who cross-dressed. While Vidal recognizes that cross-dressing does allow a certain degree of agency within a power hierarchy, he concludes his essay by arguing that no matter what *persona* any subject employs in order to negotiate power, sooner or later the mask must be removed and the truth must be told: A truth that inevitably leads to domination and oppression. Vidal concludes his essay by saying,

> Once discovered, she [Sor Juana] had no other option but to return to her gender identity and find some other way to have full access to an intellectual lifestyle, which she did by becoming a nun, living in the routines of the convent, within the Church—the most fundamental institution in the Spanish colonial order. (49)

Vidal ignores the complexities of Sor Juana's return to the institutional order. While it could be argued that she eventually succumbs to its claims over her body and mind in her epistle "Yo la peor de todas," it could also be argued that her ability to "write like a man" creates a *persona* and a place for herself within the discursive structure of the Church by allowing her to maintain control over artifice via language. However, she is only able to control her appearances by leaving some portion of herself beyond the grasp of the Church and its laws. Coming into full presence of the law—and whether or not such an act is possible is a debate that will have to be side-barred here—would erase any potential place, albeit invisible, from which Sor Juana, Sarduy, or anyone else might articulate a revolutionary difference.

Vidal, similar to other cultural critics, questions whether Sarduy's cross-dressing or any artifice can be used as a valid ground upon which to construct Latin American or any identity since, "After all, once the male transvestite finishes his spectacular extravaganza, he will have to undress, remove his make-up, and at some time return to his regular work unless he is a professional entertainer. Identification as a professional entertainer certainly disqualifies him as a macro-cultural metaphor" (49). This understanding of artifice and masks doesn't recognize the fact that, given the state of modern politics, one might be hard pressed to find any political figure or any cultural metaphor that is not without its entertainment value or its baroque surface.[2] This aside, Vidal, like other critics, wants to render everything visible, to make the truth known for all to see so that the structures of power might be known and changed for the better. However, by shedding light on what is hidden, by forcibly undressing Sor Juana or Sarduy and showing them for what they "truly" are, he also renders them ineffectual, leaving them no place to hide from the glare of the searchlight on top of the panopticon. Without wanting to, by revealing the truth critics enact a function similar to the one criticized by Mary Louis Pratt in her analysis of "imperial eyes." Once something is seen for what it is, we think we understand it and can place it within a predetermined category of knowledge, there is no excess. The metaphoric folds of language have been ironed out to fully expose the truth. We see Sor Juana stripped of her artifice and place her in the category of "woman" or we see Sarduy without his extravagant *persona* and put him under the sign "man." The play of simulation and the camouflage they offered Sarduy is lost. We know where he is and, even more importantly perhaps, we know what he is. He cannot hide.

The inability to "hide" or to find some respite from the gaze of the Other as might be the case in a dictatorial regime, induces anxiety in the subject. Anxiety is not the result of distance or of lack; on the contrary, anxiety comes as a result of over proximity of the Other. We feel anxiety when there is no place for us to be in private. A simple example of this would be an acquaintance or neighbor who is always coming over and who won't leave once he or she comes into your home. No matter how much you like the person initially, if they won't allow for some distance in the relationship, you will begin to feel anxious. In George Orwell's *1984*, people lead lives filled with anxiety and stress in large part because even their most intimate actions and thoughts are public. This is what happens when we live in a society—in many respects like the current one—where there is no privacy, where our friends and neighbors bombard us constantly on Facebook and Twitter with the intimate details of their lives. If there is nothing that is "obscure," if everything is "clear" or "*claro*" then we live in a constant state of turmoil or anxiety brought on by the over proximity of the Other.

Against this, the baroque and neo-baroque emphasize the darkness, the place where it is possible to escape the gaze of the Other. The neo-baroque does this, in part, by reminding us of the limits of language and representation. In short, the neo-baroque reminds us of the constitutive lack in the symbolic order. This lack, while unsettling, also offers us respite in a society where everything is overly "clear." As Todd McGowan relates:

> With the advent of the symbol, we can put on a public persona that holds something private in reserve, hidden beneath the symbol. In this way, the symbolic order opens us a private space, a respite from its own intrusive operations. (*The End of Dissatisfaction* 25)

The line between the public and the private that has been erased creates a society in which private space appears impossible. However, by emphasizing the need for a persona when in public, the private can be concealed and afford us some respite from the anxiety induced by the over proximate Other. Interestingly, if the symbol is the persona that hides the private, then what is hidden cannot really ever be known since the symbol in the symbolic order is constructed over the abyss of the Real. The mask or symbol allows us subjectivity while at the same time protecting us from the overwhelming presence of the real. However, as it does this it also contains within itself a part of the real, the *objet petit a*, that risks the mask's ability to function. However, at the same time, engagement with that piece of the real is necessary in order to avoid stasis or what Antonio Viego calls "death."

Sor Juana encounters a mask or persona and questions its ability to fully represent her reality in one of her most famous and frequently read sonnets, Sonnet 145, sometimes titled "Procura desmentir los elogios que a un retrato de la poetisa inscribió la verdad, que llama pasión." In her poem, Sor Juana looks at a portrait of herself criticizing it as well as its reception. She tells her readers that the *retrato* is made of "falsos silogismos de colores" creating an "engaño del sentido."[3] Sor Juana warns against our taking the painting for reality. She recognizes that the painting presents a syllogistic logic that would convince us that the painting is Real but it is a reality that is created by false syllogisms and made up of the man-made artifice of colors. So, the painting is a mask, rather than reality. She shows how the painting makes reality appear better than it really is by excusing her body.[4] As she catalogues the falsity of the painting, the rejoinder is not against art or representation, but rather against our taking that representation as a total reality, "es un resguardo inútil para el hado"[5] its protection is useless against the fate of growing old and ultimate death. In effect, she is arguing that the reader/ viewer must maintain a critical distance with relationship to the text. She does this by tempering her criticisms with ironic asides. She says that it is "un vano artificio del cuidado/ es una flor al viento delicada." "A vain artifice of care/ it is a delicate flower unprotected from the wind."[6] This last line reminds the reader of other poems by famous men writers such as Garcilaso de la Vega who writes in his famous *carpe diem*, "The frozen wind will wilt the rose."[7] Sor Juana's mention of the delicate rose that is defeated by the more powerful wind creates a dialogue between her poem, Garcilaso's, and others throughout the history of poetry that use a similar image.

However, the relation she creates with the poem/poet of the past also points to a paradox within the poem itself. The wind in this case can be the (spoken) word since in classical texts the wind is often related to language, here language defeats the rose.[8] Long after the rose he and she are describing withers, the poem and its description nevertheless will exist. Also, by creating the connection to Garcilaso, she (re)writes the canon in a feminine voice by participating in its construction, but she also shows how language and poetry last even when reality, the rose, or she, do not. Sor Juana does not leave her poem as an aesthetic example. That is, the poetic word is not removed from reality, rather she constantly insists on placing it and its inner principle in relation to reality through a critical understanding of the text.

She says of the painting that it is "It is a decrepit desire and, well seen,/ it is cadaver, it is dust, it is shadow, it is nothing."[9] The "bien mirado" (here translated roughly as "well seen") can be read more than one way. It can be that, if we as viewers look at the painting well as critics, as she has done in her poem, then it will show us, especially those of us reading the poem now hundreds of years after her death, that the body represented in the painting is dust, shadow, nothing. However, the "bien mirado" can also be taken to mean that the painting itself is "well seen" or that it looks good. The last lines also are a sort of irony since they both teach the reader of the vanity of all artifice that the truth is we're getting older and are going to die, but also that the painting lives on long after its object has died. Even as it points to the lie shown in representation, it also reveals a truth if we "look well" at the poem, we are all mortal. The lines also resonate with poems by other male Spanish poets of her day. Some examples are Quevedo's "polvo enamorado" and Fray Luis de Leon's "en tierra, en polvo, en humo, en nada." Even as she criticizes the relationship of representation to reality, she nevertheless participates in the creation of the realm of artifice created by language and "deceitful colors." That is, she engages in battle of "one up-man-ship" that was going on between poets, or, at the very least, places her poem ending with the referents of life becoming "polvo" and "nada" with other poems from recognized masters that do the same. The paradoxical play of the "bien mirado" and the wind that destroys the rose even as language/ wind is used to describe it, also points to the potential poetic language has.

Sor Juana recognizes the complexity of the relationship between representation and reality, she does not opt for one over the other by creating a resolution regarding what some might see as a dialectic between two opposites. In her next two sonnets she shows how she does not completely abandon art and representation, an impossibility given that she is a poet. In her next two poems she proclaims that it is better to consume "vanities of life" than to consume "life in vanities" (Soneto 146).[10] She is quite unlike Don Quijote who is unable to adopt a critical distance from art and life and is consumed by art and unable to see the two realities of art and life. Sor Juana sees that it is possible to read and observe well (*mirar bien*) the artistic work and thereby learn something from it that might be applied to the other, mortal life. Put another way, as long as art is "bien mirado" using criticism, it can teach us something new, but we cannot and should not take it for reality, for totality or the final word. In this she is arguing for a critical distance from the work of art, but one that also recognizes it as art and not as a space of transparent representation.

In her next poem, "Moral censura a una rosa, y en ella a sus semejantes," she places the two realities of art and life in dialogue and maintains her distance from each. In this poem, which once again takes part in literary tradition by writing about the rose, she observes the rose's beauty, but it is a beauty that also teaches. The rose is "magesterial purple in beauty" and "snowy lesson to beauty."[11] In its being, the paradoxes of life and death are united "in whose being nature united/ the happy crade and the sad sepulcre."[12] Again taking part in the baroque tradition of seeing the "coffin in the cradle" she portrays the sadness that comes about with the well observed recognition of life given to her by examining a thing of beauty; that, as soon as we are born we begin to die. As she ends the poem she tells the rose that "living you trick and by dying you teach,"[13] but without its life, without its beauty in contrast to musty death, there would be nothing learned. Her poem in itself stands as a statement in favor of art, since the rose lives on along with its potential capacity to teach. However, what it teaches is not something that Sor Juana decides. As she says in her "Prólogo al lector" for her *Romances*, "In your freedom I put/ if you want to censure them; there is no understanding freer than/ human understanding" (3).[14] I take the "tú" here to be the reader, by starting off her *Romances* by telling the reader, most specifically the official censor, that he possesses a rational capacity like all humans. In fact she seems to be saying to the censor that even if he does censor her work, there is nothing freer than human understanding and this cannot be censored. Another way of looking at this is that she is telling us as readers—and the censors as well—that no one can determine which conclusions her readers will arrive at upon reading her texts. She understands that critical reason, one that every human is capable of, and is therefore "entendimiento humano," will lead to many different conclusions, even some that she may not agree with.

For Sor Juana, representation is necessary and we can learn from it so long as we don't become lost in its lies and so long as we use our critical reason. However, for Sor Juana art creates an irresolvable relationship that leads to an unknown action. On the other hand, her male counterparts use the *memento mori* in their poems to add emphasis to their *carpe diems*. As they artfully describe the beauty of their female listeners, the message is that the women should enjoy their beauty now—or let the men enjoy their beauty— before they get old and are no longer desirable to the male "I" of the poem. Sor Juana's lesson is less obvious. The painting teaches us something, it teaches us that we were once young and are getting older. The rose shows us that even in our youthful vigor and joy we are headed toward death. She tells us that by contemplating the beautiful rose we will learn something, but beyond the already known fact that we are all mortal, she does not reveal what that something is. What are we supposed to do with that knowledge? Unlike her male counterparts she is not trying to convince us to go to bed with her. As a nun, she does not tell us to become more observant in our religious beliefs and practices. Her poems point toward the tension created between eternal art and mortal life teaches us an important lesson. Unlike Sancho in *The Quijote* Sor Juana does not provide a synthesis to resolve the difference created by the antithetical opposition between painting and life, young and old rose. She seems to leave that work to our own capacity to be "bien miradores." She leaves language at its limit as potential. Language becomes alive when it is recognized as a mask that covers over something that it cannot express, it lives and offers us the possibility to escape censorship or the over proximity of the Other when we investigate its darkness, its end and our own.

Where the Enlightenment emphasizes clarity and light, the baroque often uses the visible to signal toward the obscure, what is not in the discursive frame, or perhaps toward what is located outside of the typical location of the vanishing point. In Velásquez's *Las meninas* for example, there are multiple vanishing points in the frame itself, but perhaps more importantly, the primary vanishing point is entirely outside the frame located at a spot where the look of the spectator coincides with the multiple eyes looking out from the painting. In Latin American letters, darkness, the ellipse, blank spaces and other absences riddle literary production. Looking at Gertudis Gómez de Avellaneda's "Al partir" for example, it is possible to see how the blank spaces in the poem as well as the ellipse are used to not only express the failure of any linguistic sign to communicate the extreme emotion she feels, but also to break with and reconfigure the sonnet structure even as she is writing one. Enrique González Martínez, in a poem that created an event in

Latin American letters, "Tuércele el cuello al cisne," puts an end to the flowery, over the top formal, precious beauty in the poetry of so many of the late poets of El modernismo. González writes against the "falso plumaje" of the swan and instead asks the reader to look at the knowledgeable owl who interprets the "libro del silencio."[15] He replaces evident, perceivable beauty and an over-preoccupation with the visible form with an owl reading in the darkness. But how can anyone besides an owl read in the darkness? Knowledge is something that has to be groped for, challenging our sense of mastery.

The preference for the dark or the creation of visible signs that signal toward what is indiscernible is a tendency that is common to both the neo-baroque and the baroque. Baltazar Gracían, in his *Oráculo manual y arte de prudencia* as well as in *El criticón*, tells his readers how to survive courtly life by hiding what they know rather than ostentatiously showing off their knowledge. Signs and other visible means are used to construct an artifice that attracts the interest of others in one's self. As William Egginton puts it, "What distinguishes this person, what makes him a *persona*, in other words is his ability to use the spatial play of the baroque to entice the participation of his fellow players" (60). Since the viewer is brought into the play of the visible he or she becomes part of the artifice or the work of art itself as with *Las meninas*. The play of surfaces entices rather than reveals, hides rather than displays. This aspect of the baroque has troubled critics who want truth to be displayed in all of its fullness as well as those who deny the existence of any truth whatsoever.

Gilles Deleuze argues in *The Fold: Leibniz and the Baroque* that the artistic style of the baroque is nothing more than a play of surfaces, that every interior is really just a fold in the surface and therefore is an exterior/interior. By arguing for an infinite fold rather than an interminable play of surfaces with something behind them, Deleuze misses a key aspect of the baroque by getting lost in its artifice. For the baroque there is something that is not seen, that is not brought into the light and which eludes our ability to represent it or talk about it. For the baroque, and neo-baroque artist there is still something behind the mask created by the *persona* but it is a thing that cannot be represented. The *persona* as is well known, is a word derived from the mask that Greek actors used when on stage to cover their faces and take on their role in the drama. As Egginton argues, "Everything, people included, are posited as being engaged in a constant and thoroughgoing play of appearances over against some core being of corporeal essence" (68). However, this essence upon which all *persona* are built is unattainable to the viewer and to the subject him or herself since, as Egginton argues, the *persona* signals an originary lack. In other terms, upon entering into language the subject must leave something of itself behind. That something is still there even though the symbolic order cannot contain it.

The baroque, particularly in Latin America, is structured on an engagement with darkness, with the originary lack or absence over which representation is structured. Sor Juana's use of masks and the encounters she stages between reality and representation in her work, is perhaps the first moment in Latin American letters of what is a long tradition of such an engagement with darkness. Montero's novel, as I will show in what follows, continues that legacy.

II: VICTOR GRIEG, THE BLIND SCIENTIST

In Mayra Montero's novel, *Tú, la oscuridad*, the character, Victor Grieg, is a herpetologist trained in the Western scientific tradition. As a result, he believes only what he can see clearly and distinctly. Like most scientists, he is single-minded in the pursuit to obtain his goal and to reveal the truth. His focus on the object of his journey, the blood frog, is so laser-like in its attention that he ignores the people around him unless they talk about the frog and he seems entirely blind to the devastation around him. Perhaps most chillingly, he is entirely unconcerned by the fact that by capturing what is thought to be the last known blood frog, he may contribute further to the decline of the earth's environment. Montero intercalates the tale of Victor's search with chapters that tell the life of Thierry, Victor's Haitian guide, and brief paragraphs that announce the extinction of a variety of different frogs. Though Victor is confident in his capacity as a scientist, Montero undercuts his surety, revealing to the reader that there is more to the picture than he, or perhaps we as readers, can see. In the opening scene of the novel, Montero shows how Victor's confidence leads to blindness and arrogance, which contribute to his own sense of superiority and mastery over the natural world and others, like his wife or Thierry.

In the opening paragraphs of the novel, Victor relates how Thierry is telling him of a fruit that his father gave him when he was sick. Thierry says that the fruit "it was like the flesh of a saint"[16] from which he deduces Thierry is describing a pear. After this, Victor says, "I let him talk for a while. It is impossible to think that a man like Thierry can remain silent for a long time" (13).[17] Though Victor lets Thierry speak here, he does not listen to him. The next several pages that make up the rest of the chapter are devoted to Victor telling us about his breakup with his wife, Martha. Later, Victor decides to record Thierry when he talks because he realizes that he often relates important information about frogs when he is relating other, more personal tales.

As Victor relates the end of his marriage, his faith in his own abilities as observer and someone attuned to details is evident. Proclaiming his scientific capacity he says, "When you have a profession like mine, it is really easy to capture certain signs, identify certain smells, recognize the movements previous to *amplexus* (that is what we call the sexual embrace of frogs) that is approaching" (14).[18] In spite of his ability to recognize the minute movements and odors of frogs, Victor remains blind to the fact that Martha, his wife, is growing increasingly distant from him and is getting closer to a female friend, Bárbara. He doesn't realize that she is having an affair with Bárbara until Martha returns home from Dharamsala—a trip she was supposed to take with Victor—wearing a coat made from the blue sheep, an animal of the Himalayas. Their relationship and the dissolution of his marriage come as a total surprise to Victor. His mastery over reality and his relationship, his ability to tell when things are going to happen due to his scientific eye, is completely subverted by Martha's tryst.

In his description of the coat he says that the blue sheep is the preferred meal of the snow leopard (14). Though it is perhaps a minor point, mention of the snow leopard and the blue sheep reminds the reader of the once famous travel novel by Peter Matthiessen called *The Snow Leopard* (1978). Similar to Montero's novel, Matthiessen writes of a journey with a scientist to find something that few if any have ever seen and that is now on the verge of extinction, the snow leopard. The novels are both similar in that the object of the journey in each is to find what few have seen and observe it scientifically, to make either the snow leopard or the blood frog an official part of the scientific record and thus part of our knowledge base. However, the journey to make something visible and knowable is told alongside another story that renders the scientific method suspect. Thierry and Victor are in search of what is possibly the last living blood frog, and though they find it, the novel seems to be about much more. When Montero mentions *The Snow Leopard* in the first pages of the novel, she warns the reader to not be fooled by Victor's pursuit, that we should be attentive to other signs and to the darkness itself. If not, we could suffer the same fate as Victor, we could be so confident in our abilities to notice all the signs that point toward the sexual union of frogs, but completely blind to other, perhaps more important warnings.

Unlike Matthiessen's novel where the secondary, non-scientific journey takes up almost the entire book, the development of multiple voices in Montero's novel makes the narrative less evidently unified. Where Matthiessen muses about Buddhism, meditation, and related matters as he struggles up the slopes of the Himalayas, Montero creates a novel with multiple voices that seem at first glance to be unrelated. Thierry's story of his life growing up and the intimate details of his family life seem disconnected from Victor's journey and the fragmentary scientific pronouncements concerning the extinct frogs. That said, the movement in the novel is structured nevertheless around Victor's search for the frog. The novel begins with Victor and Thierry in the mountains looking for the frog and it ends with them crossing the bay in a ferry and drowning along with the frog they have in a specimen jar. But, if we as readers focus solely on Victor's pursuit, then we are in peril of avoiding the stories that might be of as much, if not more, importance. In short if we follow his story alone, then we are in danger of being just like him and we risk a similar fate. As a neo-baroque writer, Montero includes many voices and distinct perspectives challenging us as readers to put the story together in a coherent way. However, such an enterprise also makes us aware of our own lack of mastery, of our own inability to arrive at satisfactory conclusions with regard to the novel or, perhaps, life in general. Throughout the novel she makes Victor and us aware of our own limitations due to our own prejudices created by the ideological framework we inhabit. That is to say, she makes us aware of the darkness, of what we cannot see.

One example of how Montero makes us aware of Victor's and our own limitations is when he encounters Emile Boukaka. In her representation of their encounter Montero also pokes fun at the North's sense of self-importance and, in a sense, undermines one of the pleasures readers of the global north may get from her novel by using Emile Boukaka to tell them they aren't as powerful as they think. From the beginning of his encounter with Boukaka, Victor's sense of mastery is already upset. Boukaka does not conform to the image that Victor had of him. Victor says, "I thought that Emile Boukaka was a mulatto, no one had told me, but I imagined him differently [. . .] he was really, really black" (129).[19] From the beginning Boukaka doesn't conform to the category that Victor has for scientists, that they must at least have *some* white blood in them. On the contrary, Boukaka does not seem to have even a drop of white blood in him; he is black *con ganas.* Against the racism that shapes Victor's perception of reality, Boukaka is learned and articulate by Victor's and the Western reader's standards. Boukaka has published in respectable, scientific journals and seems knowledgeable of Victor's own work. In fact, Boukaka is so erudite by Western standards that Victor has a difficult time keeping up with him. Victor says,

> I made an effort to naturally deal with the enormous quantity of facts that Boukaka provided me. I was surprised by his attention to detail, his precision and I can even say knowledge. (132)[20]

Along with the vast amounts of knowledge Boukaka is providing, the fact that the vast amounts of information are coming out of someone who Victor thinks incapable of such thinking makes his head reel. He is surprised at the attention to detail and precision, at least in part because Boukaka is black. His racism is confirmed when he says that what Boukaka is telling him could be categorized as "knowledge."

Victor's statement regarding Boukaka's "knowledge" reveals Victor's and Western science's own limitations due to how it categorizes the world and its encounters with it. What Boukaka tells Victor would normally be categorized as belief or some sort of mysticism at best. It could also be considered quaint folklore as an example of how magical realism produces a moment of nostalgia for a past the Western reader never had. The fact that Victor might consider what Boukaka is saying as knowledge raises it to a higher category than folkloric belief or mysticism. This rupture in the system of categories that Victor has been given by Western science creates further instability in Victor's perception of himself and the world.

What causes Victor so much instability is that he cannot fit either Boukaka or the knowledge that he shares into a pre-existing category. The instability Victor and the readers feel in this encounter contributes to the magical real sense of haunting that runs throughout the narrative. As Stephen Palmié relates,

> The feeling of being "haunted" arises when our everyday worlds appear uncannily bereft of their normalcy and reveal themselves as what they are: collectively instituted and maintained infrastructures of certainty [. . .] built on the systematic (and systematically necessary) forgetting, displacement, and disavowal in time and space of [. . .] powerfully estranging reminders. (11)

Victor and the reader are made aware of the ideological framework that allows us to arrive at certitude, at scientific truths. It shows how that scientific framework is built on systematic disavowals of other knowledge systems. With Boukaka's powerful presence Victor and the reader are confronted with a powerfully estranging reminder of the force of that other knowledge's presence, precision, and exactitude. This generates instability in Victor and perhaps the reader, creating an opening through which a haunting presence may appear.

The novel is filled with signs that Victor and the Western reader need to expand their categories and accept other ways of knowing. Early in the novel Victor and Thierry explore a mountain looking for a frog. Victor insists that he is close to getting the frog, but Thierry can hear voices telling him that it is time to leave. Initially we think that the voices he hears might be the result of some sort of magical real power that he has that allows him to sense the voices of zombies or something else. Later in the novel we find out that various drug lords control different mountains and it is their voices Thierry hears. We also see that the price for not listening to the voices—for not hearing them and paying them heed—can be death. So, Thierry's knowledge is extremely important to Victor's survival.

On the way down the hill they go past their encampment where Victor sees an issue of *Froglog*, an academic journal for herpetologists. Even though the journal is covered in excrement, Victor, in an act of academic narcissism, decides to stop and look at it since it contains one of his articles.

Showing an attachment typical for any academic to his work Victor tries to save the journal or at least to see his article and his name in print, but, "I couldn't even see the photo or the title of my article because they were hidden beneath the stain that the turds left" (66).[21] This is perhaps one of the more humorous moments in the novel, when Montero pokes fun at the self-important Victor and the scientific and academic community in general. But, along with the laughter we see exactly how important his knowledge is to the locals. The stains on the article tell him that the skills and knowledge that grant him authority in other places is worth nothing here. Rather than stopping for a moment of self-adulation, he better listen to Thierry and get off the mountain before the gang leader decides to kill him.

Victor's ignorance or willful blindness to his surroundings sometimes leads him to danger. For some reason Victor decides to get rid of Thierry even though he has saved his life. After the first expedition Victor decides they aren't compatible. He says that "Thierry and I weren't compatible" (87).[22] The only reason Victor gives is personal, based on emotions. Victor says that there is no "chemistry" between them and they just don't get along. Aside from that he does not explain why he feels this way about Thierry. His decision makes no sense at all; Victor provides no scientific rationale for it. Thierry knows more about the blood frog than just about anyone in Haiti including Victor himself. He also knows the island, its geography and socio-political problems, like the back of his hand. One could guess that the reason Victor does not feel comfortable with Thierry is precisely because Thierry is a threat to his own status as "the most knowledgeable expert."

When they first meet, similar to his later meeting with Boukaka, Victor is put off by Thierry's looks. He seems to be too old and weak, he is missing his teeth, and presents an overall unpleasant physical appearance. As with Bou-kaka, Victor seems overly concerned with how Thierry looks and not with how much he knows. However, Thierry shows Victor and the reader that his knowledge, and perhaps his obsession with the frog is equal to or surpasses Victor's. Thierry comes to his meeting with Victor wearing a shirt the color of the blood frog and is able to draw a perfect picture of the frog when Victor demands it as a type of test to see how much Thierry knows. When Thierry gives Victor the picture, Victor is, as in his interaction with Boukaka, taken aback by how much the seemingly decrepit Haitian knows. The picture, like Boukaka's knowledge, startles Victor due to its precision and accuracy down to the minutest detail. Victor says in astonishment after studying the picture that, "Now I was the one who had to stall for time" (36).[23] In spite of Thierry's overall excellent credentials as a guide, Victor decides to fire him. He does so at his own risk.

Moments after Victor resolves to find a different guide, we see just how obtuse he is to his surroundings and its possible dangers. He decides to walk down a street even though he sees a rather large fire that is emitting a strange odor that Victor says must be an animal. Montero gives no other indication, but the fire is most likely an incident of what was called "necklacing." The odd sounding word "necklacing" refers to a practice commonly used against detractors of Jean Claude Duvalier (aka Baby Doc) between 1986 and 1990. The *ton ton macoute* or other supporters of Baby Doc would fill a tire with gasoline, put it around the neck of their enemy and light it on fire. Victor, totally oblivious to the political realities of Haiti, walks toward the fire. Too late he decides to go in an opposite direction. Someone grabs him and the crowd beats him until he loses consciousness (87). When he awakes in a room, Thierry is standing over him, nursing him back to health.

Victor has suffered a fall caused by his hubris and as a result, he has lost any control he might have had over himself and his surroundings. The result is that the hierarchical distinction—a result of his own prejudices—that previously created a divide between him and Thierry, no longer exists. Victor has no choice but to allow Thierry to treat him with whatever non-Western cure Thierry sees fit. As he allows himself to be doctored by Thierry and feels himself returning to health, all of his doubts about Thierry as a guide or their so-called compatibility disappear. The two men are closed up together in a small room and the intimacy created by the situation creates an opportunity for the two men to share stories of their lives equally. Victor actually listens to Thierry rather than simply "letting him speak" as he does at the beginning of the novel. It is during this time that Thierry tells Victor of the secret and mysterious "Law of the Water." In exchange Victor tells Thierry more about what is equally mysterious to his Haitian guide, the ostriches that his father farms.

With the egalitarian interchange between them Montero provides her own take on magical realism, a take that echoes and expands the scope of one of the primary moments of magical realism in Latin American and Caribbean literature, the death/salvation of Mackandal in Alejo Carpentier's *El reino de este mundo*. In that scene, as I have already discussed, Carpentier tries to present the event of Mackandal's death/salvation from a bifocal perspective that allows the reader to decide for him or herself what the truth really is. In this way he creates doubt in the reader and shows how representation carries with it an ideological framework that his description places in doubt. With the interaction between Thierry and Victor, Montero gives us examples of how each man perceives the culture of the Other.

With Victor weakened from the beating he took, Thierry offers to exchange information with him. He says, "I can teach you of the 'Law of the Water' provided that you tell me about the birds your father grows" (90).[24] Previously, Victor had told Thierry about the birds and Thierry's reaction is one of total disbelief. Thierry's reaction to Victor's description of his father's ostrich farm is as if someone were to tell me that his father has a farm of five-headed beasts that fly or something similarly odd.

Now, with Victor prostrate, Thierry offers the possibility of an equal exchange of information regarding their cultural wonders and secrets. The marvel and interest that Thierry expresses upon learning about the ostrich is similar to that anyone from the West or the Global North might have when they first hear of the "Law of the Water." For Thierry, the ostrich seems to be a fantastic animal. He is intrigued by how large it is and by how many people the eggs and flesh from the bird can feed. Equally for us, the "Law of the Water" seems mysterious, perhaps even magical and unbelievable, yet it is an important part of Thierry's cultural background.

By creating a situation where characters from two different cultural backgrounds look at details in each other's stories as if they were magical, Montero upsets the traditional relationship in magical realism. Customarily magical realism places the "magical" on the side of the groups not of the Global North or with their traditions rooted in the West. Showing us Thierry's wonder at something we take for granted—something that for us is unquestionably real—Montero shows how Western truths can be seen as magical. This creates the possibility for instability in the reader and the ideological framework that gives structure to his or her reality. In the cracks created by this instability, it is possible for us to look for truths in what we may have previously thought of as "magical." Since Thierry exchanges his knowledge of the "Law of the Water" for Victor's about ostriches, Montero seems to be saying that we as readers should look at both events in a way that allows for astonishment while at the same time allowing for the possibility of their truth or reality.

The possibility that what Western science sees as magical or folklore could be raised to the category of rigorous truth or knowledge prepares Victor and the reader for the meeting with Boukaka. The Haitian doctor Emile Boukaka straddles both Western and non-Western knowledge practices. His knowledge has been officially approved by the Western, scientific community since he has an article published in the respected journal *Froglog*. Victor had read the article even before his trip to Haiti and even though it is not a very long article, Victor is so impressed by it that he makes a note of it with objective of meeting Boukaka and talking about his findings (127). Even before meeting him, Victor recognizes that he is fully knowledgeable of the scientific field of herpetology, giving Boukaka the credentials to be a respected member of the establishment. Along with his scientific knowledge, Boukaka combines his mastery of the "Law of the Water." Though Boukaka presents both types of knowledge together, and even gives more value to the "Law of the Water," Victor, and perhaps the reader along with him, is unable to accept the "Law of the Water" as a category of knowledge.

Discussing the disappearance of frogs from the face of the earth, Boukaka has an immediate explanation. He says that "Agwé Taroyo, the god of the waters, has called to the frogs requesting that they spend some time at the

bottom" (131).[25] Recognizing that Victor would find this explanation unbelievable, Boukaka says, "It seems absurd, doesn't it?"[26] but he keeps insist-
ing that his is the most rational explanation. He defends his conclusion,
pointing out the arrogance of Western science that thinks it can control
everything: "The great escape has already begun—he claimed. You all invent
excuses: acid rain, herbicides, deforestation. But the frogs disappear from
places where these things have never arrived or been a problem." (132).[27]
Western science is arrogant enough to think that it can control the world, that
even its destruction is a result of its inventions and practices. Boukaka tells
Victor and us that there is something more powerful than any of us, that we
cannot control the world; rather we are controlled by it.

Though Victor has suffered events that have created the possibility for
him to be more receptive to different types of knowledge, he initially rejects
everything Boukaka says. As I discussed earlier, one of the main reasons he
rejects Boukaka's knowledge as knowledge is because he has difficulty accepting that someone who is "negro con ganas" can be so knowledgeable.
Instead of listening attentively to Boukaka, he spends most of the conversa-
tion trying to find a category for the black scientist. But Boukaka turns the
tables on him by lumping Victor in with other Western scientists and calling
them "Ustedes," or "You people." This categorization upsets Victor momentarily, but he immediately sees that he is one of "them," the people who are
"incapable of seeing the dark side" due to the objective, pompous attitude
they take (132). Vestiges of his own grounding in the Global North, Western
science and a racist ideological framework balance his acceptance of Boukaka's knowledge, however.

When he and Thierry are leaving Victor finally finds a way to define and
categorize Boukaka within a knowledge system with which he is familiar. He
says that Boukaka is a spitting image of Theolonius Monk, the famous jazz
pianist. As Ángel A. Rivera argues with regard to Victor's observation, "Although the narrator suggests that establishing a comparison between the Haitian herpetologist and Monk is inconsequential, silence is in fact a crucial or
central compositional element in Monk's jazz style" (web). Silences like
darkness is a key component of this narrative, and here Victor is encountering a dark area of his own knowledge, a place that he refuses to look since it
denies him mastery over it. The song he says is not one that is frequently
heard, "See You Later, Beautiful Frog." But after rather extensive research, I
have found that it is a Monk song that does not exist.[28] What does it mean
that there is an absence next to the categorization of Boukaka as Monk? That
the category is under question, that his knowledge is not definitive or even
that well informed. It places under suspicion, at the very least, the limits of
his knowledge. However, it is ironic that for me his knowledge is suspect
because I did the academic thing and went searching for it. Mention of the
song made me, a jazz enthusiast, think I had encountered something that I

should know but didn't, it made me feel unsure of my knowledge just as it makes me unsure of Victor's.

As his encounter with Boukaka comes to an end, the Haitian doctor reveals to Victor and the reader a new way to think about knowledge. Boukaka says, "What I have learned I learned from books. [. . .] But what I know, everything I know, I took from fire and water, from water and flame: one puts out the other" (133).[29] Exactly what these words mean are a mystery to Victor and me. However, what the words do show is that there are other ways of knowing, other things to know that escape our abilities of comprehension due to the fact that we are located within an ideological framework that does not include them as a possible category.

Boukaka, like Thierry and the excrement-stained journal containing Victor's article, call into question and disempower Western science and with it Western instrumental reason. The explanation Western science has for the causes of global warming and the destruction of the planet—though they might be accurate—also place Western modernity at the center. Western science allows us to think that we are so powerful that we have caused the collapse of the earth and now we also have the power to save it. Boukaka thinks otherwise and tries to show Victor that he, with all of his science/knowledge and the authority it gives him, are entirely powerless to save the frogs or the earth. Certainly this is an unsettling view since there is nothing Victor or any of us can do, at least within our current framework of knowledge, which can save us. The information is even more startling since demise of the frogs could mean the end of the earth since they form an important part of the food chain.

What exactly we can do with what he tells us is unknown. After his meeting with Boukaka, Thierry and Victor talk about the interaction. The chapter ends with Victor cast into an uncharacteristic sea of doubt, "A man never knows anything, Thierry, that is his fear" (133).[30] That said, Boukaka seems to be provide a model for us to follow since he is entirely knowledgeable of both Western science as well as what we would label "local traditions," or non-Western ways of knowing. He straddles both ways of attempting to understand himself and reality. What Montero shows us is that the limits to our knowledge exclude ways of knowing that might very well save our lives or the current life on the planet. We would do well to investigate the limits of what we know and peer into the darkness.

Victor seems to change as the novel progresses. As the line I quoted above shows, he realizes the limits of his ability to know, "a man never knows anything," and is open to other ways of being and understanding. Victor's transformation is evident in two ways. The first is when he tries to write a letter to his father and the second is when he and Thierry encounter a female scientist on the mountain. Sarah is a scientist he and Thierry meet in their final, and successful, pursuit of the frog. Like Victor in the beginning of the novel, Sarah is single-minded and obsessed with finding samples of a rare plant she is searching for. When Victor and Thierry warn her that the drug lords demand that they all leave the mountain, she ignores them. She says, "I have to keep on. [. . .] Who can I bother here?" (229).[31] We aren't told what happens to her, but given the general sense of doom, shots are constantly heard in the distance, dead bodies are piling up everywhere, we can guess that she probably is killed by the gang that controls the mountain. Sarah possesses the scientific single-mindedness that allows her to focus on the object of her pursuit while ignoring the devastation and danger around her. In this she is similar to Victor at the beginning of the novel. As he passionately tries to convince her to heed Thierry's warnings we see that Victor is no longer like her, he is not as single-minded in his pursuit, he is able to see the broader picture.

Victor's change in perspective is all the more evident when he writes to his father and constantly fails to communicate. In one draft of the letter he tells his father about Thierry's obsession with ostriches as a way of telling his father that he remembers the ranch and that he thinks of his father often. As with all the other letters he writes, he balls that draft up and throws it away. In each letter he is trying to tell his father that he loves him and thinks of him often, but he cannot find the words. His writing fails to communicate his emotions, "la carta me salió tan fría," in the sense that the letter comes out too stony, retelling only cold, hard facts as in scientific writing and not the depth of his emotions. He writes many versions of the letter until he has a small mountain of torn paper around him. Finally he remembers a word game that his father taught him when he was a child to calm Victor when he had nightmares. That is what he decides to write and send to his father. Victor has realized that language is incapable of communicating everything we want it to. He is face to face with the darkness at the limits of language and knowledge.

His transformation continues as the novel approaches its end. In the chapter where he writes the letter to his father, he also writes to Vaughn Patterson to inform him about his scientific findings in Haiti. Though he finds words incapable of expressing his love for his father, he is able to write a clear, scientific letter to Vaughn Patterson. However, near the end of the novel he again tries to write to Patterson. This time he contemplates how to write a letter to a man who is entirely incapable of paying attention to anyone or anything that does not have to do with frogs. In his single-minded focus, Patterson is a paragon of scientific thought, but if Victor is to explain himself and his journey to Patterson, he will have to talk about more than just frogs. He needs to speak to him from a place outside the scientific system, one that may require metaphors and a more literary style of writing. Victor wonders how he can explain to Patterson that Haiti is not just a mountain with a frog on it, and then he lists all of the mysteries, the darknesses he has encountered.

He tells Patterson about Cito Francisque the drug lord, the various bodies he has seen hanging from trees left by rival gangs. He wonders how he can tell him about Thierry and what he has learned from him so that Patterson will listen to him. Near the end of a long list of things he cannot say, he asks how can he tell Patterson that "Haiti, was ending" and that soon it would be nothing more than a mound of bones (227).

Victor realizes that the frog, which Thierry finds shortly after Victor's interior monologue regarding his thoughts on the letter he sends to Patterson, cannot be seen as Patterson would wish, outside of the complicated context in which it is found. It cannot be fully understood unless it is taken along with everything else. Since that "everything else" is also beyond Victor's capacity to know and tell, the frog itself cannot be known. In this instance, Victor comes face to face with his own limits and with the real. He is on the verge of becoming what Badiou would call a true subject. In an effort to restore the revolutionary impulse of modernity Badiou argues in *Theory of the Subject*, that the only true subject is one that touches the real, or looks out at that thing that haunts the symbolic order and is in darkness and unsymbolizable. For Badiou, the subject is only really ever a subject when he or she engages with the limits of his or her own being. Similarly, Montero shows in her novel that in a global culture, or any culture for that matter, we must also not only realize the limits of our knowledge, but also that we should respect the darkness even as we try to engage it. This does not mean bringing what is invisible and unnamed into the light—such an enterprise would be impossible—but to engage in a dialectic interplay with it; allowing it to unsettle and disturb the neat categories that we have learned to use in our encounters with the other and ourselves.

The irony of Victor's quest is that he captures the last known example of the blood frog, making it extinct, or so it would appear. Unlike Sarah, a scientist who is searching for a plant that is dying out so that she can grow more of them, Victor will take the blood frog and put it in a specimen jar. Naming it, knowing it and possessing it results in its death. By putting it in the specimen jar and bringing it back to Vaughn Patterson, Victor will bring the existence of the blood frog to light, and it will become part of scientific knowledge. Victor's quest has not been to know more about the frog, how it survives in its native habitat and maybe to try and do something to allow it to survive, but to kill it and put it in a jar. By doing this he will also make himself famous in his academic community and be given a fellowship that will allow him do even more research. His community that values a single-minded scientific pursuit of the visible ignores the problematic context in which their quests take place. Engagement with darkness, with the unknown, would create too many complications that would unsettle and confuse the search for knowledge. Victor, with his acquisition of the blood frog has achieved the pinnacle of success and is on the verge of becoming famous at least in the limited confines of his field. However he is unaware that Dambal-lah has other ideas.

Boukaka may not have been able to tell Victor or us how to save the world, but he did give him knowledge that would have helped Victor save himself and Thierry. Once they have the frog they put it in a jar and take a ship from Jérémie to Port-au-Prince. The ship goes under and neither Victor's nor Thierry's body is found. The frog goes down with them. If Victor had paid heed to Boukaka's explanation for the disappearance of the frogs, he would have remembered that they were being called to the bottom of the ocean. By having the frog with them and crossing a body of water, they tempt the god and end up going under along with the frog. After all, we cannot save the earth if we don't save ourselves first.

The question is, how to do that, how to "save ourselves"? What I think Montero is showing us is that we need to become aware of the darkness within ourselves so that we can become true subjects in Badiou's terms. We learn how to become real subjects by engaging the lack that is within each of us. We become aware of that lack, through our interactions with others. Montero is careful not to place Thierry in the typical position of the ethnic or racial other that we see in most Hollywood films. He is not, because of his status as a Haitian at the periphery of the Global North, capable of some sort of existence or truth that is unavailable to us. Montero shows us Thierry's limitations that he must overcome in his relationship with Victor and, most particularly, in his relationship with Ganesha.

The words for the title, *Tú, la oscuridad* come from the most problematic character in the novel, Ganesha. I say she is problematic because she is the most abused by the men as a sexual object who serves only the pleasure of men. She is also abused by Montero's pen, since Montero seems to have created Ganesha as an object of the Western, orientalist gaze. Papa Cra-paud—another herpetologist—travels to Guadeloupe in search of frogs and returns with Ganesha. Thierry's story about her could be used as a textbook example of orientalism. Ganesha, as her name implies, is from a family of immigrants from India and, because of her roots, participates in customs that are strange to Thierry and the surrounding community; she constantly smells of cow urine and cooks foods that are exotic to Thierry and other Haitians. Conforming to orientalist modes of representation, Thierry describes Gane-sha's unbridled sexuality and her inability to control her desire for other men. Such is her animalistic desire that Papa Crapaud has to put barbed wire on the windows to keep her in and men out. But even that is not enough. While Crapaud is away, she offers herself to Thierry and they have sex. Montero describes Ganesha through Thierry's eyes with little if any criticism of his perspective. Ganesha is left in the darkness created by Thierry's own orien-talist gaze; she is shown to the reader only as a wild, sexual animal. His description of her seems an exaggeration, but we are told little else about her.[32]

Though all we get is a troubling and limited view of Ganesha, her presence haunts the text. Along with giving the novel its title, her words are repeated several times throughout the novel and are the last we hear Thierry speak. As if to signal the impartial knowledge we have of Ganesha, the title contains only part of the entire quote that she originally spoke in French, "You, darkness that envelops the spirit of those who ignore your glory" (239).[33] These words relating the power of darkness return to Thierry haunting him at the end of the novel. He says that the ghost of the now dead Ganesha whispers them in his ear, "I only remember her prayer, Ganesha was dead and her ghost/phantasm came to blow them into my ear" (132).[34] Thierry says that he hears the words repeatedly now and that he will hear them when he dies. After he dies he says that he will see everyone he has ever known and, he hopes, all of those who loved him. Then he will repeat Ganesha's words and "Then they will give me light" (132).[35] Light will come to him after he passes over into the absolute darkness of death. Thierry does not tell us who the "they" are; he leaves it up to us to decide. Perhaps it is something only he will know after he is dead. What Thierry does tell us is that what was once darkness or obscured will be made visible. At last, after death, there will no longer be any limits on his knowledge.

Ganesha's words also point toward the darkness, what cannot be understood or clearly perceived. The unseen presence of Ganesha whispers into Thierry's ear, telling him of the power of what has been cast into darkness by the brilliant light of science and Western modernity. What is now in darkness will envelop and defeat those who ignore its glory. Similar to the way that Ganesha's ghost—now in darkness—haunts Thierry, so will everything else that has been ignored or unseen by science's light. It is also a reminder of the dialectic created by Western modernity itself and the so-called underside. This "underside" that has been placed in the darkness by the light of Western reason is a place from which a different type of knowledge can be articulated, it is the second center of the ellipse in Sarduy's articulation of the baroque; it's there, we just cannot see it. Trinh T. Minh-ha argues in favor of encounters with darkness when she says, "Knowledge leads no more to openings than to closures. The quest for knowledge and power makes it often difficult to admit that enlightenment (as exemplified by the West) often brings about endarkenment" (40). The very act of casting light creates its opposite, darkness. Each closure that knowledge creates, leads to its eventual undoing, to another opening up. Trinh argues for a new type of knowledge acquisition, one that is no longer the accumulation of information into an archive giving power to a few, but "the term of an ongoing unsettling process" (40). She is arguing for the continuation of the dialectic process, one that seeks closure only to be disrupted and re-opened. She is arguing like Montero for an engagement with darkness.

Listening to Montero's words in Ganesha's mouth, the danger the analyst or interpreter of the novel must resist is that of imitating Victor the scientist by diving into the darkness in an effort to shed some light on an unknown, concealed fact. The Western scientist would think that once the fact is brought to light that it forms part of a category and advances our knowledge in the march of progress. The critic, analyst, interpreter, and scientist must avoid the desire ingrained in him by his milieu to fully enlighten this formerly dark or unknown thing, to conquer it, to gain mastery over it. The challenge is to avoid bringing the presence Thierry senses of Ganesha's ghost into the full light of knowledge making it all too present thereby committing violence against it and rendering it powerless, lifeless, like a frog in a jar.

Being able to see something, whether it is our bodies or what is in front of us, gives us the sense that we have mastery over it, that we have power over it. Our emphasis on seeing what is in the light decreases our sense of what is cast into the darkness by the beam of light we are projecting.[36] Montero's challenge here is against the entire discourse of Western modernity that reduces the subject to what he can see. As Lacan says, "The whole of science is based on reducing the subject to an eye" (*Seminar I* 80). Though vision serves an important function in everything, from the construction of our own subjectivity to the understanding of our surroundings, our perspective is also limited in its capabilities. The sense of mastery, this sense of presence that the eye gives us is disrupted by other presences in Montero's narrative. She shows us things that haunt our imagined authority over any situation even the sense of control we have over ourselves.

With the emphasis on darkness at the end of this novel, Montero seems to return to *El reino de este mundo*. If the utopia promised by political revolution is not possible in the kingdom of this world, neither is full and complete knowledge of our others or ourselves. What is left in darkness will always come back to envelop those who decide to ignore its presence, destroying them, leaving them, their sense of mastery, their ideological fantasy, in ruins. However, what is in darkness is also without form, it remains as something about which we cannot speak with any degree of satisfaction. We can only speak in symbols and codes that relay what we sense in half-truths. It is knowledge that is entirely unknowable until after death when we will be face to face with what we see through a glass darkly: And maybe not even then. We have no choice but to remain in the light, in the land of the living, in the kingdom of this world, while still looking toward what we cannot see no matter how unsettling it may be.

NOTES

1. In fact, there are other correlations that could be made. Both writers are exiles and live— or lived in the case of Carpentier—in a somewhat undetermined state. Carpentier traveled between Paris and Havana. Montero lives in Puerto Rico, an Island country whose status is largely undecided and has been called a "floating island" by writers like Rosario Ferré. I think many would probably consider Montero a Puerto Rican writer. Though the themes of her novels deal with topics that are more pan-Caribbean and global than other writers. Her latest novel, *El caballero de la flauta* (2012) has her characters traveling to Cadiz and Russia. In this way she is not unlike current writers in Latin America like Jorge Volpi who place there stories in locations outside of their home country.

2. As is evident throughout my study, my major argument with cultural critics is their belief in the ability to arrive at some type of language that is not in some way metaphoric, that there is a language that is capable of communicating the real in all of its fullness. Once again, Vidal seems to argue that entertainers are not political and that it is possible to have a politics without metaphor, that speaks the real truth.

3. The translations are "false syllogisms of color" and "trick of sense."

4. "[. . .] de los años los horrores/ y venciendo del tiempo los rigores/ triunfar de la vejez y del olvido."

5. "[. . .] it is a useless protection from destiny."

6. "[. . .] con falsos silogismos de coloreses cauteloso engaño del sentido."

7. "[. . .] marchitará la rosa el viento helado."

8. The quote "Verba volant, scripta manent" that is used to refer to the relationship between language and history is now taken to mean that the spoken word flies away and dies while the written word remains. However, in antiquity, and perhaps during the times of Sor Juana, the word flying away in the wind meant that it was released into the wind and would live forever and, perhaps change forever, while the written word remained the same and would eventually decay and die.

9. "[. . .] un afán caduco y, bien mirado,/ es cadáver, es polvo, es sombra, es nada."

10. This translates to "vanidades de la vida" and "que la vida en vanidades."

11. The translations are "magisterio purpúreo en la belleza" and "enseñanza nevada."

12. "[. . .] en cuyo ser unió naturaleza/ la cuna alegre y triste sepultura."

13. "[. . .] viviendo engañas y muriendo enseñas."

14. "En tu libertad te pongo,/ si quisieras censurarlos [. . .] No hay entendimiento más libre que/ el entendimiento humano."

15. The translations are "false feathers" and "book of silence."

16. "[. . .] era como carne de santa."

17. "[. . .] lo dejé hablar un rato. Es imposible pretender que un hombre como Thierry permanezca callado mucho tiempo."

18. "Cuando se tiene una profesión como la mía, es facilísimo captar ciertas señales, identificar ciertos olores, reconocer ciertos movimientos previos al *amplexus* (así llamamos el abrazo sexual entre las ranas) que se."

19. "Pensé que Emile Boukaka era mulato, nadie me lo había dicho, pero lo imaginaba de otro modo [. . .] era negro con ganas."

20. "[. . .] hice un esfuerzo por manejar con naturalidad la enorme cantidad de datos de que me proveía Boukaka. Me asombró su capacidad para el detalle, su precisión, puedo decir que su sabiduría."

21. "Ni el foto ni el título de mi escrito se podían ver, ocultos como estaban bajo la mancha que dejaron los mojones. Desestí rescatar nada más."

22. "Thierry y yo no habíamos congeniado."

23. "[. . .] era yo en ese momento quien intentaba ganar unos minutos."

24. "Le puedo enseñar la Ley del Agua con tal de que usted me cuente lo de los pájaros que cría su padre."

25. "Agwé Taroyo, el dios de las aguas, ha llamado a las ranas para que se vayan por un tiempo al fondo."

26. "Parece absurdo, ¿no?"

27. "Ya empezó la gran huida—recalcó—Ustedes se inventan excusas: la lluvia ácida, los herbicidas, la deforestación. Pero las ranas desaparecen de lugares donde no ha habido nada de eso."

28. Among other sources, I consulted his discography found here: http://www.jazzdisco.org/thelonious-monk/discography/.

29. "Lo que he aprendido lo aprendí en los libros. [. . .] Pero lo que sé, todo lo que sé, lo saqué del fuego y del agua, del agua y la candela: una apaga a la otra."

30. "Un hombre nunca sabe nada, Thierry, ése es su espanto."

31. "Tengo que seguir [. . .] ¿a quién puedo molestar aquí?"

32. When I taught this novel in a class consisting of all female students, they had a hard time believing that the novel in general and the Ganesha episodes in particular were written by a woman. Montero is really adept at inhabiting and telling stories from the perspective of her others.

33. "Tú, la oscuridad que envuelve el espíritu de aquellos que ignoran tu gloria."

34. "Me acordé tan sólo de su rezo, Ganesha estaba muerta y su fantasma vino a soplarme al oído."

35. "Entonces ellas me darán la luz."

36. Lacan in *Seminar I* says, "the sight alone of the whole form of the human body gives the subject an imaginary mastery over his body" (79).

Works Cited

Acosta, Ivonne. *La mordaza: Puerto Rico 1948–1957*. Río Piedras: Editorial Edil, 1998.
Anderson, Benedict. *Imagined Communities: Reflections on the Origin and Spread of Nationalism*. London: Verso, 1991.
Arriví, Francisco. *Vejigantes*. Río Piedras: Editorial Cultural, 1970.
Badiou, Alain. *Being and Event.* Oliver Feltham translator. London: Continuum, 2006.
———. *Conditions.* Steven Corcoran translator. London: Continuum, 2008.
———. *Theory of the Subject*. Bruno Bosteels translator, 2009.
Benítez Rojo, Antonio. *El mar de las lentejas*. Spain: Plaza y Janes Bibloteca Letras del Exilio, 1984.
———. *La isla que se repite: el caribe y la perspectiva posmoderna*. Hanover, NH: Ediciones Norte, 1996.
Boothby, Richard. *Death and Desire: Psychoanalytic Theory in Lacan's Return to Freud*. New York: Routledge, 1991.
Bruce-Novoa, Juan. "Metas monológicas, estrategias dialógicas: La literatura chicana." *Cuadernos Americanos*. 55 (January–February) 1996: 183–197.
———. "Pancho Villa: Post-Colonial Colonialism, or the Return of the Americano." *Kritikos*. 2 (March 2005): 1–11.
Buck-Morss, Susan. *Hegel, Haiti, and Universal History*. Pittsburgh: Pittsburgh University Press, 2009.
Carpentier, Alejo. *Obras completas*. 7 Volumes. México: Siglo XXI Editores, 1983.
———. ¡Ecue yamba O! In *Obras Completas*. Vol. 1.
———. El reino de este mundo. In *Obras Completas*. Vol. 2.
———. El siglo de las luces. Ambrosio Fornet editor. Madrid: Cátedra, 1988.
———. "Del folklorismo musical." *Obras Completas.* Vol. 13.
———. Los pasos perdidos. In *Obras Completas*. Vol. 2.
———. *La novela actual en vísperas de un nuevo siglo y otros ensayos*. México: Siglo XXI, 1981.
———. "Prólogo al Reino de este mundo." In *Obras Completas*. Vol. 2.
———. "Problemática de la actual novela latinoamericana." En "Tientos y diferencias." En *Obras completas*. Vol. 13.
Carnegie, Charles V. *Postnationalism Prefigured: Caribbean Borderlands*. New Jersey: Rutgers University Press, 2002.
Castillo, David. *Baroque Horrors: The Roots of the Fantastic in the Age of Curiosities*. Ann Arbor: Michigan University Press, 2010.
Cavafy, C. P. "Ithaca." *Complete Poems*. David Mendelsohn translator. New York: Knopf, 2012. 13–15.

Celorio, Gonzalo. *Ensayo de contraconquista*. México: Tusquets Editores, 2001.

Chow, Rey. "How (the) Inscrutable Chinese Led to Global Theory." *PMLA* 116. 1. Special Topic: Globalizing Literary Studies. (Jan, 2001): 69–74.

———. *The Age of the World Target: Self Referentiality in War, Theory, and Comparative Work*. Durham: Duke University Press, 2006.

Copjec, Joan. *Imagine There is No Woman: Ethics and Sublimation*. Boston: MIT University Press, 2002.

———. *Read My Desire: Lacan Against the Historicists*. Cambridge, MA: October Books, 1994.

———. "The Sartorial Superego." *October*. 50 (Autumn 1989): 56–95.

Dávila, Arlene. *Sponsored Identities: Cultural Politics in Puerto Rico*. Philadelphia: Temple University Press, 1997.

Davis, Lennard J. *Obsession: A History*. Chicago and London: University of Chicago Press, 2008.

Díaz del Castillo, Bernal. *Historia verdadera de la conquista de la Nueva España*. Miguel León-Portilla editor. Spain: Crónicas de América, 1984.

Díaz, Roberto Ignacio. *Unhomely Rooms: Foreign Tongues in Spanish American Literature*. Lewisburg, Bucknell University Press, 2002.

Deleuze, Gilles. *The Fold Leibniz and the Baroque*. Minneapolis: University of Minneapolis Press, 2003.

Deleuze, Gilles, and Felix Guatarri. *A Thousand Plateaus: Capitalism and Schizophrenia*. Brian Matsumi translator and editor. Minneapolis: University of Minneapolis Press, 1987.

Derrida, Jacques. *Dissemination*. Barbra Johnson translator. Chicago: University of Chicago Press, 1983.

D'haen, Theo. "Cultural Memories, Literary Forms, Caribbean Revolutions." *Caribbean Interfaces*. Lieven d'Hust editor. Amsterdam: Rodopi, 2007. (169–183)

Díaz Quiñones, Arcadio. *El arte de bregar: ensayos*. San Juan: Ediciones Callejón, 2000.

Dubois, Laurent. *Avengers of the New World*. Cambridge: Belknap Press of University of Harvard, 2004.

DuBois, W. E. B. *The Souls of Black Folk*. Delaware: Dover, 1994.

Duchesne Winter, Juan. "Presentación: Puerto Rico Caribe." *Puerto Rico Caribe: Zonas Poéticas del Trauma*. Spec. Issue of *Revista Iberoamericana*. Spec. Ed. Juan Duchesne Winter. Issue of *Revista Iberoamericana*. 75.229 (oct-dic 2009): 933–941.

Duffy Burnett, Christina, and Burke Marshall, eds. *Foreign in a Domestic Sense: Puerto Rico, American Expansion and the Constitution*. Durham/London: Duke University Press, 2001.

Dussel, Enrique. *The Invention of the Americas: Eclipse of the Other and the Myth of Modernity*. Michael D. Barber translator. New York: Continuum, 1995.

Egginton, William. "Of Baroque Holes and Baroque Folds." In *Hispanic Baroques: Reading Cultures in Context*. Nicholas Spadaccini and Luis Martín-Estudillo editors. Nashville: Vanderbilt University Press, 2005. (55–71)

Eliade, Mircea. *The Myth of the Eternal Return or Cosmos and History*. Willard R. Trask translator and editor. New Jersey: Princeton University Press, 1971.

Eréndira. Dir. Ruy Guerra. Perf. Irene Papas, Claudia Ohana and Michael Lonsdale. Les Films du Triangle. 1984. VHS.

Erickson, Daniel. *Ghosts, Metaphor and History in Toni Morrison's* Beloved *and Gabriel García Márquez's* One Hundred Years of Solitude. New York: Palgrave MacMillan, 2009.

Fama, Antonio. "Ficción, historia y realidad: Pautas para una teoría de la novela según Carpentier." *Revista Iberoamericana* (enero-marzo 1991) 64 (154): 135–149.

Faris, Wendy B. *Ordinary Enchantments: Magical Realism and the Remystification of Narrative*. Nashville: Vanderbilt University Press, 2004.

Fernández, Ronald. *The Disenchanted Island: Puerto Rico and the United States in the Twentieth Century*. New York: Praeger, 1992.

Figueroa, Victor. "The Kingdom of Black Jacobins: C. L. R. James and Alejo Carpentier on the Haitian Revolution." *Afro-Hispanic Review*. 25.2 (Fall 2006): 55–71.

Flores, Juan. *From Bomba to Hip Hop: Puerto Rican Culture and Latino Identity*. New York: Columbia University Press, 2000.

————. "The Insular Vision: Pedreira and the Puerto Rican Misère." In *Divided Borders: Essays on Puerto Rican Identity*. Houston: Arte Público Press, 1993. 13–57.

Flores, Juan, and George Yúdice. "Living Borders/ Buscando America: Languages of Latino Self Formation." *Social Text* (1990) 8.2: 57–84.

Fuguet, Alberto, and Sergio Gómez. *McOndo*. Barcelona: Grijalbo Mondadori, 1996.

Fusco, Coco. *English is Broken Here: Notes on Cultural Fusion in the Americas*. New York City: New Press, 1995.

Foucault, Michel. *The Order of Things: An Archaeology of the Human Sciences*. R. D. Lang editor. New York: Vintage, 1970.

García Canclini, Néstor. *La globalizaciión imaginada*. Buenos Aires: Paidos, 1999.

García Márquez, Gabriel. *Cien años de soledad*. New York: Vintage, 2002.

————. *La increíble y triste historia de la cándida Eréndira y de su abuela desalmada*. Barcelona: Mondadori, 2000.

————. "Un hombre muy viejos con unas alas enormes." In *La increíble y triste historia de la cándida Eréndira y de su abuela desalmada*. Barcelona: Mondadori, 2000.

García Ramis, Magali. *Felices días tío Sergio*. San Juan: Editorial Cultural, 2005.

Gates, Henry Louis. *Loose Canons: Notes on the Culture Wars*. New York: Oxford University Press, 1992.

————. *The Signifying Monkey: Theory of Afro-American Literary Criticism*. New York: Oxford University Press, 1988.

Gaylord, Mary Malcolm. "Don Quixote's New World of Language." *Cervantes: Bulletin of the Cervantes Society of America*. (2007 Spring); 27 (1): 71–94.

Gelpi, Juan. *Paternalismo y literatura en Puerto Rico*. San Juan: Editorial University Press, 1993.

Gherovici, Patricia. *The Puerto Rican Syndrome*. New York: Other Press, 2003.

Gilroy, Paul. *The Black Atlantic: Modernity and Double Consciousness*. Cambridge: Harvard University Press, 1993.

González, José Luis. "El país de los cuatro pisos." In *El país de los cuatro pisos y otros ensayos*. San Juan: Ediciones Huracán, 1989.

González Echeverría, Roberto. *Alejo Carpentier the Pilgrim at Home*. Ithaca, NY: Cornell University Press, 1977.

————. "Ultimos viajes del peregrino." *Revista Iberoamericana*. (enero-marzo 1991) 64 (154): 119–134.

Hardt, Michael, and Antonio Negri. *Empire*. Cambridge: Harvard University Press, 2000.

————. *Multitude: War and Democracy in the Age of Empire*. New York: Penguin University Press, 2004.

Hegel, G. W. F. *Philosophy of History*. J. Sibree translator. Lexington: Philospher's Stone, 2009.

Hutcheon, Linda. *A Theory of Parody: The Teachings of Twentieth Century Art Forms*. Urbana: Illinois University Press, 2000.

"Is the Spirit of Competition the Soul of Yoga?" *New York Times*. "Fashion and Style Section" November 19, 2009. http://www.nytimes.com/2009/11/19/fashion/19fitness.html?_r=1& scp=1&sq=competitive%20yoga&st=cse

James, C. L. R. *The Black Jacobins: Toussaint L'Ouverture and the San Domingo Revoultion*. New York: Vintage, 1989.

Jameson, Fredrick. *The Ideologies of Theory—Essays 1971–1986: Volume 2—Syntax of History*. Minneapolis: University of Minneapolis Press, 1988.

————. "Notes on Globalization as a Philosophical Issue." In *The Cultures of Globalization*. Masao Miyoshi editor. Durham: Duke University Press, 1998. 54–77.

Jay, Martin. *Downcast Eyes: The Denigration of Vision in Twentieth Century French Thought*. Berkeley: University of California Press, 1993.

Katz, Friedrick. *The Secret War in Mexico: Europe, the United States and the Mexican Revolution*. Translated portions Loren Goldner. Chicago and London: University of Chicago Press, 1981.

Kuhn, Thomas. *The Structure of Scientific Revolutions*. Chicago: University of Chicago Press, 1962.

Lacan, Jacques. "Of the Gaze as Objet Petit a." In *The Seminar of Jacques Lacan: Book XI The Four Fundamental Concepts of Psychoanalysis*. 67–122.

———. "On a Question Prior to Any Possible Treatment of Psychosis." *Ecrits*. Bruce Fink translator. New York: W.W. Norton, 1999. (445–488).

———. *The Seminar of Jacques Lacan: Book XI The Four Fundamental Concepts of Psychoanalysis*. Alan Sheridan translator. New York: Norton, 1981.

———. *The Seminar of Jacques Lacan X: Anxiety 1962–1963*. Unedited Manuscripts. Cormac Gallagher translator. Eastborne UK: Anthony Rowe Ltd, n.d.

Larrain, Jorge. *El concepto de la ideología V. 1–3*. Santiago, Chile: LOM Editores, 2007.

Levinson, Brett. *Secondary Moderns: Mimesis, History, and Revolution in Lezama Lima's American Expression*. Lewisburg, PA: Bucknell University Press, 1996.

Lezama Lima, José. *La expresión americana*. Chile: Editorial Universitaria, 1969.

Lima, Lázaro. *The Latino Body: Crisis Identities in American Literary and Cultural Memory*. New York: New York University Press, 2007.

Llorens Torres, Luis. "El grito de Lares: Drama histórico-poético en tres actos y en prosa y en verso." *Obras completas Tomo II Prosa y teatro*. Hato Rey, PR: Editorial Cordillera, 1969. 212–343.

Laó-Montes, Agustin. "Afro-Latinidades: Bridging Blackness and Latinidad." *Technofuturos: Critical Interventions in Latino Studies*. Nancy Raquel Mirabal and Agustin Laó-Montes, eds. Lanham: Lexington Books, 2007. 117–140.

Marting, Diana E. "The End of Eréndira's Prostitution." *Hispanic Review* 69.2 (Spring 2001): 175–190.

Matthiessen, Peter. *The Snow Leopard*. New York, Penguin, 2008.

Marqués, René. *La carreta: Drama en tres actos*. Río Piedras, PR: Editorial Cultural, 1983.

———. "El puertorriqueño dócil." Ed. Unknown. *Ensayos 1953–1971*. Spain: Editorial Antillana, 1972. 151–216.

Martin, Gerald. *Gabriel García Márquez: A Life*. New York: Knopf, 2008.

Martínez-San Miguel, Yolanda. *Caribe Two Ways: Cultura de la migración en el Caribe*. San Juan: Ediciones Callejón, 2003.

Marx, Karl. *The German Ideology: Parts I and III*. R Pascal editor and translator. New York: International Publishers, 1967.

McClintock, Anne. *Imperial Leather: Race, Gender, and Sexuality in the Colonial Conquest*. New York: Routledge, 1995.

McGowan, Todd. "Condemned to the Absolute or How Hegel Can Help Us Across Borders." *Journal of the Midwestern Language Association*. 30 (Spring 1997): 114–130.

———. *The End of Dissatisfaction?: Jacques Lacan and the Emerging Society of Enjoyment*. Albany: SUNY University Press, 2004.

———. *The Real Gaze: Film Theory After Lacan*. Albany: SUNY University Press, 2007.

Menton, Seymore. *Historia verdadera del realism mágico*. México: Fonda de Cultura Económica, 1998.

———. *Latin America's New Historical Novel*. Austin: Texas University Press, 1993.

Mills, Moylan C. "Magic Realism, García Márquez, and Eréndira." *Latin American Film Quarterly* 17.2 (1989): 113–122.

Mignolo, Walter. *The Idea of Latin America*. Malden, MA: Blackwell Publishing, 2005.

———. *Local Histories/Global Designs*. New Jersey: Princeton University Press, 2000.

Mohr, Nicolasa. "Puerto Rican Writers in the United States, Puerto Rican Writers in Puerto Rico: A Separation Beyond Language." *Americas Review* 15.2 (1987): 87–92.

Moreiras, Alberto. "Hegemonía y subalternidad." En *Nuevas perspectivas desde/sobre América Latina: El desafío de los estudios culturales*. Mabel Moraña y John Beverley editores. Pittsburgh: Pittsburgh University Press, 2002. (157–71)

———. *The Exhaustion of Difference: The Politics of Latin American Cultural Studies*. Durham: Duke University Press, 2001.

Moreno, Marisel. "Family Matters: Revisiting La gran familia puertorriqueña in the Works of Rosario Ferré and Judith Ortíz Cofer." *Centro de Estudios Puertorriqueños Journal*. 22.2 (Fall 2010): 75–105.

Mulvey, Laura. "Visual Pleasure and Narrative Cinema." Robert Stam and Toby Miller editors. *Film and Theory an Anthology*. Malden, MA: Blackwell Publishing, 2000. 483–94.

Muertas de Juárez, Las. Dir. Enrique Murillo. Perf. Claudia Bernal, Carlos Cardán and Eleazar García jr. Laguna Productions. 2002. DVD.

Negrón Muntaner, Francés. *Brincando el charco*. New York: Hipspic Productions: Distributed by Women Make Movies, 1994. Video Cassette.

Neroni, Hilary. "Jane Champion's Jouisance: Holy Smoke and Feminist Theory." In *Lacan and Contemporary Film*. Todd McGowan and Sheila Kunkle, eds. New York: Other Press, 2004. 209–232.

Ortega y Gasset, José. *La deshumanización del arte*. Madrid: Revista de Occidente, 1925.

Ortiz Cofer, Judith. *In the Line of the Sun*. Athens: University of Georgia, 1989.

————. *The Meaning of Consuelo*. New York: Farrar, Strauss, and Giroux, 2003.

Ortiz, Fernando. *Contrapunteo cubano del Tabaco y el azúcar*. Enrico Mario Santi editor. Madrid: Cátedra, 2002.

Palmié, Stephan. *Wizards and Scientists: Explorations in Afro-Cuban Modernity and Tradition*. Durham: Duke University Press, 2002.

Pabón, Carlos. *Nación Postmortem: Ensayos sobre los tiempos de insoportable ambigüedad*. San Juan: Ediciones Callejón, 2003.

Pancrazio, James J. *The Logic of Fetishism: Alejo Carpentier and the Cuban Tradition*. Lewisburg: Bucknell University Press, 2004.

Parkinson, Zamora. *The Inordinate Eye: New World Baroque and Latin American Fiction*. Chicago: University of Chicago Press, 2006.

————. "Swords and Silver Rings: Magical Objects in the Work of Jorge Luis Borges and Gabriel García Márquez." In *A Companion to Magical Realism*. Stephen M. Hart and Wen-Chen Ouyang editors. Woodbridge, UK: Tamesis, 2005. (28–45)

Paravisini-Gebert, Lizabeth. "The Haitian Revolution in Interstices and Shadows: A Re-Reading of Alejo Carpentier's *The Kingdom of This World*." *Research in African Literatures*. (2004 Summer); 35 (2): 114–27.

Pedreira, Antonio S. *Insularismo: Ensayos de interpretación puertorriqueña*. Spain: Plaza Mayor, n.d.

Pieterse, Jan Nederveen. *Globalization and Culture: Global Mélange*. New York: Rowman & Littlefield, 2003.

Pratt, Mary Louise. *Imperial Eyes: Travel Writing and Transculturation*. London: Routledge, 1992.

Quijano, Anibal. "Colonidad y modernidad-racionalidad." En *Los Conquistadores*. H. Bonilla editor. Bogotá: Tercer Mundo, 1992. 437–447.

Quijano, Anibal, and Immanuel Wallerstein. "Americanity as a Concept, or the Americas in the Modern World System." 134 *ISSA1* (1992): 549–547.

Quesada, Carmen Cañete. "José Lezama Lima y su noción de "teleología insular": Lectura del Coloquio con Juan Ramón Jiménez." *Afro Hispanic Review*; 25, 2; (Fall 2006); 33–54.

Rama, Angel. "Los procesos de transculturación en la narrative latinoamericana." *La novella en América Latina: Panoramas 1920–1980*. Veracruz: Universidad Veracruzana, 1982. 203–233.

Ranciere, Jacques. *Dissensus: On Politics and Aesthetics*. Steve Corcoran translator. New York: Continuum, 2010.

Reyes, Israel. *Humor and the Excentric Text in Puerto Rican Literature*. Gainesville: University of Florida Press, 2005.

Ríos Ávila, Rubén. "A Bite of the Visible." N.A.

————. *La raza cómica del sujeto en Puerto Rico*. San Juan: Ediciones Callejón, 2002.

————. "Queer Nation." *Revista Iberoamericana*. Puerto Rico Caribe: Zonas Poéticas del Trauma. Spec. Issue of *Revista Iberoamericana*. Spec. Ed. Juan Duchesne Winter. Issue of *Revista Iberoamericana*. 75.229 (oct-dic 2009): 1129–1138.

Rivera, Angel A. "Silence, Voodoo, and Haiti in Mayra Montero's *In the Palm of Darkness*." Web Accessed on August 13, 2013.

Robinson, Randall. *Unbroken Agony: Haiti From Revolution to the Kidnapping of a President*. New York: Basic Civitas Books, 2008.

Rodríguez Mangual, Edna. *The Construction of an AfroCuban Cultural Identity.* Chapel Hill: University of North Carolina Press, 2004.

Sánchez González, Lisa. *Boricua Literature: A Literary History of the Puerto Rican Diaspora.* New York: New York University Press, 2001.

Santner, Eric. "Terry Schiavo and the State of Exception." http://www.press.uchicago.edu/Misc/Chicago/05april_santner.html . Accessed on July 24, 2012.

Santiago Díaz, Eleuterio. *Escritura afropuertorriqueña y modernidad.* Pittsburgh, PA: Instituto Internacional de Literatura Iberoamericana, Universidad de Pittsburgh, 2007.

Santiago Díaz, Eleuterio, and Ilia Rodríguez. "Desde las fronteras raciales de dos casas letradas: Habla Piri Thomas." Puerto Rico Caribe: Zonas Poéticas del Trauma. Spec. Issue of *Revista Iberoamericana.* Spec. Ed. Juan Duchesne Winter. Issue of *Revista Iberoamericana.* 75.229 (oct-dic 2009): 1199–1219.

Santos, Daniel. "Lamento borincano." Daniel Santos: Lamento borincano. (original Rec. Date not known). Orfeón, 1991.

Sarduy, Severo. *Barroco.* Buenos Aires: Editorial Sudamericana, 1974.

———. *La simulación.* Caracas, Venezuela: Monte Avila Editores, 1982.

Sklodowska, Elzbieta. "Viajes sin salvoconducto: imágenes de Haití en la narrativa de Alejo Carpentier y Antonio Benítez Rojo." *Moderisms and Modernities: Studies in Honor of Donald L. Shaw.* Susan Carvalho editor. Newark: Juan de la Cuesta Press, 2006. (223–262).

Smith, Verity. "Ausencia de Toussaint: interpretación y falseamiento de la historia en *El reino de este mundo.*" *Historia y ficción en la narrative hispanoamericana.* Roberto González Echeverría compilador y prólogo. Venezuela: Monte Avila Editores, 1984. (275–286).

Stevens, Camilla. "The Haunted Puerto Rican Stage: Lucy Boscana in La carreta and Vejigantes." *Latin American Theatre Review.* Fall (2004): 5–22.

Terada, Rei. *Looking Away: Phenomenality and Dissatisfaction Kant to Adorno.* Cambridge, MA: Harvard University Press, 2009.

Thomas, Katherine. "Hippolytus in Haiti: Classical Myth in Carpentier's *El reino de este mundo.*" *Publication of the Afro-Latin American Research Association.* (2005) 9: 47–54.

Torres, Arlene. "*La gran familia puertorriqueña 'ej prieta de beldá.'*" ("The Great Puerto Rican Family is Really Black.") *Blackness in Latin America and the Caribbean: Social Dynamics and Cultural Transformations.* Arlene Torres and Norman E. Whitten Jr. editors and introduction. Indianapolis: Indiana University Press, 1998. 287–306.

Trinh, Thi Minh-Ha. *Woman, Native, Other: Writing Postcoloniality and Feminism.* Bloomington: Indiana University Press, 1989.

Trouillot, Michel-Rolph. *Silencing the Past: Power and the Production of History.* Boston: Beacon Press, 1995.

Valdez, Michael Moses. "Magical Realism at World's End." *Literary Imagination: The Review of the Association of Literary Scholars and Critics.* 3.1 (2001), 105–133.

Vasconcelos, José. *La raza cósmica: misión de la raza iberoamericana.* México, DF: Espasa Calpe, 1966.

Vega, Ana Lydia. "Pollito/ Chicken." Carmen Lugo Filippi and Ana Lydia Vega. *Vírgenes y mártires.* San Juan: Editorial Cultural, 2002. 73–80.

———. "Sálvese quien pueda: La censura tiene auto." *El Mundo.* Suplemento "Puerto Rico Ilustrado. (18 de diciembre 1988): 20.

———. "Sobre tumbas y héroes (Folletín de caballería boricua). Pasión de historia y otras historia de pasión. Buenos Aires: Ediciones La Flor, 1987. 101–145.

Vega, Garcilaso de la. "Soneto XXIII En tanto que de rosa y azucena." http://users.ipfw.edu/jehle/poesia/entantoq.htm. Accessed July 24, 2012.

Vélez, Diana. "'Pollito/ Chicken': Split Subjectivity, National Identity and the Articulation of Female Sexuality in a Narrative by Ana Lydia Vega." *Americas Review* 14.2 (1986): 68–73.

Vidal, Hernán. "Aesthetic Categories as Empire Administration Imperatives: The Case of the Baroque." In *Hispanic Baroques: Reading Cultures in Context.* Nicholas Spadaccini and Luis Martín-Estudillo editors. Nashville: Vanderbilt University Press, 2005. 20–54.

———. "Restaurar lo político, imperativo de los estudios literarios y culturales latinoamericanistas." In *Nuevas perspectivas desde/sobre América Latina: El desafío de los estudios culturales*. Mabel Moraña y John Beverley editors. Pittsburgh: Instituto Internacional de Literatura Iberoamericana, University of Pittsburgh, 2002. 139–146.

Viego, Antonio. *Dead Subjects: Toward a Politics of Loss in Latino Studies*. Durham: Duke University Press, 2007.

White, Hayden. *The Tropics of Discourse Essays in Cultural Criticism*. Baltimore: Johns Hopkins University Press, 1986.

———. *Metahistory the Historical Imagination in 19th Century Europe*. Baltimore: Johns Hopkins University Press, 1975.

Williams, Raymond. *Marxism and Literature*. Oxford: Oxford University Press, 1977.

Williams, William Carlos. "Landscape with the Fall of Icarus." http://english.emory.edu/classes/paintings&poems/williams.html. Accessed July 24, 2012.

Xenophon. *Anabasis: The March Up the Country*. H. G. Dayknes translator. Texas: El Paso Norte Press, 2007.

Yúdice, George. *The Expediency of Culture in the Global Era*. Durham: Duke University Press, 2003.

Zimmermann, Warren. *First Great Triumph: How Five Americans Made Their Country a World Power*. New York: Farrar, Straus, and Giroux, 2002.

Žižek, Slavoj. "Che Vuoi?" *The Sublime Object of Ideology*.

———. *For They Know Not What They Do: Enjoyment as a Political Factor*. New York: Verso, 1991.

———. *First as Tragedy, Then as Farce*. New York: Verso, 2009.

———. *How to Read Lacan*. New York: W.W. Norton and Company, 2006.

———. "Hermeneutic Delirum." *Lacanian Ink*. 34 (Fall 2009); 138–151.

———. *Less than Nothing: Hegel and the Shadow of Dialectical Materialism*. New York: Verso, 2012.

———. *The Sublime Object of Ideology*. New York: Verso, 1997.

———. *Tarrying With the Negative: Kant, Hegel, and the Critique of Ideology*. Durham: Duke University Press, 1993.

———. *The Ticklish Subject: The Absent Center of Political Ontology*. London: Verso, 1999.

Index

About the Author

John V. Waldron is an associate professor of Spanish, global studies, and Latin American and Caribbean studies at the University of Vermont. He graduated with a PhD in Spanish from the University of California, Irvine. He teaches classes on Latin American and global cinema and literatures. He has published articles on the literature of Puerto Rico, Mexico, Cuba, and their diasporas.